30 Mock Tests for Olympiad CLASS 6

Science | Mathematics | English
Logical Reasoning | GK | Cyber

DISHA™
Publication Inc

DISHA Publications Inc.

45, 2nd Floor, Maharishi Dayanand Marg,
Corner Market, Malviya Nagar, new Delhi -110017
Tel: 49842349/ 49842350

Typeset By

DISHA DTP Team

CONTENTS

English

Mathematics

Science

General Knowledge

Logical Reasoning

Cyber

ENGLISH

OLYMPIAD

Mock Test 1

Name : __________
Number of Questions : 50

Max. Marks : 50
Time : 2 Hours

There is no negative marking in the test.

DIRECTIONS (Qs. 1 to 11): Choose the best option to fill in the blanks.

1. He liked my painting at first __________.
   (a) glance (b) see
   (c) sight (d) view
2. Gradually the forests are __________. Humankind is being very hard on them.
   (a) decreasing (b) circulating
   (c) growing (d) cutting
3. What's happening? Why are you making so much__________?
   (a) noise (b) voice
   (c) play (d) music
4. The expert _____tried to cite many cases to prove his point.
   (a) lawyer (b) mechanic
   (c) student (d) plumber
5. The number of girls is ____than the number of boys in my class.
   (a) fewer (b) lesser
   (c) less (d) little
6. During the interrogation I didn't remember_____, my mind went blank.
   (a) something (b) anything
   (c) everything (d) nothing
7. We must not eat ____much sugar, it is not good for our health.
   (a) too (b) very
   (c) so (d) not
8. He had been complaining of fever for a long time. After a number of tests, he was ______ with malaria.
   (a) discovered (b) diagnosed
   (c) explored (d) suffering
9. They always keep calculating lions' ______.
   (a) people (b) population
   (c) numbers (d) cubs
10. During summers we must drink a ______of water, it prevents dehydration.
    (a) much (b) too much
    (c) lot (d) very much
11. You ______ take your goggles, as it is cloudy.
    (a) need not
    (b) could not
    (c) must not
    (d) may not

Space for Rough Work

DIRECTIONS (Qs. 12 to 14): How many words are wrongly spelt in the sentences given below?

12. He wanted to go to the beech but his freinds wanted to go somewhere else.
    (a) 2 (b) 3
    (c) 1 (d) None
13. Weather the parents should intervene when there children are scolded by there teachers is a difficult morale question.
    (a) 1 (b) 4
    (c) 3 (d) 2
14. Keep your things safe, because if you lose them, you'll be in big truble.
    (a) 1 (b) 3
    (c) 2 (d) None

DIRECTIONS (Qs. 15 to 23): From the given options, choose the best answer to complete each sentence.

15. You must ____ before it starts raining.
    (a) left (b) leave
    (c) have left (d) will leave
16. If you _____ press this red button, the alarm bell will start ringing.
    (a) would (b) could
    (c) will (d) can
17. I finished the work _____ you told me to do.
    (a) which (b) that
    (c) who (d) where
18. Everyone praised him for his perseverance ________ Ram did not praise him.
    (a) so (b) as
    (c) but (d) and
19. 'Get the taste of one's own medicine' would mean ________.
    (a) reveal a secret
    (b) better than everybody else
    (c) stay away or avoid someone
    (d) get the ill-treatment which one gave others
20. Resha and Kiya can't stand each other as ________________.
    (a) one of them has to sit
    (b) they thoroughly dislike each other
    (c) they bend down
    (d) they sit and talk
21. If bread is to sandwich, cotton is to ____________.
    (a) dress (b) plant
    (c) polyester (d) colour
22. He _____ the news of the terrorist attack on the border.
    (a) made (b) broke
    (c) take (d) make
23. We must ____a room for everyone's views.
    (a) keep (b) make
    (c) take (d) have

DIRECTIONS (Qs. 24 to 25): Rearrange the following sentences to form a meaningful paragraph.

24. I. The simple device that made faraway things look nearer.
    II. A telescope is one of humankind's most important inventions.
    III. It changed our view of Earth and our place in the universe forever.

Space for Rough Work

IV. When man started using a telescope to look up the sky,

(a) I, II, III, IV (b) II, I, IV, III

(c) III, I, IV, II (d) II, III, IV, I

25. I. The study of English language reveals a history of versatility.

II. Language is a means by which we can communicate our ideas to others.

III. Any language evolves through time.

IV. It has adopted many languages to become what it is today.

(a) II, III, I, IV (b) II, I, IV, III

(c) IV, I, II, III (d) III, II, I, IV

DIRECTIONS (Qs. 26 to 27): Choose the best option to fill in the blanks.

26. Abraham Lincoln did what he thought was ____ for his country.

(a) best

(b) more better

(c) better

(d) good

27. He has been without work ____ a year.

(a) of (b) at

(c) on (d) for

DIRECTIONS (Qs. 28 to 30): Find the odd one out.

28. Obey, Follow, Consent, Avoid, Comply, Observe, Yield

(a) Follow (b) Consent

(c) Avoid (d) Yield

29. Literate, Learned, Educated, Scholarly, Ignorant, Erudite

(a) Literate (b) Educated

(c) Scholarly (d) Ignorant

30. Beautiful, Hideous, Pretty, Handsome, Delicate

(a) Hideous (b) Beautiful

(c) Handsome (d) Delicate

DIRECTIONS (Qs. 31 to 35): Read the table given below and answer the questions that follow. Choose the answers from the options given below.

SERIAL NO.	COUNTRY	SEX RATIO
1.	China	944
2.	India	933
3.	USA	1,029
4.	Brazil	1,025
5.	Pakistan	938
6	Russian Federation	1,140
7.	Japan	1,041
8.	Nigeria	1,016
9.	Indonesia	1,004
10.	Bangladesh	953
11.	World	986

31. Which one of the following statements is false?

(a) All the developing countries have low sex ratio.
(b) Russian federation has the highest sex ratio.
(c) Bangladesh is ahead of India.
(d) Pakistan has the lowest sex ratio.

32. Sex ratio is measured as the number of females per _____ males.
(a) ten (b) ten thousand
(c) thousand (d) none

33. Low sex ratio is not an indicator of ______.
(a) practice of female infanticide
(b) sex discrimination
(c) stereotype against women
(d) lack of education

34. Federation here would mean ____.
(a) a football federation
(b) a federation of states joined together
(c) an organization
(d) a government

35. We can see that in general the sex ratio all over the world is low; how do you think we can work towards making it equal?
(a) By educating people
(b) By giving more rights to women
(c) By making the girls more powerful
(d) By stopping female infanticide

DIRECTIONS (Qs. 36 to 45): Read the following questions and choose their answer from the options given below.

36. Sam: Why are you_____________ so much? Are you not well?
Brian: Yes, I have fever.
(a) sleeping (b) studying
(c) working (d) happy

37. Rohan: Our answers were similar but he was given more marks than me.
Gautam: ______________
(a) That's good.
(b) That's not enough.
(c) That's unfair.
(d) That's average.

38. Sam: He is never late for his work.
Forge: ____________________
(a) He is very timely.
(b) He is very orderly.
(c) He is very punctual.
(d) He comes very regular.

39. Kavita: I couldn't understand what you said. ___________________
(a) Could you please repeat?
(b) Couldn't you speak slower?
(c) Could you speak lowly?
(d) Could you speak gradually?

40. Viren: I was trying your number. But I couldn't _________ through.
(a) got (b) get
(c) arrange (d) phone

41. What is the indirect speech of the sentence given below?
Direct speech: Sam said, "I am going tomorrow."
Indirect speech: ______________
(a) Sam said that he was going tomorrow.
(b) Sam said that he is going tomorrow.
(c) Sam said that he will be going tomorrow.
(d) Sam said that he has to leave tomorrow.

Space for Rough Work

42. The doctor said to the patient, ______________

 (a) "How are you feeling today?"
 (b) "What is your condition today?"
 (c) "What is your sickness?"
 (d) "How can I treat you today?"

43. Sweta said to her father, "Have you invited our relatives for the party?"
 Father: ____________________

 (a) Yes, I have.
 (b) Yes, I could not.
 (c) They seem to be busy.
 (d) I am too occupied.

44. The inspector said to the witness, "Can you __________them?"

 (a) discover (b) recognise
 (c) remember (d) recall

45. Mr. Pathak said to the students, "Do you know that you will be required to fill in the examination ______ today?"

 (a) document (b) set
 (c) form (d) paper

DIRECTIONS (Qs. 46 to 50): Given below is an advertisement. Have a look at it and answer the questions that follow.

46. What is meant by alchemy?

 (a) It is a chemical science that claims to change ordinary into special.
 (b) An art that beautifies things.
 (c) A process of making watches.
 (d) A machine to design watch chains.

47. Which of the following is the antonym of automatic?

 (a) Electronic
 (b) Electrical
 (c) Manual
 (d) Mechanical

48. A country's name is mentioned below the brand 'RADO'. Why?

 (a) Because it is available only in Switzerland.
 (b) Because it is manufactured there.
 (c) Because it is manufactured specifically for Swiss people.
 (d) Because it is a copyright of Switzerland.

49. Findout the word in the advertisement that is the opposite of archaic?

 (a) Alchemy (b) Plasma
 (c) Modern (d) Metallic

50. Imagine a life without watch. What would you use to know the time?

 (a) Would look at the sky and tell the time.
 (b) Would look at the sun and tell the time as people did in older times.
 (c) Would wake up and know it was morning.
 (d) Would sleep in the dark and wake up in the morning.

Space for Rough Work

OLYMPIAD Mock Test 2

Name : ________
Number of Questions : 50

Max. Marks : 50
Time : 2 Hours

There is no negative marking in the test.

DIRECTIONS (Qs. 1 to 11): Choose the best option to fill in the blanks.

1. Head Office has expressed ______ about what is happening here.
   (a) concern (b) concept
   (c) confidence (d) compromise
2. He learnt driving _____ he was in California.
   (a) during (b) since
   (c) when (d) for
3. Seema is a very good _____. She speaks too good.
   (a) listener (b) orator
   (c) dancer (d) vocalist
4. He _______ from his house in search of truth.
   (a) sets in (b) sets
   (c) set up (d) set out
5. He always ____ for not doing his work.
   (a) makes causes
   (b) makes excuses
   (c) refuses
   (d) makes pauses
6. He ate up the whole _____ of grapes.
   (a) bundle (b) bunch
   (c) stack (d) group
7. Have you ever seen a _____ of leopards? I saw when I was on an African Safari.
   (a) pride (b) leap
   (c) group (d) herd
8. A _____ gathers and communicates public information.
   (a) journalist (b) reporter
   (c) writer (d) detective
9. I wanted to scream but my _____ cords seem to be frozen.
   (a) vocal (b) neck
   (c) voice (d) noise
10. I discussed the problem ____ my friends.
   (a) to (b) with (c) of (d) for
11. There is such a contrast _____ them!
   (a) among (b) between
   (c) to (d) in

DIRECTIONS (Qs. 12 to 14): How many words are wrongly spelt in the sentence given below?

12. My uncel knows intersting facts about the world's oceans.
   (a) 1 (b) 2 (c) 3 (d) 5

Space for Rough Work

13. Ashish wanted to know the prise of the new car.
    (a) 1 (b) 2 (c) 3 (d) None
14. Adrian pored his cup of coffee to help him fight his fatige.
    (a) 1 (b) 3 (c) 2 (d) None

DIRECTIONS (Qs. 15 to 20): Choose the best answer to complete each sentence from the options given.

15. I warned him of the risk involved in the trek ____ he decided to go.
    (a) but (b) and
    (c) still (d) when
16. Priya ____ the head girl of the school.
    (a) choose (b) refused
    (c) was elected (d) resented
17. Nobody has ever known him tell a lie. He is ______________
    (a) as gentle as a lamb.
    (b) as honest as the day is long.
    (c) as busy as a beaver.
    (d) as honest as the sun.
18. Harry is sure to ruin his lungs. He ____________
    (a) smokes like a chimney.
    (b) eats like a bird.
    (c) smells like a furnace.
    (d) sits there like a bump on the log.
19. A good judge never jumps _____the conclusion.
    (a) at (b) to (c) on (d) for
20. ____ you have the determination, you can go ahead.
    (a) If (b) But
    (c) As (d) Hence

DIRECTION (Q. 21): Choose the word that is not synonymous with the rest of the words.

21. Tranquil, Peaceful, Serene, Soothing, Idyllic, Irritating
    (a) Idyllic (b) Serene
    (c) Soothing (d) Irritating

DIRECTION (Q. 22): Match the following idioms with their meanings.

22.

A	Put one's foot down	1	Extremely happy
B	Cat's whiskers	2	Reveal a secret unintentionally
C	Spill the beans	3	Be very firm when opposed
D	On cloud nine	4	Better than everyone else

	A	B	C	D		A	B	C	D
(a)	3	4	2	1	(b)	4	3	1	2
(c)	3	2	4	1	(d)	3	4	1	2

DIRECTIONS (Qs. 23 to 27): Read the following report carefully and answer the questions that follow. Choose the answers from the options given below.

BDK Public School, Noida: A four-day long programme was held which focussed on environmental issues. A special assembly was conducted on the importance of proper planning to save earth from the clutches of unplanned human activities. The proceedings of the day included tree plantation programme where the young learners sowed their actual future in the soil. Students also pledged to avoid wastage of resources. Short, crisp and concise one minute talk on the strategies to enhance life on earth exposed the communicative skills of the students.

23. What according to you are environmental issues?
    (a) Issues relating to pollution.
    (b) Issues relating to deforestation.
    (c) Issues relating to endangered wildlife.
    (d) All of the above
24. What is the meaning of the phrase 'sowed their future in soil'?
    (a) They sowed their books in soil.
    (b) They sowed their certificates in soil.
    (c) They sowed trees.
    (d) They started with a new venture to ensure their future.
25. Find out a word from the above report that is synonymous to clutch.
    (a) Brush (b) Clench
    (c) Concise (d) Crisp
26. What does the word crisp mean here?
    (a) Spicy (b) Very
    (c) Short (d) Messy
27. What do you think can be a cause for rising depletion of the environment?
    (a) Increasing use of chemicals to meet the demands of overgrowing population.
    (b) Over plantation of trees occupying a lot of space meant for humans.
    (c) Overproduction of animals putting pressure on the resources.
    (d) None of the above

DIRECTIONS (Qs. 28 to 37): For the given situtations, choose the most appropriate expression from the options.

28. Betty: Go away. I don't want any stranger in my house.
    Stranger: ________
    (a) I am David. I am your cousin.
    (b) You can't do that.
    (c) I am your only friend.
    (d) You are quite fortunate to have me in your house.
29. The hospital is ____________clean bandages and medicines.
    (a) short cut (b) short of
    (c) in short (d) in short supply
30. Saira: You've just got a new job. You'll have to work very hard.
    Her Friend:________________
    (a) I can't work hard. It's a waste of time.
    (b) I don't mind hard work. The experience will help me in my career.
    (c) Why are you telling me this?
    (d) Hard work is of no use. I will not join the job.
31. Advice that you will give to students appearing for an examination.
    ____
    (a) You must write in bold letters.
    (b) You must write in capital letters.
    (c) You must answer all the questions.
    (d) You must write all the correct answers.
32. You want to congratulate your friend on his achievement. How will you do it?
    ____
    (a) Congratulations! I wish I could do it.
    (b) Congratulations! That's a great achievement!
    (c) Wow! But your score is not very good.
    (d) Alas! That was great!

Space for Rough Work

33. How will you interrupt two people discussing some issue? ________
 (a) Will you both keep quiet and let me speak.
 (b) May I have your attention?
 (c) May I interrupt?
 (d) That's not fair! Give me a chance to speak.

34. Imagine yourself going to a sweet shop. You want to try some sweets. How will you ask the shopkeeper? ________
 (a) Can I taste this?
 (b) Please give me the honour to taste this.
 (c) Do you think I should taste this?
 (d) You have to allow me to taste this.

35. Sita: Did you like your gift?
 Rita: ________
 (a) No, thanks.
 (b) Yes, thanks for that wonderful gift.
 (c) Thanks, I don't mind.
 (d) It wasn't that good.

36. You liked somebody's song performance, how will you react? ________
 (a) Wow! (b) Eureka!
 (c) Euphoria! (d) Encore!

37. You are staying in a hotel. You want to order some food. How will you order it? ________
 (a) Hello, I wanted to place an order for dinner.
 (b) Hello, please get my order.
 (c) Hello, some food please.
 (d) Hello, is that room service? I wanted to place an order for dinner.

DIRECTIONS (Qs. 38 to 42): Read the following chart and answer the questions that follow. Choose the answers from the options given below.

(I) A survey was conducted on student preference with respect to the most popular means of communication among them. Surprisingly, the students didn't seem much interested in traditional means of communication. Only 7% were interested in writing letters to their friends or kins as compared to those who preferred e-mails.

(II) However, the chief competition is between users of Instant Messenger and those of Emails. The users of tax line as a medium of communication are only marginal. There are supporters of text messaging also. Overall, the survey had a mixed response from the students.

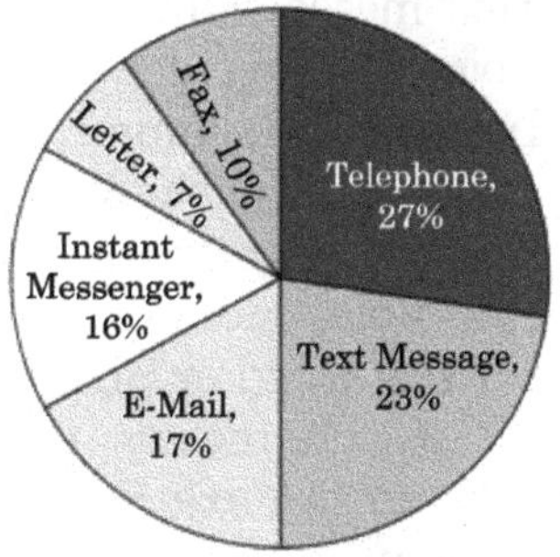

(III) The students informed that out of the choices given in the servey questionnaire, they have indicated the most preferred option. But, most of the students are of the view that video calling needs to be mentioned in the questionnaire as it is the most effective and most popular means of communication. Further, voice messages are the second most preferred means of communication.

38. Which means of communication is liked by more than one-fourth of the students?
    (a) Telephone (b) Text message
    (c) E-mail (d) Fax
39. Which means of communication is liked by exactly one-tenth of the students?
    (a) Letter (b) Fax
    (c) E-mail (d) Letters
40. What is the overall response of the students to the survey?
    (a) Biased (b) Unbiased
    (c) Mixed (d) None of these
41. What is the correct order of the medium of communication in decreasing order of preference?
    (a) Voice message, Text message, Instant Messenger, Fax
    (b) Text message, Instant Messenger, Voice message, Fax
    (c) Instant Messenger, Fax, Voice message, Text message
    (d) Text message, Instant Messenger, Fax, Voice message
42. Pick out the word or phrase from the passage which means the same as 'study' (used in Para 1).
    (a) Survey
    (b) Popular
    (c) Communication
    (d) Kins

DIRECTIONS (Qs. 43 to 50): Read the passage given below and fill in the blanks from the options given below.

The Met says that the Monsoon this year could prove to be (1) _____normal, about 93% of the long-period average. A firmer assessment will be available only later. Most certainly, poor rains will not be (2)____news. At the same time, there is no cause for panic. If (3)_____favours us, the _(4)_________of even the subnormal rains that materialise could be such as to minimise the (5)_______. For another, food (6)______are (7)______high enough to preclude any major worry on the availability of (8)________.

43. Choice the right option for (1)
    (a) above (b) below
    (c) about (d) somehow
44. Choice the right option for (2)
    (a) good (b) bad
    (c) better (d) best
45. Choice the right option for(3)
    (a) nature (b) luck
    (c) goodluck (d) times
46. Choice the right option for (4)
    (a) pouring (b) distribution
    (c) division (d) spread
47. Choice the right option for (5)
    (a) damage (b) rains
    (c) floods (d) drought
48. Choice the right option for (6)
    (a) stacks (b) stocks
    (c) sacks (d) heaps
49. Choice the right option for(7)
    (a) still (b) not
    (c) about (d) so
50. Choice the right option for (8)
    (a) water (b) cereals
    (c) wheat (d) rice

Space for Rough Work

OLYMPIAD Mock Test 3

Name : ________

Number of Questions : 50

Max. Marks : 50

Time : 2 Hours

There is no negative marking in the test.

DIRECTIONS (Qs. 1 to 14): Choose the correct option to fill in the blanks.

1. We can meet the doctor only ______ six in the evening.
   (a) around (b) at
   (c) by (d) before
2. The earthquake in Nepal took place______2015.
   (a) at (b) in
   (c) during (d) since
3. My teacher knows interesting facts _____animals.
   (a) about (b) over
   (c) of (d) by
4. Dry weather conditions are unsuitable ________ cultivating paddy.
   (a) for (b) of
   (c) in (d) by
5. Let them rest a little, for they have _____ finished painting the wall.
   (a) rarely (b) softly
   (c) only (d) just
6. He addressed the Minister __________.
   (a) sadly (b) politely
   (c) carefully (d) quickly
7. The expedition through the old city was held up because of _____ delays in the delivery of food supplies.
   (a) several (b) any
   (c) much (d) every
8. The hostess _____the guests to sit down.
   (a) ordered (b) invited
   (c) resented (d) forced
9. The teacher _____ him to go and polish his shoes right away.
   (a) requested (b) ordered
   (c) dragged (d) invited
10. They have laid the foundation stone at the proposed_______.
    (a) cite (b) site
    (c) sight (d) ground
11. Every time the stand up clown did something hilarious, the audience____________.
    (a) laughed
    (b) became delighted
    (c) was sad
    (d) wanted to leave

Space for Rough Work

12. "Let someone off" would mean ______
    (a) let down
    (b) let go
    (c) lessen or become less intense
    (d) excuse or punish someone very lightly
13. My mother______ me to study hard.
    (a) help (b) made
    (c) let (d) refused
14. We ____________ to protect our environment at any cost.
    (a) have (b) has
    (c) are (d) must

DIRECTIONS (Qs. 15 & 16): How many words are wrongly used in the sentences given below?

15. Both of them right articles for newspapers.
    (a) 3 (b) 1
    (c) 2 (d) None
16. They complemented the winner.
    (a) 1 (b) 2
    (c) 3 (d) None

DIRECTIONS (Qs. 17 to 24): From the given options, choose the best answer to complete the sentence.

17. Rashi was driving a car______ looked really old.
    (a) that (b) which
    (c) who (d) whom
18. The last we _____from him was on Sunday.
    (a) hear (b) will hearing
    (c) heard (d) herd
19. There are __________books that it becomes difficult to decide which one to buy.
    (a) huge (b) so many
    (c) so much (d) so many good
20. People living in _____ suffer from many ailments.
    (a) gutters (b) slums
    (c) houses (d) rooms
21. The movie was not at all interesting, the storyline was ______________.
    (a) run-out-of
    (b) run-of-the-mill
    (c) on-the-run
    (d) the run
22. He is such a coward, he is ____________.
    (a) yellow bellied
    (b) blue bellied
    (c) red-bellied
    (d) spineless
23. He is driving for the first time, keep your ___________.
    (a) fingers crossed
    (b) hands crossed
    (c) nails crossed
    (d) eyes closed
24. He has a keen interest in birds. He wants to become a/an __________.
    (a) bird catcher
    (b) bird watcher
    (c) ornithologist
    (d) pilot

DIRECTION (Q. 25): Choose the word that is not synonymous with the given word.

25. LEARNED
    (a) Hideous (b) Scholarly
    (c) Erudite (d) Intellectual

DIRECTIONS (Qs. 26 to 30): Read the following passage and answer the questions that follow. Choose the answers from the options given below.

Space for Rough Work

Albert Einstein (In a letter to M.K. Gandhi)

You have shown through your works, that it is possible to succeed without violence, even with those who have not discarded the method of violence. We may hope that your example will spread beyond the borders of your country, and will help to establish an international authority, respected by all, that will take decisions and replace war conflicts.

26. Find out a word from the above letter that is the opposite of agreement.
    (a) Conflict
    (b) Decision
    (c) Adjustment
    (d) Correspondence
27. Why do you think Albert Einstein wrote this letter to Gandhiji?
    (a) To praise him of his efforts towards non-violence
    (b) To suggest him ways to follow non-violence
    (c) As a gesture of formality
    (d) To join him in his struggle
28. As hoped by Einstein an international authority to resolve international disputes has been set-up. What is the name of that authority?
    (a) United Nations
    (b) International league
    (c) SAARC
    (d) World Peace Organization
29. Which of the following statements is false?
    (a) Gandhiji used non-violence despite violence from the other side.
    (b) Gandhiji used non-violence till the other person was also not violent.
    (c) Einstein wanted an international organisation to be set up to resolve conflicts.
    (d) All of the above
30. According to you what should be done in an event of conflict?
    (a) We should retaliate to show the other person that it's not easy to confront us.
    (b) We should try to resolve the conflict by peaceful means.
    (c) War is the only answer.
    (d) Non-violence is the thing of the past, now we have nuclear weapons.

DIRECTIONS (Qs. 31 to 39): Choose the best alternative to complete the following sentences.

---

31. Leave your shoes outside in the Sun so that ________________
    (a) they can absorb sunlight.
    (b) they can dry.
    (c) they can become loose.
    (d) they help you run.
32. Please hurry up for your school or ________________
    (a) you will reach late.
    (b) you are late.
    (c) you cannot be late.
    (d) the school will remain closed.
33. Despite his best efforts to conceal his anger, ________________
    (a) we could detect that he was very happy.
    (b) he failed to give us an impression of his agony.

Space for Rough Work

(c) he could succeed in doing it easily.
(d) people came to know that he was annoyed.

34. Dennis: I love Harry Potter.
Martha: ________________
(a) Wow! Why do you?
(b) Wow! How could you?
(c) Wow! I love it too!
(d) Wow! But it's boring.

35. Ben: Could you please move? You are standing on my toes.
Kevin: ________________
(a) Oh really! I didn't know that.
(b) Show me, I want to see.
(c) Sorry! I didn't see it.
(d) Oh! But I didn't hurt anyone.

36. Mother: I am going out.
Smith: When will you be back?
Mother: ________________
(a) Why should I tell you?
(b) I'll be back by 5:30.
(c) You can't ask me that.
(d) I will come as per my convenience.

37. 'Even if it rains, I shall come' means ________________
(a) if I come, it will not rain.
(b) if it rains, I shall not come.
(c) I will certainly come whether it rains or not.
(d) whenever there is rain I shall come.

38. She never visits any zoo because she is strong opponent of the idea of ________________
(a) setting the animals free into forest.
(b) holding the animals in captivity for our joy.
(c) feeding the animals while others are watching.
(d) going out of the house on a holiday.

39. I felt somewhat more relaxed ________________
(a) but tense as compared to earlier.
(b) and tension-free as compared to earlier.
(c) and tense as compared to earlier.
(d) as there was already no tension at all.

DIRECTIONS (Qs. 40 to 44): Read the newspaper article and answer the questions that follow. Choose the answers from the options given below.

Rama Das, 11, is a fearless little girl from Jharkhand. She says that one afternoon her small brother suffered a severe electric shock when he touched a switch board that had a damaged lead. Her mother and grandmother, trying to pull him away, were also hurt. Rama, remembering that plastics are bad conductors, pulled the plug out of the socket and so saved three lives.

40. Who was the first person to suffer electric shock?
(a) Rama's mother
(b) Rama's aunt
(c) Rama's brother
(d) Rama

41. What had gone wrong with the switch board?
(a) Water had gone inside it.
(b) Its lead was damaged.
(c) Its wires were exposed.
(d) Fire had damaged its lead.

42. What should be done to save one from electric shocks?
    (a) We should never touch naked wires.
    (b) We should never touch electric appliances.
    (c) We should start using battery operated appliances.
    (d) None of the above
43. While plastics are bad conductors, then why do we cover the electric wires with plastic?
    (a) Copper wires will not look good.
    (b) To prevent electric current passing from the wires to human body.
    (c) To differentiate between the different sources of power.
    (d) None of the above
44. With the repeated outcry over shortage of electric power, what can we do to conserve power?
    (a) Put off the lights while leaving a room.
    (b) Unplug things when not using them.
    (c) Increase the use of solar energy as a source of power.
    (d) All of the above

DIRECTIONS (Qs. 45 to 50): Read the passage given below and fill in the blanks from the options given below.

Courage is ______ (1) _____ to fear, mastery of fear. Consider the flea incomparably the bravest of all creatures of God, if ignorance of fear was _________ (2) _________. _____ (3) _________you are asleep or awake he will attack you, caring nothing for the fact that in ________(4)_______ you are to him as are the massed armies of earth to a suckling child; he lives both day and night and all days and nights in the very lap of peril and the immediate presence of death, and _______(5)____ is no more afraid than is the man who walks the _________ (6)______ of the city that was threatened by an earthquake ten centuries before.

45. Choose the correct option for (1).
    (a) reluctance
    (b) resistance
    (c) mastery
    (d) hatred
46. Choose the correct option for (2).
    (a) courage (b) fearless
    (c) insult (d) sad
47. Choose the correct option for (3).
    (a) Whether (b) Weather
    (c) Even (d) Since
48. Choose the correct option for (4).
    (a) courage
    (b) strength
    (c) health
    (d) cowardice
49. Choose the correct option for (5).
    (a) but (b) yet
    (c) still (d) despite
50. Choose the correct option for (6).
    (a) road (b) street
    (c) houses (d) feet

Space for Rough Work

OLYMPIAD Mock Test 4

Name : __________
Number of Questions : 50

Max. Marks : 50
Time : 2 Hours

There is no negative marking in the test.

DIRECTIONS (Qs. 1 to 14): Choose the most appropriate option to fill in the blanks.

1. Mr. Harris usually goes to office_____ car.
   (a) by (b) through
   (c) with (d) on
2. Have you out ______ the invitations for the party yet?
   (a) posted (b) sent
   (c) dispatched (d) delivered
3. When that old man died, he gave______ all his property to a charity for orphans.
   (a) away (b) out
   (c) on (d) off
4. There were _____mistakes this time.
   (a) fewer (b) less
   (c) better (d) few
5. On my way back home, I stopped ______groceries for my house.
   (a) buy (b) to buy
   (c) buying (d) bought
6. I wish he could _______my problem.
   (a) state (b) understand
   (c) read (d) write
7. Do you expect me to ________to him for his mistakes?
   (a) forget (b) apologise
   (c) forgive (d) grab
8. Nobody died in the accident, but a lot of people were __________.
   (a) damaged (b) spoiled
   (c) injured (d) broken
9. He would not have been late for the exam, if he _____________earlier.
   (a) leaving (b) left
   (c) has left (d) had left
10. I wish I _____ go out.
    (a) could have (b) will
    (c) could (d) can
11. Where has he ____? He should have come hours ago.
    (a) went (b) gone
    (c) going (d) goes
12. He decided not to jump at the last minute because he might________ himself.
    (a) have hurt
    (b) hurted
    (c) had hurt
    (d) has been hurt

Space for Rough Work

13. Jenny ______studies, so her grades are getting worse day by day.
    (a) hard (b) hardly
    (c) late (d) lately
14. I am bored. I think I should go and_____some programme on television.
    (a) look (b) see
    (c) watch (d) watch at

DIRECTIONS (Qs. 15 to 17): How many words are wrongly spelled in the sentences given below?

15. Mr. Stevenson was always fare in his judgements.
    (a) 1 (b) 2
    (c) 3 (d) None
16. He has gone to the docter for a helth check up.
    (a) 1 (b) 2
    (c) 3 (d) None
17. Mr. Davis works as an astraunot.
    (a) 1 (b) 2
    (c) 3 (d) 4

DIRECTIONS (Qs. 18 to 28): From the options given below, choose the best answer to complete the sentence.

18. He has gone on a business_______to Tokyo.
    (a) trip (b) journey
    (c) voyage (d) travel
19. I never drive to work, I ________ walk.
    (a) seldom (b) often
    (c) always (d) sometimes
20. Do you want me to __________ you to go to the doctor tomorrow? You forgot your appointment last week.
    (a) remember (b) memorise
    (c) remind (d) remember me
21. Tata steel was _____in 1907 by the Tatas.
    (a) fined (b) found
    (c) founded (d) find
22. The miser gazed _________ at the pile of gold coins in front of him.
    (a) avidly (b) admiringly
    (c) thoughtfully (d) earnestly
23. She dances _______. She can pursue a career in dancing.
    (a) good (b) so well
    (c) very good (d) very well
24. I saw a _______ of cows in the field.
    (a) group (b) herd
    (c) swarm (d) flock
25. "The state will not bear any breach of law" would mean_____________.
    (a) zero tolerance
    (b) no tolerance
    (c) zero bearance
    (d) forbearance
26. When Rita and Seema started fighting, it brought the meeting to an abrupt __________.
    (a) conference (b) condition
    (c) conclusion (d) halt
27. The grapes are now _________ enough to be picked.
    (a) ready (b) mature
    (c) ripe (d) advanced
28. This is the _______place I have ever been to.
    (a) beautifulest
    (b) most beautiful
    (c) more beautiful
    (d) beautiful

DIRECTIONS (Qs. 29 & 30): From given options, choose the word that is not synonymous with the words given below.

29. Adulation, Praise, Tribute, Commendation, Blandishment, Hatred.
    (a) Blandishment
    (b) Commendation
    (c) Hatred
    (d) Tribute
30. Amazing, Breathtaking, Stunning, Horrendous, Astounding, Stupend-ous.
    (a) Horrendous (b) Astounding
    (c) Stunning (d) Stupendous

DIRECTIONS (Qs. 31 to 35): Read the passage given below and answer the questions that follow. Choose the answers from the options given below.

It was Sunday and the school was closed. All the children were having a holiday. It was a fine day. The Sun was shining bright and the birds were singing.

Jack, of course, longed to go swimming like the other boys in his neighbourhood. But Tom came out with a heavy heart. He held a long brush in one hand and in the other he had a bucket of limestone solution. His father had told him to whitewash the fence of the house.

Jack looked sadly at the fence. 'How high it is', he thought. Indeed, the height of the fence was about ten feet and it was 25 yards long. Jack dipped the brush into the bucket and drew it slowly across the fence. It made a very small white patch. Tom sat down and sighed heavily. Jack picked up his brush once again. He saw Harry coming down the street. Jack pretended not to notice him. He worked harder than ever. Harry was eating a muffin. He looked extremely happy.

Harry came up to jack. He rubbed his eyes. 'Why! Jack', he cried in astonishment, you're working!' Jack did not reply. He went on with his work. He seemed very interested in his work. 'Jack you're working!' Harry repeated. 'Oh! It's you, Harry. I didn't see you. 'This isn't work', Jack said and he went on whitewashing. 'Whitewashing is fun. Have you ever whitewashed a fence'? To this Harry replied, 'Well no! I haven't.' For a long time, Harry stood there watching Jack. Jack paid no attention to him and continued with the whitewashing. At last Harry said, 'Let me whitewash a little!' 'Oh no, Harry! I'm going to make this fence look beautiful. 'I find it really interesting' replied Jack. 'Let me do just a little', begged Harry. Jack said; No I'm sorry, Harry but I can't. If you do it, you'll make a mistake. You'll spoil everything'. 'I will not make any mistake. I'll be careful. You can have my muffins, if you let me!' Slowly and unwillingly, Jack gave the brush to Harry. Harry worked hard. Jack stood close by, watching him work while eating his muffins.

31. What did Jack want to do on a Sunday?
    (a) Paint the fence
    (b) Sleep till late
    (c) Go for swimming
    (d) Play cricket
32. What was he doing with limestone solution?
    (a) Cleaning the house
    (b) Doing some experiment
    (c) Painting the fence
    (d) None of these

Space for Rough Work

33. How do you know that it was a fine day?
    (a) It was not raining.
    (b) It was Sunday afternoon.
    (c) The Sun was shining and the birds were singing.
    (d) It was a holiday.

34. Why did Jack sigh down heavily?
    (a) Because he was told to paint the fence
    (b) Because he realised that painting the fence would take a very long time
    (c) Because his friends refused to take him along for swimming
    (d) Because his mom had not given him food

35. Why do you think Jack pretended to be interested in painting?
    (a) He wanted Harry to become interested in painting and make him do it.
    (b) Actually while painting he developed an interest for the task.
    (c) He wanted his friends to give up going to swimming.
    (d) None of these

DIRECTIONS (Qs. 36 to 40): Choose the word which is OPPOSITE in meaning to each of the underlined word.

36. His description of the event was rather <u>pejorative.</u>
    (a) laudatory (b) derogatory
    (c) predictive (d) adusive

37. Observing his agitation, we tried to <u>propitiate</u> the speaker.
    (a) provoke (b) placate
    (c) prohibit (d) facilitate

38. Muskan's <u>ubiquitous</u> smile helped to cheer us up in times of misery.
    (a) small (b) rare
    (c) common (d) frequent

39. Evidence of his moral <u>turpitude</u> influenced the committee's decision about his promotion.
    (a) courage
    (b) baseness
    (c) timidity
    (d) honourableness

40. Efforts at managing differences have, till date, been more <u>episodic</u> than otherwise.
    (a) intermittent
    (b) eventful
    (c) continous
    (d) half-hearted

DIRECTIONS (Qs. 41 to 50): For the given situations, choose the most appropriate expression.

41. Meena said, 'Rahul is an actor, isn't he?'
    Tina : ____________________
    (a) No, he is a carpenter.
    (b) Yes, he has acted in many popular plays.
    (c) How do I know that?
    (d) He doesn't look like an actor.

42. Harry: 'Where are all my papers?'
Samir:____________________
(a) They must be somewhere on the table.
(b) You don't know?
(c) Nobody knows anything about them.
(d) I am not supposed to know.

43. Seema: Are you scared of ghosts?
Geeta: ____________________
(a) Why should I tell you?
(b) No, I don't believe in ghosts.
(c) No, I am scared of them
(d) No, I am not scared of ghosts.

44. Ajay: Wow! I didn't know you could sing so well.
Raj: ____________________
(a) I knew it already.
(b) Thanks for the compliment.
(c) I think I am the best singer.
(d) But it is of no use.

45. Someone asks you the way, and you do not know the way to that particular place. How will you tell that person?
(a) Go past that building.
(b) I am sorry, I don't know.
(c) I can't tell you, it's not easy.
(d) Come with me I will show you the way.

46. Ken: 'Are you going to the supermarket?'
Ren:______________
Ken: Can you pick up a few things for me?
(a) No, I am not going there.
(b) Yes, I would be going in a little while.
(c) It's not easy to go there.
(d) Why don't you go?

47. Ginni: Mom, where are you going?
Mother: ____________________
Ginni: I have my coaching at 4:30.
(a) Why? What happened?
(b) I am not going anywhere.
(c) I will not tell you.
(d) Why? You want to come?

48. Kelly: Is it raining outside?
Fen: ____________________
Kelly: Okay, then we can go out.
(a) No, it isn't.
(b) Yes, it's raining heavily.
(c) Yes, it is hazy.
(d) No, it's pouring.

49. Receptionist: Hello Sir, how can I help you?
Guest:____________________
(a) You cannot help me.
(b) I am helpless.
(c) Yes, I wanted a room in your hotel.
(d) Yes, I am looking for a house.

50. Manager: Let us find a solution to this problem.
Colleague: ____________________
(a) No, we can't do anything.
(b) Let's work towards it.
(c) Let's not waste time and start.
(d) Yes, we can do it.

Space for Rough Work

OLYMPIAD Mock Test 5

Name : __________
Number of Questions : 50

Max. Marks : 50
Time : 2 Hours

There is no negative marking in the test.

DIRECTIONS (Qs. 1 to 11): Choose the best option to fill in the blanks.

1. This sounds to be a dangerous plan; you ___________ get into serious problem.
   (a) shall (b) will
   (c) shoulder (d) might
2. The children eagerly look forward _____ Teacher's Day.
   (a) to (b) for
   (c) into (d) in
3. The issue of global warming _____ become a serious threat for the entire world.
   (a) has (b) have
   (c) had (d) having
4. _____ you have fever, you should consider going to the doctor.
   (a) Since (b) Before
   (c) If (d) After
5. Tomorrow's meeting is very important; you ____ be on time.
   (a) might (b) may
   (c) must (d) can
6. On Sundays, I _______ go for match practice a little late.
   (a) will (b) can
   (c) should (d) must
7. This park is the_______of the four other parks in this area.
   (a) big (b) bigger
   (c) biggest (d) most big
8. He is _____ rude. He doesn't realise it.
   (a) sometimes (b) at times
   (c) never (d) seldom
9. Let us talk _______ someone else.
   (a) about
   (b) to
   (c) for
   (d) on
10. The coach congratulated the football team ______ winning the world cup.
    (a) for (b) to
    (c) on (d) in

Space for Rough Work

11. Long ago, man started domesticating animals _____ cultivating plants for food.
(a) but (b) and
(c) since (d) for

DIRECTIONS (Qs. 12 to 14): How many words are wrongly spelt in the sentences given below?

12. The car manufactring industry has shown fenominal growth in ricent years.
(a) 1 (b) 2
(c) 3 (d) None
13. He likes to peal the apples before he eats them.
(a) 1 (b) 2
(c) 3 (d) 4
14. He will start going to collage next year.
(a) 1 (b) 2
(c) 3 (d) None

DIRECTIONS (Qs. 15 to 24): Choose the best answer to complete each sentence from the options given.

15. Thousands of people have sent _________ for the victims of the earthquake.
(a) money
(b) wealth
(c) health
(d) cheques
16. Mother Teresa never spoke harshly to anyone. She was always ________ with everybody.
(a) gentle (b) mild
(c) soft (d) arrogant
17. I don't have much _______ to read these days.
(a) time (b) sport
(c) money (d) training
18. Weather reports say it is the ______ rains we have had for six years.
(a) best (b) worst
(c) bad (d) good
19. There are __________ marbles in the box that it is difficult to count them.
(a) so much (b) so many
(c) such a huge (d) so strong
20. Please _____________ the fire after you have cooked food.
(a) light
(b) extinguish
(c) assemble
(d) put off
21. Let's give Ravi a box of _________ on his birthday.
(a) food
(b) chocolates
(c) mud
(d) marbles
22. The clerk took a loan from the bank _____ renovate his house.
(a) to (b) for
(c) so (d) so that

Space for Rough Work

23. The cricketer was groaning in pain ___________ he had sprained his ankle.
    (a) so (b) because
    (c) since (d) as
24. The tenant ___________ the rent since last few months.
    (a) has not paid
    (b) has not been paying
    (c) did not pay
    (d) did not pay

DIRECTIONS (Qs. 25 to 27): Read the passage and fill in the blanks from the options given below.

Mother Teresa set (1)_____an order of nuns called the Sisters of Charity. The nuns of this order have lived in Kolkata for years in a small house. They visited the slums and the railway stations. The look after the abandoned children. They have brought them to their home and (2) ___________care of them. They have (3)___________ that being unwanted is the worst disease that any human being can suffer from.

25. Choice the right option for (1)
    (a) out (b) up
    (c) after (d) for
26. Choice the right option for (2)
    (a) take (b) took
    (c) has taken (d) are taking
27. Choice the right option for (3)
    (a) repented (b) realised
    (c) believed (d) thought

DIRECTIONS (Qs. 28 to 30): Read the sentences given below and fill in the blanks with appropriate words.

28. He _______rushed to the hospital to see his wife.
    (a) suddenly
    (b) eagerly
    (c) hurriedly
    (d) None of the above
29. After winning the match, Ram felt as if he was on top of the___________.
    (a) cloud nine
    (b) moon
    (c) sun
    (d) world
30. I have worked very hard but the ____ test will come when we sit for the assessment.
    (a) acid
    (b) base
    (c) final
    (d) ultimate

DIRECTIONS (Qs. 31 to 35): Read the letter given below and answer the questions that follow. Choose the answers from the options given below.

Dear Rohit,

I know you will be surprised to know that I am on a trip to the North-East (Gangtok) and I am really enjoying the lovely and adventurous journey. The plan for Gangtok was so spontaneous that we decided about it a day before the departure. We have spent a night in Kolkata, where we took a ride in the trams. Darjeeling is one of the best places I have ever visited. The monasteries and the gardens here are beautiful. At present I am at Gangtok, the capital of Sikkim. It is truly a mystical wonderland, nestling in the heart of Himalayas. I wish you were here too, though I know that you could not get a leave from your office. I hope you will be joining me on my next vacation. Convey my regards to uncle and aunty.

Yours lovingly,

Bimal

31. What is Bimal enjoying in Darjeeling?
    (a) The trams
    (b) A ride in the metro
    (c) The beautiful gardens and monasteries.
    (d) Parks and historical monuments.
32. Where is Gangtok?
    (a) Darjeeling
    (b) Kolkata
    (c) Sikkim
    (d) None of the above
33. Where is Bimal writing this letter from?
    (a) Gangtok (b) Darjeeling
    (c) Kolkata (d) Himalayas
34. Nestling in Himalayas means____________
    (a) birds having their nest in Himalayas.
    (b) amidst the Himalayan ranges.
    (c) sleeping in Himalayan hotels.
    (d) None of the above
35. Why didn't Arun go with Bimal?
    (a) Because he did not like the place
    (b) Because he could not get leave from work
    (c) Because he wanted to go somewhere else
    (d) Because he was not on good terms with Rohit

DIRECTIONS (Qs. 36 to 40): Read the following chart and answer the questions that follow.

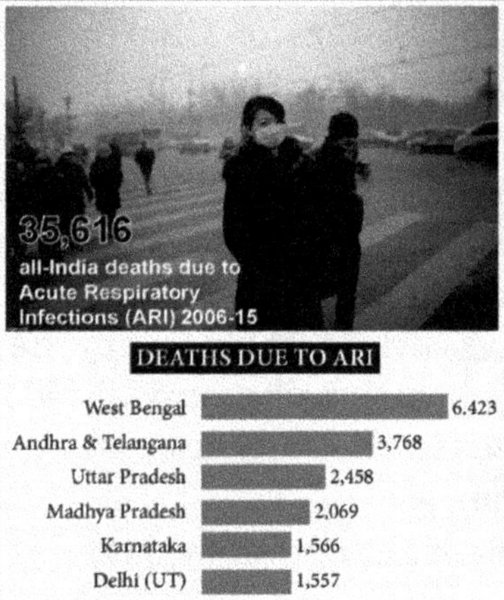

REPORTED CASES OF ARI

Year	Cases (in cr)
2006	2.61
2007	2.61
2008	2.74
2009	2.82
2010	2.61
2011	2.63
2012	3.16
2013	3.17
2014	3.48
2015	1.27*

*till May, 2015

36. Which of the following states reported highest number of deaths due to ARI?
    (a) Delhi
    (b) West Bengal
    (c) Madhya Pradesh
    (d) Karnataka

37. Which of the following statements is false?
    (a) Telengana became a state in January 2014.
    (b) Telengana has more than ten districts.
    (c) Madhya Pradesh is ahead of Delhi in deaths due to ARI.
    (d) All India death tolls due to ARI are approximately 35,000.
38. What is the full form of ARI?
    (a) All Respiratory Infections
    (b) Air Respiratory Infections
    (c) Acute Respiratory Infections
    (d) Adverse Respiratory Infections
39. The report presents the deaths in________.
    (a) thousands (b) hundreds
    (c) lakhs (d) crores
40. What can be the probable cause for respiratory infections?
    (a) Environmental pollution
    (b) Contaminated air caused by pollution from vehicles and industries
    (c) Smoke from cigarettes
    (d) All of the above

DIRECTIONS (Qs. 41 to 50): For the given situations, choose the most appropriate expression.

41. Nisha: Why are you in such a hurry today?
    Vibha: ____________________
    Nisha: Don't be late; she must be waiting for you there.
    (a) My sister is waiting for me to go home from college.
    (b) I am always in a hurry.
    (c) Going home is not tough as I will go by a cab.
    (d) That's my choice.
42. Aman: Where were you on Tuesday? I had come to your house and found it locked.
    Sameer: ____________________
    Aman: Great! How was it? Hope you enjoyed it.
    (a) I had gone out with my dog.
    (b) I'd gone with my family to watch 'Spiderman'.
    (c) I'd gone to see my grandmother.
    (d) My house is always locked.
43. Harish: I have bought a new house in the countryside.
    Navin: ____________________
    Harish: Thanks! Do come and visit us.
    (a) Wow! I want to buy a new house too.
    (b) Why did you buy a new house?
    (c) Congratulations!
    (d) Oops! Good you bought a new house.

Space for Rough Work

44. Vikram: Leena has eaten too much, and she wants to eat more.
Hitin: Okay, I will ____________
(a) stop her from eating.
(b) tell her to eat some more food.
(c) tell her to go out.
(d) tell her to serve me some food.

45. You seem to be tired, because_______
(a) you worked hard today.
(b) you slept for too long.
(c) you are eating too much.
(d) you watched a movie.

46. Host: What would you like to take?
Guest:_____________
(a) How do I know?
(b) It's your choice.
(c) Something cold, please.
(d) No, thanks.

47. Harry: My house is near that park.
Frazer:___________________
(a) I live in a big city.
(b) I don't know that park.
(c) I live next to that building.
(d) So is mine.

48. Some elderly lady is standing and talking to her friend, and you need to go past her, what will you say?
(a) May I beg your pardon, I am in a hurry.
(b) Excuse me, may I get past?
(c) Get aside I am in a hurry.
(d) Please move, I am in a hurry.

49. Customer: How much is this for?
Shopkeeper: _______________
(a) It is for ₹180.
(b) I am not keen on selling it.
(c) Why do want to buy it?
(d) Why are you asking the price?

50. Monika: It's my birthday tomorrow and I am throwing a party. Will you come?
Fenny: ___________________
(a) I'll surely come.
(b) I don't know.
(c) Yes, but it's too late.
(d) Yes, but I am not sure.

Space for Rough Work

MATHEMATICS

OLYMPIAD

Mock Test 1

Name : ________ **Max. Marks : 50**

Number of Questions : 50 **Time : 2 Hours**

There is no negative marking in the test.

1. Find the difference between largest and smallest 5 digit number.
   (a) 89900 (b) 89999
   (c) 89998 (d) All of these
2. Keeping the place of 6 in the number 6350947 same, the smallest number obtained by rearranging other digits is.
   (a) 6975430 (b) 6043579
   (c) 6034579 (d) 6034579
3. Find the surface area of a chalk box whose length, breadth and height are 10cm, 6cm and 3cm respectively.
   (a) 117 cm^2 (b) 275 cm^2
   (c) 216 cm^2 (d) All of these
4. The ratio between the rates of walking of A and B is 2 : 3 and therefore A takes 10 minutes more than the time taken by B to reach the destination. If A had walked at double the speed, then in what time would he have covered that distance?
   (a) 9 min. (b) 14 min.
   (c) 15 min. (d) 19 min.
5. If the denominator of a fraction is 1 more than thrice its numerator and if the numerator is increased by one and denominator is reduced by two then its value is 0.5. Find the fraction.
   (a) $\frac{1}{2}$ (b) $\frac{4}{13}$
   (c) $\frac{3}{10}$ (d) $\frac{2}{7}$
6. Vishal jogged around a rectangular field 4 times. If the rectangular field was 135 m long and 78 m wide, then how far did Vishal jog?
   (a) 426 m (b) 852 m
   (c) 1278 m (d) 1704 m
7. Mother asked Neelu and her brother to pick stones from the wheat. Neelu picked one fourth of the total stone in it and her brother also picked up one fourth of the stones. What fraction of the stone did both pick up together ?

Space for Rough Work

(a) $\frac{1}{6}$ (b) $\frac{1}{2}$

(c) $\frac{3}{4}$ (d) $\frac{5}{2}$

8. Cost of 1 dozen pens is ₹180 and cost of 8 ball pens is ₹56. Find the ratio of cost of a pen to the cost of a ball pen.
(a) 7 : 8 (b) 15 : 7
(c) 7 : 17 (d) 15 : 8

9. Measure of angle ∠ACD in the given figure is

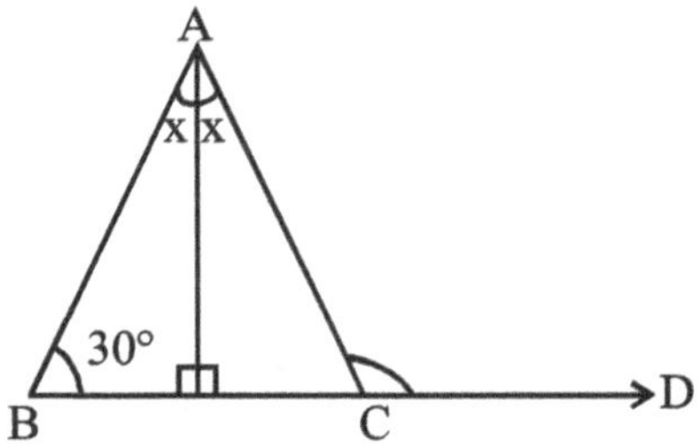

(a) 130° (b) 120°
(c) 150° (d) 115°

10. A bus was carrying 27 passengers. At the bus stop, 6 passengers alighted and 9 boarded the bus. How many passengers were there in the bus after the stop?
(a) 26 (b) 27
(c) 30 (d) 28

11. Mr. Tan gives $\frac{2}{5}$ of his monthly salary to his parents and $\frac{3}{5}$ of his remaining salary to his children. He keeps the rest for himself. What fraction of his monthly salary does he keep for himself.

(a) $\frac{6}{25}$ (b) $\frac{8}{25}$ (c) $\frac{6}{50}$ (d) 0

12. Consider the following two statements.
Statement 1: The division of two unlike terms, without constant can not be reduced to its lowest term.
Statement 2: The product of two unlike terms is square of each of the term.
(a) Statement 1 and 2 are true
(b) Statement 1 is true and 2 is false
(c) Statement 1 is false and 2 is true
(d) All of these

13. Roman numeral for the greatest three digit number is
(a) IXIXIX (b) CMIXIX
(c) CMXCIX (d) CMIIC

14. The smallest number of 4-digits exactly divisible by 12, 15, 20 and 35 is
(a) 1000 (b) 1160
(c) 1260 (d) None of these

15. The circle has :
(a) one line of symmetry
(b) two lines of symmetry
(c) three lines of symmetry
(d) many lines of symmetry

16. Find the area of the figure shown below.

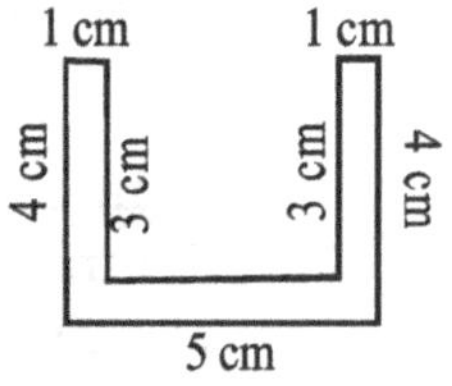

(a) 9 sq cm
(b) 10 sq cm
(c) 11 sq cm
(d) 15 sq cm

Space for Rough Work

17. The value of $-8 - 2 [6 + 4\{7 - (2.8 + 1.4)\}]$ is :
(a) -34.4 (b) -42.4
(c) $+42.4$ (d) -34.4

18. Three boys step off together from the same spot. Their steps measure 63 cm, 70 cm and 77cm, respectively. What is the minimum distance each should cover, so that all can cover the distance in complete steps?
(a) 8228 (b) 2116
(c) 4320 (d) 6930

19. On a straight road four cities are there A, B, C and D

Distance between B and D is 39 km, between A and C is 27 km and between C and D is 15 km. How far is A from B?
(a) 6 km (b) 3 km
(c) 24 km (d) 12 km

20. Read the following statements carefully and choose the correct option.
(i) Value of $\frac{0.216+0.064}{0.36+0.16-0.24}$ is 1.
(ii) If $4.175 = \frac{1}{0.2395}$ then the value of $\frac{1}{0.0004175}$ is equal to 2935.
(iii) Value of $[0.9 - \{2.3 - 3.2 - (7.1 - 5.4 - 3.5)\}]$ is 0.
(a) (i) and (ii) are true while (iii) is false.
(b) (i) and (iii) are true while (ii) is false.
(c) (ii) and (iii) are true while (i) is false.
(d) All the given (i), (ii) and (iii) are true.

21. Mean of a set of observations is the value which
(a) occurs most frequently
(b) divides observation into two equal parts
(c) is a representative of the whole group
(d) is the sum of observations

22. Read the information about the given figure and choose the false statement.

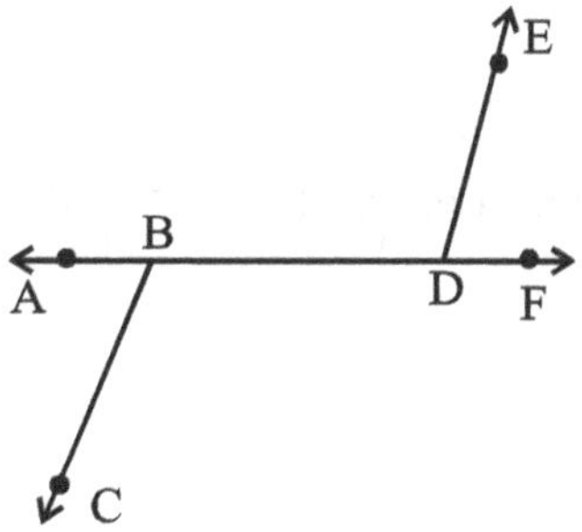

"$\angle ABC = 30°$, $\angle EDF = (40 - x°)$ and $\angle ADE = 13x + 20°$ ".
(a) $\angle ABC = \angle EDF$
(b) $\angle DBC + \angle EDF = 180°$
(c) $BC \parallel DE$
(d) $\angle BDE$ and $\angle DBC$ are supplementary angles.

23. Observe the figure carefully and answer the question. In the given figure, O and P are the centres of two

Space for Rough Work

equal three-quarter circles. The length of OP is 14 cm. The perimeter of the figure is $\left(\text{use} = \pi = \frac{22}{7}\right)$

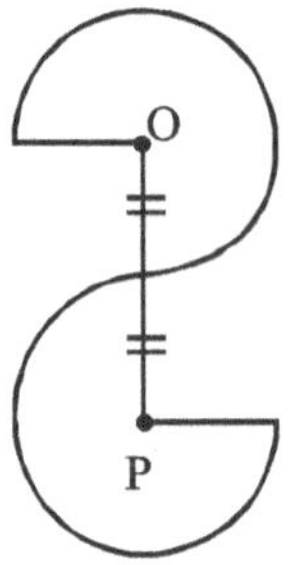

(a) 50 cm (b) 94 cm
(c) 49 cm (d) 95 cm

24. What is the value of $\left(\frac{3}{4} \times \frac{1}{4}\right) \div 3$?

(a) $\frac{3}{16}$ (b) $\frac{6}{25}$
(c) $\frac{16}{25}$ (d) $\frac{1}{16}$

25. The H.C.F of three numbers is 24. If they are in the ratio 35 : 55 : 77, then the numbers are ________, ________ and ________
(a) 280, 440, 615
(b) 105, 175, 231
(c) 900, 1400, 1900
(d) 840, 1320, 1848

26. The product of the polynomials, $(3u^2v - 5uv^2)$ and $\left(\frac{1}{5}u^2 + \frac{1}{5}v^2\right)$ is
(a) $\frac{3}{5}u^4v - u^3v^2 - uv^4 + \frac{3}{5}u^2v^3$
(b) $\frac{u^4v}{5} - 2uv^2 + u^2v^3 - \frac{5uv^4}{3}$
(c) $\frac{3u^4v}{5} - 4v^2 + 4u^2v^3 - \frac{5uv^4}{3}$
(d) $\frac{3u^4v}{5} - u^3v^2 + u^2v^3 - 5uv^4$

27. Sohan was putting covers on his note books. He put one fourth of the covers on Monday. He put another on fourth on Tuesday and the remaining on Wednesday. What fraction of the covers did he put on Wednesday ?

(a) $\frac{1}{4}$ (b) $\frac{1}{2}$
(c) $\frac{3}{4}$ (d) $\frac{2}{5}$

28. Namita travels 20km 50m everyday. Out of this she travels 10 km 200 m by bus and the rest by auto. How much distance does she travel by auto ?
(a) 7.326 km (b) 9.850 km
(c) 11.260 km (d) 12.540 km

29. The ratio of the heights of A and B is 4 : 3. If B is 1.2 m tall, then the height of A is.
(a) 0.9 m (b) 1.8 m
(c) 1.6 m (d) None of these

Space for Rough Work

30. 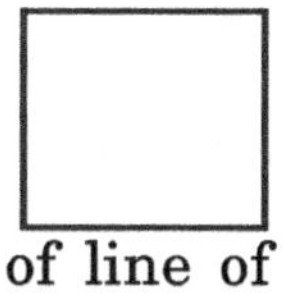

The number of line of symmetries that the given figure have :

(a) 4 (b) 2
(c) 3 (d) 1

31. The length of a rectangle is $\frac{6}{5}$th of its breadth. If its perimeter is 132 m, its area will be ______.

(a) 1,080 m^2 (b) 640 m^2
(c) 1,620 m^2 (d) 2,160 m^2

32. The measure of an angle is $\frac{4}{5}$ times of its complement. Find the angle.

(a) 40° (b) 50°
(c) 60° (d) 70°

33. The difference of L.C.M. and H.C.F. of the numbers 40,240 and 480 is equal to twice a number. Find the number.

(a) 340 (b) 440
(c) 220 (d) 880

34. The number 45682 rounded off the nearest hundred is ____.

(a) 40000 (b) 45,700
(c) 46,000 (d) 45,000

35. A piece of wire $\frac{7}{8}$ metre long broke into two pieces. One piece was $\frac{1}{4}$ metre long. The length of other piece is.

(a) $\frac{1}{4}$m (b) $\frac{3}{4}$m
(c) $\frac{6}{8}$m (d) $\frac{5}{8}$m

36. Read the table and fill in the blanks with the value of A, B and C.

Time	Distance travel by Karan	Distance travel by Kriti
2 hrs	8 km	6 km
1 hr	4 km	B
4 hrs	A	C

(a) A = 16 km; B = 6 km; C = 12 km
(b) A = 20 km; B = 3 km; C = 12 km
(c) A = 16 km; B = 3 km; C = 12 km
(d) A = 16 km; B = 3 km; C = 14 km

37. The temperature dropped 15 degrees in the last 30 days. If the rate of temperature drop remains the same, how many degrees will the temperature drop in the next ten days ?

(a) 5 (b) 10
(c) 15 (d) 18

DIRECTIONS (Qs. 38 to 40) : Read the passage(s) given below and answer the questions that follow.

Passage

- A combination of locks requires 3 numbers to open
- The second number is 2d + 5 greater than the first number.
- The third number is 3d – 20 less than the second number.

Space for Rough Work

• The sum of the three numbers is 10d + 9.

38. The first number is
   (a) 3d – 11 (b) 2d + 19
   (c) 3d – 7 (d) 5d – 11

39. Sum of first and third number is
   (a) 5d + 11 (b) 3d + 7
   (c) 5d – 11 (d) 6d + 5

40. Algebraic expression for clue number obtained in second clue
   (a) Second number = First number + 2d + 5
   (b) Second number = First number – (2d + 5)
   (c) First number = Second number + 2d + 5
   (d) None of these

   Choose the correct algebraic expression for the second number

41. In the adjoining figure which fraction of the whole is represented by the shaded portion ?

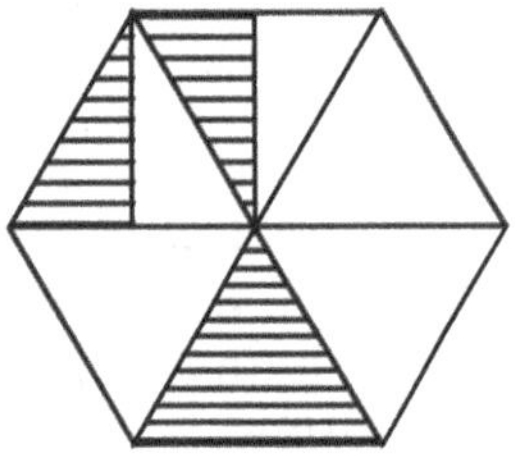

   (a) $\frac{3}{12}$ (b) $\frac{1}{4}$
   (c) $\frac{1}{3}$ (d) $\frac{3}{8}$

42. x% of y + y% of x =
   (a) 3% of xy
   (b) 2% of xy
   (c) 5% of xy
   (d) 1% of xy

43. Find the remaining part of the whole number on subtracting $\frac{5}{6}$ from the smallest whole number other than 0.
   (a) 0 (b) $\frac{2}{3}$
   (c) $\frac{1}{6}$ (d) $\frac{2}{6}$

44. When a number is divided by 125, the remainder is 82. When the same number is divided by 25, the remainder will be
   (a) 8 (b) 9
   (c) 6 (d) 7

45. Consider the following statements.
   (i) If L.C.M. of two numbers 6 and 8 is 24, then their H.C.F. is 2.
   (ii) First number × second number = L.C.M × H.C.F

   Which of the above statement(s) is /are correct?
   (a) Only (i)
   (b) Only (ii)
   (c) Both (i) and (ii)
   (d) Neither (i) nor (ii)

46. The average speed of a truck is 80 km/hr, the total distance covered in t hours is 240 km, then t is ....
   (a) 3 hours (b) 4 hours
   (c) $\frac{1}{2}$ hours (d) $4\frac{1}{2}$ hours

Space for Rough Work

47. First, second and the third terms of a proportion are 5, 120 and 40. Then the fourth term is
(a) 89 (b) 480
(c) 960 (d) 98

DIRECTIONS (Qs. 48 to 50): Following pictograph represents some surnames of people listed in the telephone directory of a city.

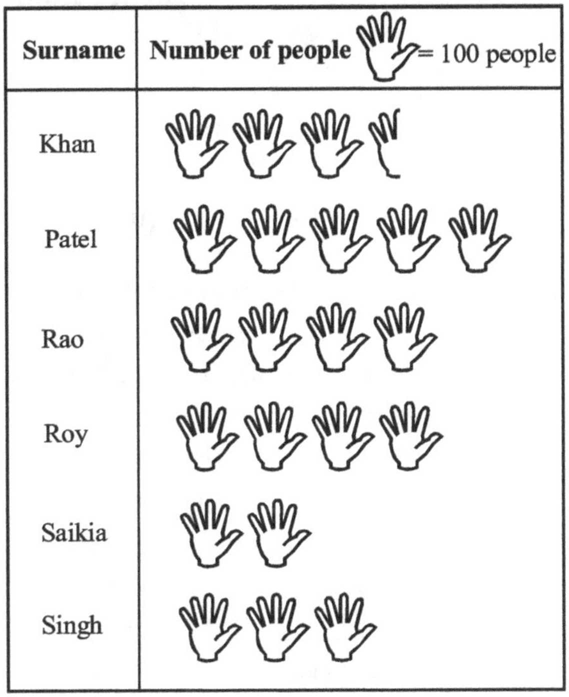

Observe the pictograph and answer the following questions:

48. How many people have surname 'Roy'?
(a) 400
(b) 500
(c) 300
(d) 450

49. Which surname appears the maximum number of times in the telephone directory?
(a) Roy
(b) Patel
(c) Khan
(d) Rao

50. Which two surnames appear an equal number of times?
(a) Singh, Roy
(b) Khan, Singh
(c) Patel, Khan
(d) Rao, Roy

Space for Rough Work

OLYMPIAD

Mock Test 2

Name : ________ **Max. Marks : 50**

Number of Questions : 50 **Time : 2 Hours**

There is no negative marking in the test.

1. If 63.3605 = 6A + 3B + 3C + 6D + 5E, then the value of 4A + 7B + 6C + D + 3E is
   (a) 47.6003 (b) 4.7603
   (c) 147.6003 (d) 47.603

2. Consider the following statements,
   Statement 1: Whole numbers and fractional numbers both can be represented on the number line.
   Statement 2: Only whole numbers can be represented on the number line.
   Which one of the following options is correct about the above statement?
   (a) Statement 1 is true and 2 is false
   (b) Statement 1 is false and 2 is true
   (c) Both statements are false
   (d) Both statements are true

3. Simplify the (34 + 20) × 2 and find the multiplicative inverse of the resulting simplification.
   (a) $\frac{2}{108}$ (b) $\frac{1}{108}$
   (c) $\frac{3}{108}$ (d) All of these

4. A number when divided by the sum of 555 and 445 given two times their difference as quotient and 30 as remainder. The number is
   (a) 220030 (b) 22030
   (c) 1220 (d) 1250

5. Find the missing length of the following figure.

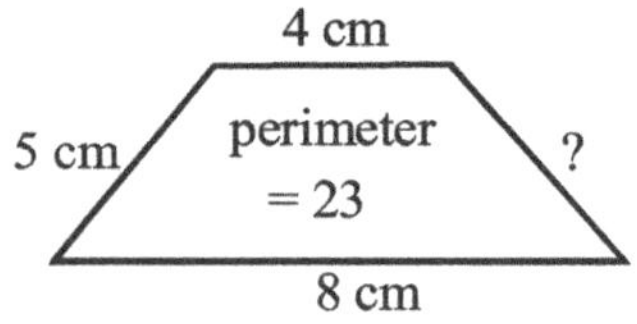

   (a) 6 cm (b) 4 cm
   (c) 2 cm (d) 5 cm

Space for Rough Work

6. If $a = 3, b = 5, c = b - a$, then which of the following expressions represent 10 ?
   (a) (a + c) × b (b) (a + b) – c
   (c) (b + c) + a (d) (a – b) + c
7. Express 54 km/h in metre/second.
   (a) 7 (b) 9 (c) 15 (d) 27
8. Add the following expression, 6x – 3by + 4cz, 7by – 8ax – 5cz and 9cz – 2by + 2ax?
   (a) x – 2by + 8cz – 6ax
   (b) 6x + by + 8cz – 6ax
   (c) 6x + 2by + 8cz – 6ax
   (d) All of these
9. In the given measure, measure of ∠b and ∠x are

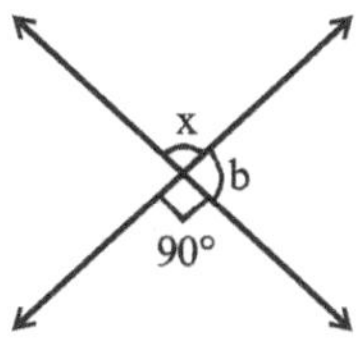

   (a) ∠x = 90°, ∠b = 60°
   (b) ∠x = 90°, ∠b = 30°
   (c) ∠x = 90°, ∠b = 90°
   (d) ∠x = 90°, ∠b = 180°
10. The ratio of the number of sides of a square to the number of edges of a cube is
   (a) 1 : 2 (b) 3 : 2
   (c) 4 : 1 (d) 1 : 3
11. In a box, the ratio of red marbles to blue marbles is 7 : 4. Which of the following could be the total number of marbles in the box?
   (a) 18 (b) 19
   (c) 21 (d) 22
12. Three tankers contain 403 litres, 434 litres and 465 litres of diesel, respectively. The maximum capacity of a container that can measure the diesel of the three containers exact number of times is.
   (a) 31 litres
   (b) 27 litres
   (c) 42 litres
   (d) 62 litres
13. Sarita bought $\frac{2}{5}$ metre of ribbon and Lalita $\frac{3}{4}$ metre of ribbon. What was the total length of the ribbon they bought?
   (a) $1\frac{3}{20}$ m
   (b) $2\frac{1}{20}$ m
   (c) $1\frac{1}{20}$ m
   (d) $3\frac{5}{20}$ m

Space for Rough Work

14. Consider the statement: Ratio of breadth and length of a hall is 2 : 5. Complete the following table that shows some possible breadths and lengths of the hall.

Breadth of the hall in metres	10	A	40
Length of the hall in metres	25	50	B

(a) A = 20; B = 100

(b) A = 50; B = 120

(c) A = 20; B = 80

(d) A = 10; B = 50

15. Read the following statements carefully and choose the correct option.

(i) : On the average, John uses 12.5 litres of petrol a day, then in 2 weeks he uses 180 litres of petrol.

(ii): A motorist travelled 204 km in 4 hours, then his average speed is 51 km/hr.

(a) (i) is true only
(b) (ii) is true only
(c) Both (i) and (ii) are true
(d) Neither (i) nor (ii) is true

16. Find the area of shaded portion if radii of inner and outer circle are 210 mm and 224 mm respectively.

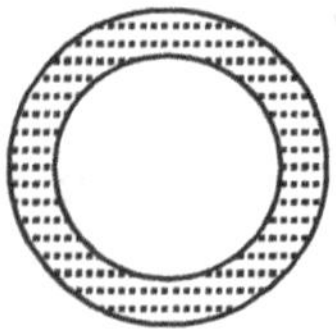

(a) 19096 sq. mm
(b) 47040 sq. mm
(c) 13860 sq. mm
(d) 21624 sq. mm

17. Given below a procedure to make a bar graph.

Choose the correct order of steps by choosing the correct option.

Step (A) Draw and label the scale on the vertical and horizontal axis.

Step (B) Draw bars of equal widths from the zero of the horizontal scale and leave the same amount of space between bars.

Step (C) Use the data from the table to choose an appropriate scale.

Step (D) List the each item and locate the points on the graph.

(a) ABCD
(b) CBAD
(c) CADB
(d) CABD

Space for Rough Work

18. Subtract $\frac{2}{5}$ from $\frac{5}{7}$.

(a) $\frac{11}{35}$ (b) $\frac{3}{7}$

(c) $\frac{7}{5}$ (d) $\frac{35}{11}$

19. The expression $10(a + 3) - 2a = 18 + 3a$ is true for how many values of a.

(a) 2 (b) 3

(c) 0 (d) 1

20. Which of the following figures represent equivalent fractions ?

(a) 

(b) 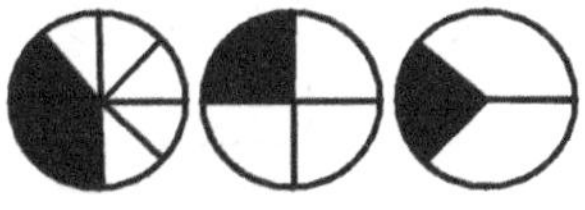

(c) 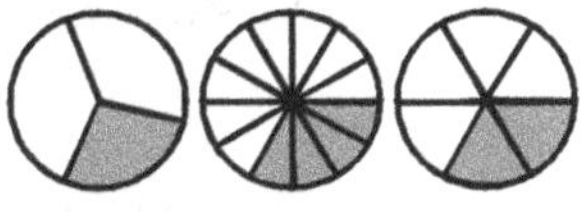

(d) 

21. What is the missing term in the following product?
$(2a^3-3)(5a^3-2) = 10a^6 +$ ________ $+ 6$

(a) $16a^3$ (b) $-16a^3$

(c) $19a^3$ (d) $-19a^3$

22. Choose the correct option whether the statements are true or false.

(i) 0 is a solution of the equation $x + 1 = 0$

(ii) The equation $x + 1 = 0$ and $2x + 2 = 0$ have the same solution.

(iii) If m is a whole number, then 2m denotes a multiple of 2.

(a) FFT (b) FTT

(c) TFT (d) TTF

23. If a bus travels 160 km in 4 hours and a train travels 320 km in 5 hours at uniform speeds, then the ratio of the distances travelled by them in one hour is

(a) 1 : 2 (b) 4 : 5

(c) 5 : 8 (d) 8 : 5

24. Naina was given $1\frac{1}{2}$ piece of cake and Najma was given $1\frac{1}{3}$ piece of cake. Find the total amount of cake given to both of them.

(a) $2\frac{5}{6}$ piece (b) $3\frac{1}{4}$ piece

(c) $7\frac{1}{3}$ piece (d) $2\frac{2}{7}$ piece

Space for Rough Work

DIRECTION (Q. 25) : Match Column-I with Column-II and select the correct answer using the codes given below the columns.

25.

Column-I	Column-II
(A) $\frac{2}{5}\%$ as a decimal form	(p) 4.5
(B) 25% of 75 is	(q) 0.03
(C) Average of first eight natural numbers	(r) 18.75
(D) $\frac{135}{45}\%$ as decimal form is	(s) 0.004

(a) A → s; B → r, C → p; D → q
(b) A → r; B → p, C → q; D → s
(c) A → s; B → r, C → q; D → p
(d) A → q; B → s, C → p; D → r

26. The Bar graph shows the sale of maths books in a bookshop for the first six months.

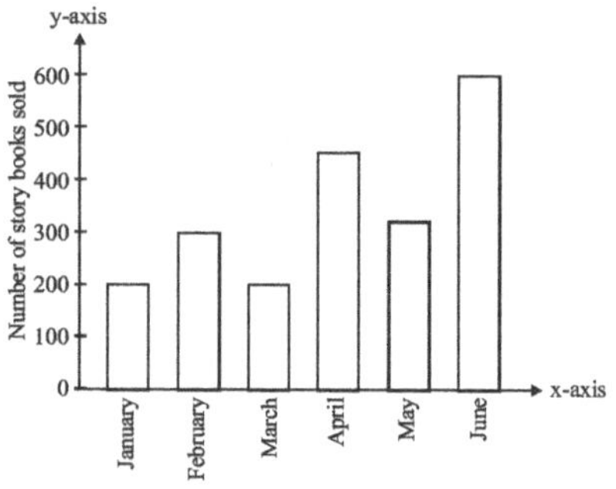

In which month was the sale of maths books 75% of the sale of books in June?
(a) March
(b) April
(c) May
(d) February

27. What number should replace the question mark ?

(a) 10878 (b) 10899
(c) 10879 (d) 12879

28.

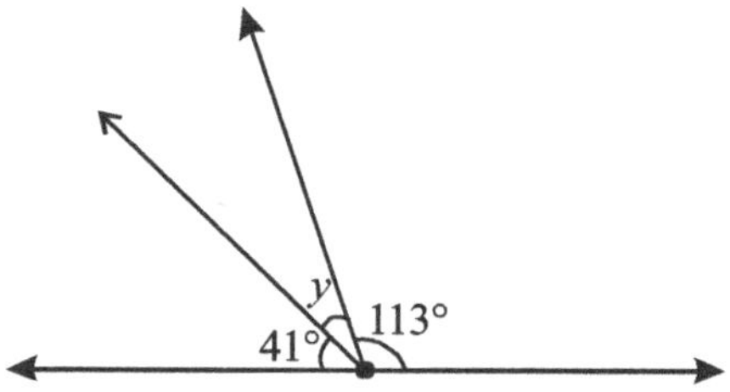

Find the value of angle y in the above figure.
(a) 26° (b) 39°
(c) 47° (d) 53°

29. At 4:20, what is the type of angle is formed between the two hands of the clock ?
(a) An obtuse angle
(b) An acute angle
(c) A right angle
(d) A straight angle

Space for Rough Work

30. The sum of two numbers is 19 and one of the numbers is one more than twice the other. Represent this statement in the form of an equation using variable x.
(a) $x(2x+1)=19$
(b) $x+(2x+1)=19$
(c) $x+(2x-1)=19$
(d) $x \div (2x-1)=19$

31. Write a pair of fractions whose sum is $\frac{7}{11}$ and difference is $\frac{2}{11}$.
(a) $\frac{3}{11}$ and $\frac{4}{11}$ (b) $\frac{9}{22}$ and $\frac{5}{22}$
(c) $\frac{2}{11}$ and $\frac{5}{11}$ (d) $\frac{5}{22}$ and $\frac{7}{22}$

32. In the given figures which of the following is a regular polygon?

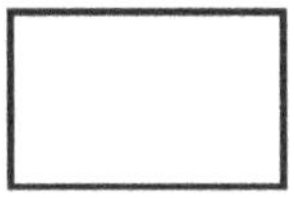

(i)

(ii)

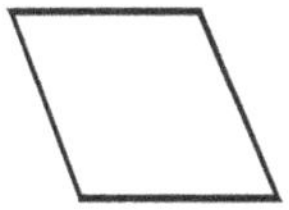

(iii)

(iv)

(a) (i) (b) (ii)
(c) (iii) (d) (iv)

33. Multiply,
$(a^2+ab+b^2)(a^2-ab-b^2)$
(a) $a^4-a^2b^2-2ab^3-b^4$
(b) $6a^2b-3ab+10a-25$
(c) $5a-3a^2+6$
(d) All of these

34. In a garden, the ratio of the number of children to the number of women is 9 : 2. If there are 84 more children than women then find the number of children in the garden.
(a) 108 (b) 120
(c) 156 (d) 182

35. Which of the following words will read the same when placed in front of the horizontal mirror?
(a) HIDE (b) CAKE
(c) SOON (d) SOUR

36. Gorang purchased 2 kg 280 g apples, 3 kg 375g bananas, 225 g grapes and 5 kg 385 g oranges. Find the total weight of fruits purchased by Gorang in kg.
(a) 11.575 kg
(b) 11.265 kg
(c) 13.265 kg
(d) 15.265 kg

37. If a bicycle wheel has 48 spokes, then the angle between a pair of two consecutive spokes is
(a) $\left(5\frac{1}{2}\right)^\circ$ (b) $\left(7\frac{1}{2}\right)^\circ$
(c) $\left(\frac{2}{11}\right)^\circ$ (d) $\left(\frac{2}{15}\right)^\circ$

Space for Rough Work

DIRECTIONS (Qs. 38 to 40): Read the passage given below and answer the question that follows:

Passage

Read the information given below carefully and answer the questions that follows.

In the national park there is a pond whose water level is monitored by a scale as shown below

38. The maximum water level of the pond is 1 m. In the summer the level reduced by $\frac{2}{5}$ m. Thus, ______ is the fraction of the water level in the pond in the summer.

(a) $\frac{1}{5}$ (b) $\frac{3}{5}$

(c) $\frac{7}{5}$ (d) $\frac{5}{2}$

39. Which of the following represents the correct representation of the fraction obtained above?

(a) 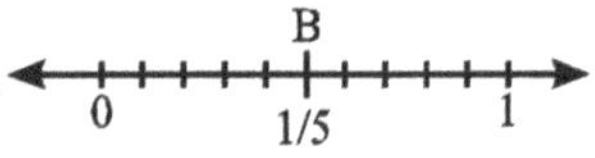

(b) 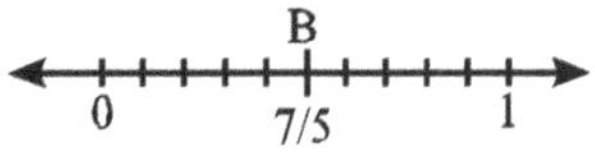

(c) 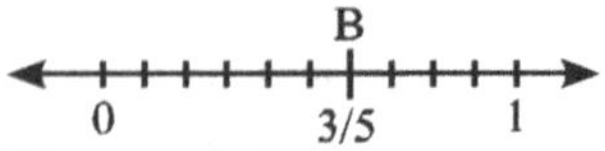

(d) None of these

40. The level of water in the pond went up by $\frac{1}{5}$ m from the point B due to rain. So, ________ is the fraction of the water level in the pond in the rainy season.

(a) $\frac{5}{4}$ (b) $\frac{4}{5}$ (c) $\frac{6}{5}$ (d) $\frac{5}{6}$

41. What number comes next in the sequence below?

3624, 4363, 3644, 4563, 3664, ?

(a) 4763 (b) 3763

(c) 3624 (d) 6763

42. The perimeter of rectangular garden is 70 m. If the length is 18 m, find its breadth.

(a) 10 m (b) 12 m

(c) 14 m (d) 17 m

43. How many triangles can be seen in this drawing?

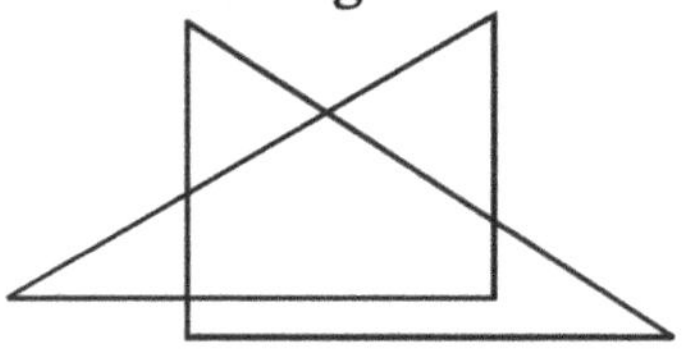

(a) 3 (b) 5

(c) 6 (d) 7

Space for Rough Work

44. In a quadrilateral ABCD, $\angle A + \angle C = 180°$ then $\angle B + \angle D =$
(a) 360° (b) 100°
(c) 180° (d) 80°

45. The H.C.F of three numbers is 24. If they are in the ratio 35 : 55 : 77, then the numbers are _________, _________ and _________
(a) 280, 440, 615
(b) 105, 175, 231
(c) 900, 1400, 1900
(d) 840, 1320, 1848

46. Floor of a room measures 4.5 metres × 3 metres. Find the minimum number of complete square marble slabs to equal size required to cover the entire floor.
(a) 5 (b) 6
(c) 7 (d) 8

47. The sum of two integers is 47. If one of the integers is –24, find the other.
(a) –46 (b) 65
(c) 71 (d) –71

48. The marks (out of 10) obtained by 28 students in a Mathematics test are listed as below:
8, 1, 2, 6, 5, 5, 0, 1, 9, 7, 8, 0, 5, 8, 3, 0, 8, 10, 10, 3, 4, 8, 7, 8, 9, 2, 0, 5
The number of students who obtained marks more than or equal to 5 is
(a) 13 (b) 15
(c) 16 (d) 17

49. Cost of fencing around a square field is ₹12000. If the cost of fencing per metre is ₹30, find the area of the square field.
(a) 10000 sq. m.
(b) 15000 sq. m.
(c) 20000 sq. m.
(d) 25000 sq. m

50. The line plot below shows how students scored on last week's maths test.

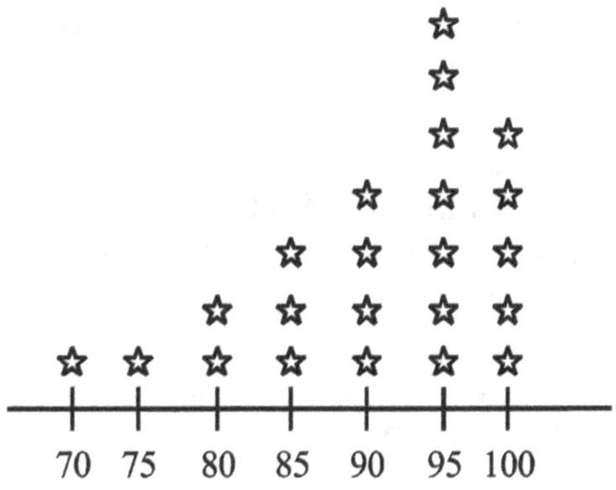

KEY : ☆ = 1 student
How many students scored 95 or higher on the test ?
(a) 5 students (b) 7 students
(c) 12 students (d) 16 students

Space for Rough Work

OLYMPIAD

Mock Test 3

Name : ________ **Max. Marks : 50**

Number of Questions : 50 **Time : 2 Hours**

There is no negative marking in the test.

1. Allen gives Mike 123 millions and after a month, Mike returns him 67,735. How much more money Mike should return him to equal the amount?
   (a) 122 millions + 932 thousands + 265
   (b) 12 lakhs + 93 thousands + 265
   (c) 12 crores + 29 lakhs + 32 thousands + 265
   (d) Both (a) and (c)

2. A figure is formed by putting two squares one on the other as shown below.

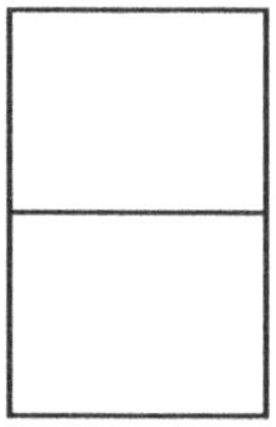

   If the length of each side of the two squares is 8 cm, then the perimeter of the formed figure is
   (a) 56 cm (b) 64 cm
   (c) 32 cm (d) 48 cm

3. If one-third of y is subtracted from its half find the result.
   (a) $\frac{-y}{6}$ (b) $\frac{y}{5}$
   (c) $\frac{y}{6}$ (d) $\frac{2y}{6}$

4. Add $\frac{2}{5}$ and $\frac{3}{7}$.
   (a) $\frac{21}{29}$ (b) $\frac{31}{37}$ (c) $\frac{29}{35}$ (d) $\frac{29}{37}$

5. If x, y and z are three numbers such that L.C.M. (x, y) = y and L.C.M. (y, z) = z, then the L.C.M. of x, y, z is
   (a) x (b) y
   (c) z (d) $\frac{x+y+z}{3}$

Space for Rough Work

6. What is the multiplicative inverse of –15 ?

(a) $\frac{1}{15}$ (b) $\frac{2}{15}$

(c) $\frac{3}{15}$ (d) $-\frac{1}{15}$

7. Riya spent ₹34.60 on purchasing a basket. How much money is left if she had ₹100?

(a) ₹65.40 (b) ₹10.50

(c) ₹65.10 (d) ₹50.75

8. Find the area of the shaded portion in the figure.

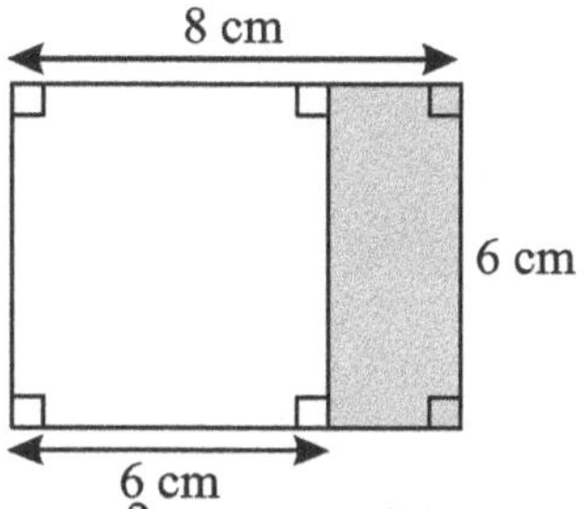

(a) 12 cm^2 (b) 20 cm^2

(c) 36 cm^2 (d) 48 cm^2

9. Flights to Mumbai leave every 5 hours. At the information counter I learnt that the flight took off 25 min before. If the time now is 10 : 45 a.m, what is the time for the next flight?

(a) 4 : 10 a.m. (b) 2 : 20 a.m.

(c) 4 : 20 p.m. (d) 3 : 20 p.m.

10. Read the following statements carefully and choose the correct option.

(i) Ratios 2:4 and 12:24 are equivalent ratios.

(ii) A team won 6 games out of 10. The ratio of the games won to the games lost is 3:2.

(a) Only (i) is true.

(b) Only (ii) is true.

(c) Both (i) and (ii) are true.

(d) Neither (i) nor (ii) is true.

11. The perimeter of a square and an equilateral triangle are same. If the side of an equilateral triangle is 8 cm, what is the area of the square?

(a) 16 sq. cm (b) 8 sq. cm

(c) 24 sq. cm (d) 36 sq. cm

12. If $\frac{3}{5}$ of the property costs ₹15,000 what is the cost of $\frac{1}{2}$ of it ?

(a) ₹7500 (b) ₹12500

(c) ₹25000 (d) ₹10000

13. Which shape has only one line of symmetry?

(a) 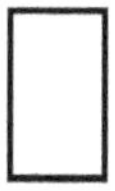 (b) 

(c) 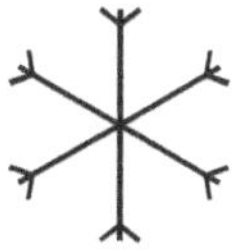 (d) 

Space for Rough Work

14. Five square flower beds each of size 2 m dug on a piece of land 15 m long and 10 m wide. Find the area of the remaining part of land.
(a) 170 sq.m (b) 210 sq.m
(c) 230 sq.m (d) 130 sq.m

15. Rani had ₹48.50. She bought an ice cream for ₹20.50 and a chocolate for ₹10.50. Find the amount left with her.
(a) ₹20.75 (b) ₹10.25
(c) ₹17.50 (d) ₹23.25

16. Divide ₹600 among Rehana and Rashmi in the ratio of 2 : 3.
(a) ₹220, ₹380 (b) ₹240, ₹360
(c) ₹120, ₹480 (d) ₹150, ₹450

17. Nandini's house is $\frac{9}{10}$ km from her school. She walked some distance and then took a bus for $\frac{1}{2}$ km to reach the school. She walked for:
(a) $\frac{2}{5}$ km (b) $\frac{1}{7}$ km
(c) $\frac{7}{8}$ km (d) $\frac{4}{5}$ km

18. Convert $\frac{3}{12}$ into a decimal fraction.
(a) 3.12 (b) 0.75
(c) 0.25 (d) 1.25

19. Read the following statements carefully and choose the correct option.
(i) Distance travelled by car A at the speed of 52 km/hr in 3 hours is 156 km/hr.
(ii) Distance travelled by car B at the speed of 58 km/hr in 3 hours is 174 km/hr.
(a) Only (i) is true
(b) Only (ii) is true
(c) Both (i) and (ii) are true
(d) Neither (i) nor (ii) is true

20. In the given figure AB = BC and AD = BD = DC.
The number of isosceles triangles in the figure is

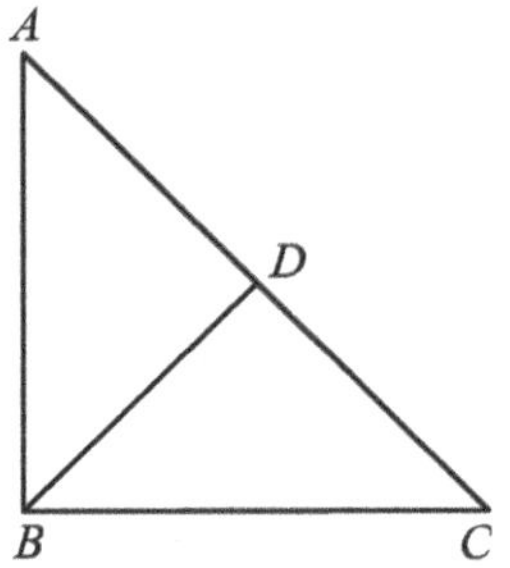

(a) 1 (b) 2
(c) 3 (d) 4

21. The measure of an angle is $\frac{4}{5}$ times its supplement. Find the angle.
(a) 100° (b) 80°
(c) 110° (d) 70°

Space for Rough Work

22. Mother wants to divide ₹56 among her daughters Parul and Priyam in the ratio of their ages. If Parul is 9 years old and Priyam is 15 years old, find the amount each one of these get.
(a) ₹25, ₹31 (b) ₹21, ₹35
(c) ₹16, ₹40 (d) ₹20, ₹36

23. Which of the following statements is/are correct?
(1) The diagonals of a rectangle are perpendicular.
(2) The diagonals of a rhombus are equal.
(3) Every square is a rhombus.
(4) None of these
(a) only 1 (b) only 3
(c) 1 and 2 (d) all 1, 2, and 3

24. A and B are two positive integers such that AB = 64. Which of the following is not the correct value of A + B?
(a) 65 (b) 16
(c) 35 (d) 20

25. 10 – x means
(a) 10 is subtracted x times
(b) x is subtracted 10 times
(c) x is subtracted from 10
(d) 10 is subtracted from x

26. In the given figure, line AB || line CD, m∠ABF = 45° and m∠CFD = 110° then find m ∠FDC

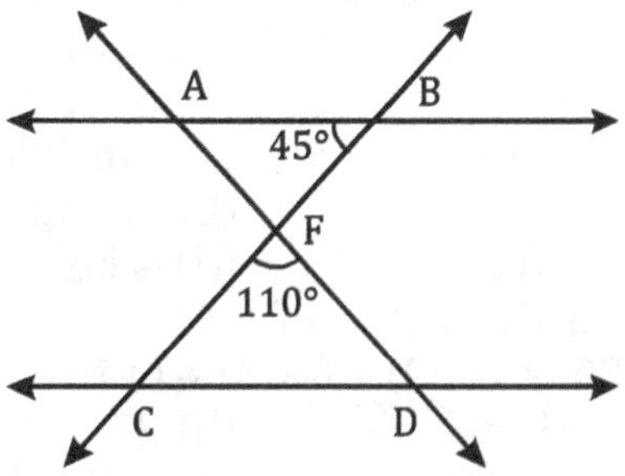

(a) 45° (b) 25°
(c) 35° (d) 30°

27. Samson travelled 16.52 km by bus, 31.46 km by auto rickshaw and walked 1.45 km. Find the total distance covered by him.
(a) 49.430 km
(b) 39.430 km
(c) 47.430 km
(d) 54.760 km

28. A taxi driver filled his car petrol tank with 40 litres of petrol on Monday. The next day, he filled the tank with 50 litres of petrol. If the petrol costs ₹44 per litre, how much did he spend in all on petrol?
(a) ₹4240 (b) ₹3960
(c) ₹2620 (d) ₹5130

29. The cost of 500 kg of wheat is ₹1756. Find the cost of 125 kg of such wheat?
(a) ₹439 (b) ₹450
(c) ₹480 (d) All of these

Space for Rough Work

30. A box of medicine contains 2,00,000 tablets each weighing 20 mg. What is the total weight of all the tablets in the box in gram and in kilogram?
(a) 2 kg (b) 2.5 kg
(c) 3.5 kg (d) 4 kg

31. Find the value of
$(-30) + (-20) + (-63) + (+75) + (65)$.
(a) 21 (b) 27
(c) 25 (d) – 27

32. The first, third and fourth terms of a proportion are 18, 27 and 36 respectively. Find the second term.
(a) 72 (b) 24
(c) 54 (d) 9

33. Which of the following letters have both horizontal and vertical lines of symmetry?
(a) X (b) E
(c) M (d) K

34. Find the ratio of the shaded portion to the unshaded portion in figure.

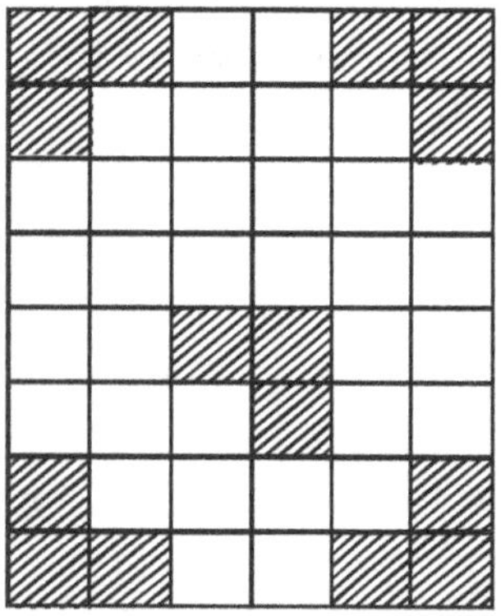

(a) 5 : 11 (b) 20 : 7
(c) 15 : 11 (d) 15 : 40

35. Find the value of $\angle a - \angle b$ in the adjoining figure.
(a) 50°
(b) 70°
(c) 10°
(d) 60°

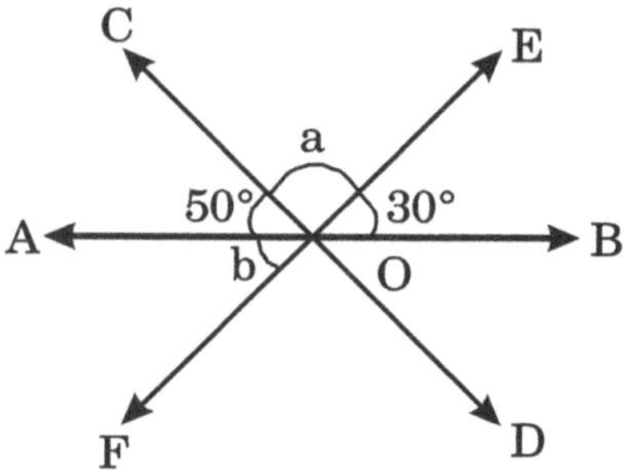

36. The number of times an observation is repeated in a data is called ______.
(a) Frequency
(b) Sample
(c) Pie chart
(d) None of these

37. Two buses travel to a place at 45 km/hr and 60 km/hr respectively. If the second bus takes $5\frac{1}{2}$ hrs less than the first for the journey, the length of the journey is
(a) 900 km
(b) 945 km
(c) 990 km
(d) 1350km

Space for Rough Work

DIRECTIONS (Qs. 38 to 40) : Read the passage(s) given below and answer the questions that follow.

Passage

Following is the arrangement of various rooms in a house.

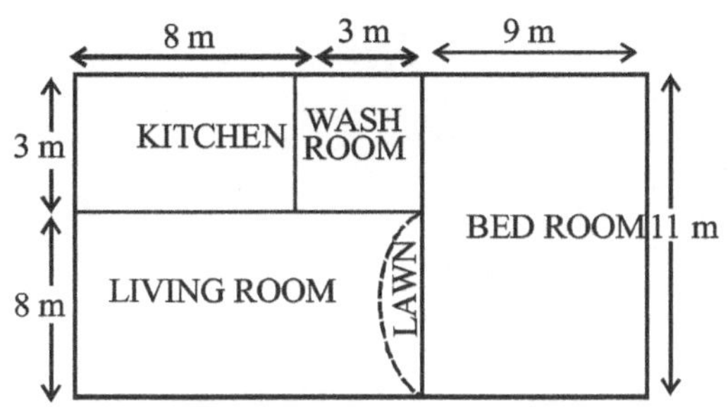

Answer the following questions.

38. Perimeter of floor of wash room is
    (a) 4 m (b) 3 m
    (c) 12 m (d) 7 m
39. Area of bed room is
    (a) 20 m^2
    (b) 99 m^2
    (c) 88 m^2
    (d) 72 m^2
40. If Mr. Verma wants to construct a lawn from the portion of living room then the perimeter of lawn is
    (a) 12 m (b) 5 m
    (c) 12.5 m (d) 5.12 m
41. Find L.C.M of 40, 48 and 45.
    (a) 560 (b) 720
    (c) 920 (d) 1000
42. By splitting the following figure into rectangles, find the area (units given are in cm).

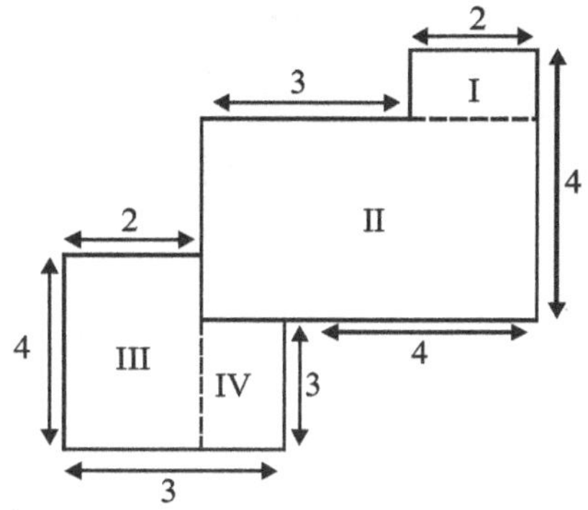

    (a) 19 sq. cm
    (b) 25 sq. cm
    (c) 28 sq. cm
    (d) 34 sq. cm
43. Fill up _______ with appropriate numeral.

$$\frac{3}{4} = \frac{21}{\square}$$

    (a) 48
    (b) 20
    (c) 16
    (d) 28

Space for Rough Work

Match Column-I with Column-II and select the correct answer using the codes given below the columns.

44. **Column-I** **Column-II**

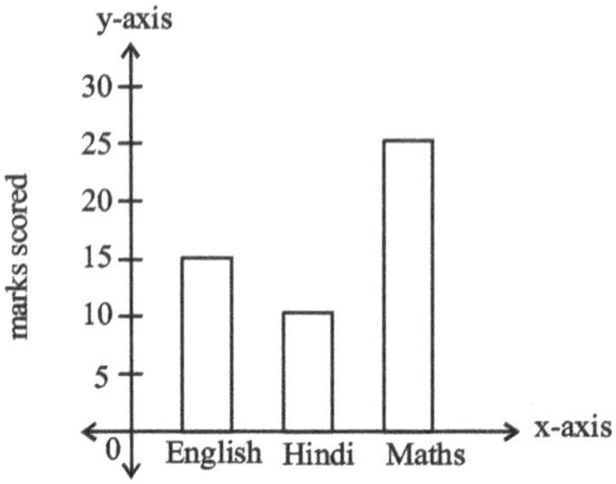

A.	The horizontal line in the graph is called	(i)	Maths
B.	The vertical line in the graph is called	(ii)	Hindi
C.	Highest marks are scored in the subject	(iii)	x-axis
D.	Least marks scored in the subject	(iv)	y-axis

(a) A → (iv); B → (iii); C → (ii); D → (i) (b) A → (iv); B → (iii); C → (i); D → (ii)

(c) A → (iii); B → (iv); C → (ii); D → (i) (d) A → (iii); B → (iv); C → (i); D → (ii)

45. In the adjoining figure, line P || line Q and line M and N are transversals. As per information in figure, find $m\angle a + m\angle b$.

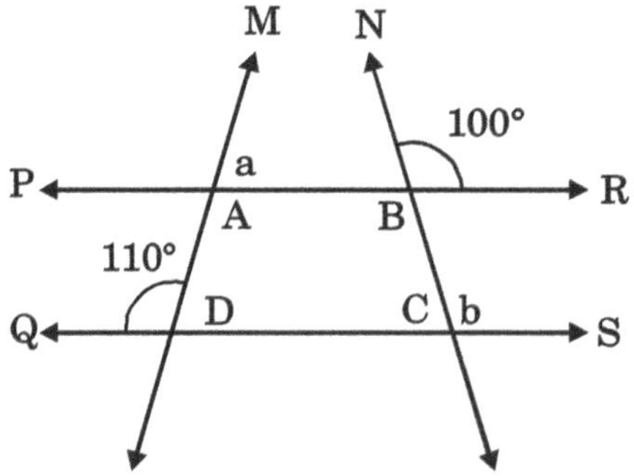

Space for Rough Work

(a) 225° (b) 90°
(c) 180° (d) 170°

46. An electric pole casts a shadow of length 20 m at a time when a tree 6 m high casts a shadow of length 8 metre. Find the height of the pole.
(a) 28 m (b) 21 m
(c) 18 m (d) 15 m

47. A bus travels 120 km in 3 hrs How long will it take to travel 360 km ?
(a) 11 hrs (b) 6 hrs
(c) 9 hrs (d) 8 hrs

DIRECTIONS (Qs. 48-50) : Read the passage(s) given below and answer the questions that follow.

Let us see what information do we get from the given pictograph made by Mr. Rai to show the number of cars passed on a road during a particular time interval.

1figure of car = 100 cars

48. How many cars passed through the road on Monday?
(a) 200 (b) 500
(c) 700 (d) 900

49. On which day maximum number of cars were passed?
(a) Monday (b) Tuesday
(c) Wednesday (d) Thursday

50. How many more cars passed on Monday in comparison with the number of cars passed on Tuesday?
(a) 100 (b) 150
(c) 200 (d) 300

Space for Rough Work

OLYMPIAD Mock Test 4

Name : ________ **Max. Marks : 50**

Number of Questions : 50 **Time : 2 Hours**

There is no negative marking in the test.

1. Find the product of $(2x + 4y)(3x - 2y)$.
   (a) $6x^2 + 8xy - 8y^2$ (b) $x^2 - 8xy - 8y^2$
   (c) $8x^2 - xy - 8y^2$ (d) All of these
2. The sum of two integers is – 396. If one of them is 64, determine the other.
   (a) –560 (b) –460
   (c) 460 (d) 540
3. Find the side of the square whose perimeter is 80 cm.
   (a) 20 cm (b) 30 cm
   (c) 32 cm (d) 40 cm
4. Which of the following statements is not true?
   (a) The HCF of two distinct prime numbers is 1
   (b) The HCF of two co-prime numbers is 1
   (c) The HCF of two consecutive even numbers is 2
   (d) The HCF of an even and an odd number is even.
5. The average speed of a truck is 80 km/hr, the total distance covered in t hours is 240 km, then t is ....
   .
   (a) 3 hours (b) 4 hours
   (c) $\frac{1}{2}$ hours (d) $4\frac{1}{2}$ hours
6. Find the greatest number that will divide 328, 436 and 544 leaving remainder 7, 8 and 9 respectively.
   (a) 205 (b) 157
   (c) 107 (d) 207
7. Which of the following would come in place of the question mark (?) in the following letter number series ?
   1, 5, 7, 14, 18, 20, 40, 44, 46, ?
   (a) 48 (b) 50 (c) 52 (d) 92
8. Read the statements given below carefully and choose the correct answer.
   (i) If a = – 2 and b = 5 then out of 2a + 3b, 2b – a, a – b and $a^2 - b^2$ only $a^2 - b^2$ has the least value.

Space for Rough Work

(ii) Anshi celebrated her 16th birthday x years ago. She would be (16 + x + z) years old in z year time.
(a) (i) is true while (ii) is false.
(b) (i) is false while (ii) is true.
(c) (i) and (ii), both are true.
(d) (i) and (ii), both are false.

9. Smallest four digit number is divided by smallest prime number. Find the predecessor of the quotient.
(a) 500 (b) 499
(c) 501 (d) 599

10. Find the value of $-12 -[(-15) + (-2) -3]$.
(a) 14 (b) −8 (c) 10 (d) 8

11. The length, breadth and height of a room are 8 m 25 cm, 6 m 75 cm and 4 m 50 cm, respectively. Determine the longest tape which can measure the three dimensions of the room exactly.
(a) 12 cm (b) 75 cm
(c) 90 cm (d) 140 cm

12. An office opens at 9.00 a.m. and closes at 5.30 p.m. With a lunch interval of 30 minutes, what is the ratio of lunch interval to the total period in the office?
(a) 1 : 19 (b) 2 : 19
(c) 1 : 17 (d) 2 : 17

13. A crate contains 400 eggs, 8 dozen eggs were found spoiled. Find the percentage of good eggs in the crate.
(a) 24% (b) 36%
(c) 52% (d) 76%

14. The greatest number which always divides the product of the predecessor and successor of an odd natural number other than 1, is
(a) 6 (b) 4 (c) 16 (d) 8

15. Range is defined as the difference between the ____ and _____ values of a data.
(a) lowest, mean
(b) highest, median
(c) lowest, highest
(d) highest, lowest

16. An animal shelter has 20 dogs, 25 cats, and 30 monkeys. What is the ratio of the number of monkeys to the number of cats to the number of dogs?
(a) 4:5:6 (b) 5:6:4
(c) 6:5:4 (d) 6:4:5

17. The perimeter of a rectangle is 36 cm. The measure of its length and breadth are natural numbers. How many such rectangles are possible ?
(a) 2 (b) 8 (c) 9 (d) 18

18. In the adjoining figure, A, B, C and D are mid points of PS, PQ, QR, RS respectively. The length and breadth of rectangle PQRS are 25 cm and 18 cm respectively. Find the area of shaded portion.

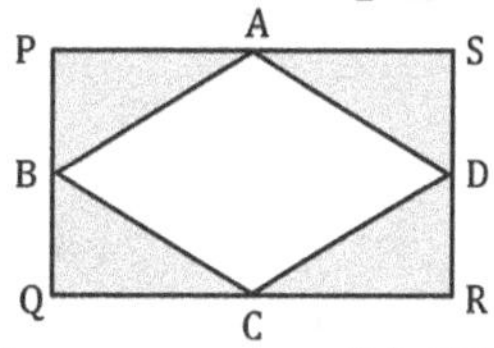

(a) 450 sq. cm (b) 112.5 sq. cm
(c) 350 sq. cm (d) 225 sq. cm

Space for Rough Work

19. In which subject did Rajeev obtain the highest percentage? Maths : 325 out 500, English : 240 out of 400, Geography : 84 out of 150, Science : 132 out of 200.
 (a) Maths (b) English
 (c) Science (d) Geography

20. A rectangular field is 90 m by 70 m. A man walks round it at the rate of 4 km per hour. What time will he take in making 5 rounds?
 (a) 20 minutes (b) 24 minutes
 (c) 34 minutes (d) 42 minutes

21. The number of angles in Fig. is

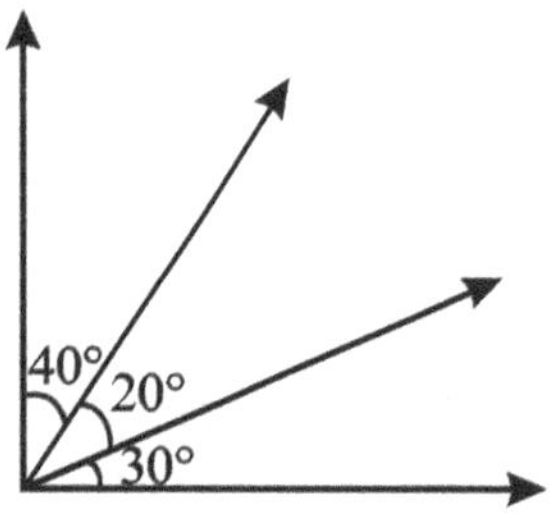

 (a) 3 (b) 4
 (c) 5 (d) 6

22. One of the angles of a triangle is equal to the sum of the other two. What is the angle?
 (a) 60° (b) 80°
 (c) 90° (d) 100°

23. Consider the following statements.
 (i) Every number is a factor of itself.
 (ii) Every number is a multiple of itself.

 Which statement is the correct?
 (a) Only (i)
 (b) Only (ii)
 (c) Both (i) and (ii)
 (d) Neither (i) nor (ii)

24. LCM of two numbers is 180. Then which of the following is not the HCF of the numbers?
 (a) 45 (b) 60
 (c) 75 (d) 90

25. Out of $-\frac{5}{11}, -\frac{5}{12}, -\frac{5}{17}$, which is the greatest.
 (a) $-\frac{5}{11}$ (b) $-\frac{5}{12}$
 (c) $-\frac{5}{17}$
 (d) Cannot be compared

26. From a square sheet of paper a circle of maximum possible size is cut. The area of the remaining portion is
 (a) Equal to $\frac{1}{4}$ the area of the circle.
 (b) Greater than $\frac{1}{4}$ the area of the circle
 (c) Less than $\frac{1}{4}$ the area of the circle
 (d) None of these

Space for Rough Work

27. The centroid divides the median in the ratio of ____.
(a) 3 : 1 (b) 2 : 1
(c) 1 : 2 (d) 1 : 1

28. Simplify : 80 –[20 – {175 ÷ 5 –(28 – 16 ÷ 4)÷ 6}]
(a) 96 (b) – 52
(c) 91 (d) 44

29. The age ratio of Peter and his father is 2 : 5. Find the age of Peter if his fathers age is 40 years?
(a) 17 (b) 16
(c) 18 (d) 19

30. Simplify: $2+2+\div\left\{2+2\div\left(2+\frac{2}{3}\right)\right\}$
(a) $\frac{13}{5}$ (b) $\frac{11}{5}$
(c) $\frac{30}{11}$ (d) $\frac{1}{5}$

31.

Column-I		Column-II
(A) The length and width of a tape are 2 m and 28 cm, ratio of length and breadth is	(p)	5 : 2
(B) Ratio of 60 hrs to 600 min is	(q)	6 : 1
(C) Simplest form of the ratio 125 : is	(r)	50 : 725
(D) In the word ENGLISH the ratio of number of consonants to number of vowels	(s)	5 : 1

(a) A – p; B – r; C – q; D – s (b) A – r; B – q; C – s; D – p
(c) A – q; B – p; C – r; D – s (d) A – s; B – r; C – p; D – q

32. Which of the following number is completely divisible by 6.
(a) 4535467 (b) 6979956 (c) 6978956 (d) None of these

33. The HCF and LCM of two numbers are 13 and 1989 respectively. If one of the numbers is 117, determine the other.
(a) 532 (b) 369 (c) 156 (d) 221

34. Divide 0.0211788 by 0.333
(a) 63.6 (b) 6.36 (c) 0.636 (d) 0.0636

35. Sachin purchased 50 dozen bananas for ₹ 150. Five dozen bananas could not be sold because they were rotten. At what price per dozen should Sachin sell the remaining bananas so that he makes a profit of 20%?
(a) ₹3.50 (b) ₹3.75 (c) ₹4 (d) ₹4.5

Space for Rough Work

36. Multiply 3a + 2b and 5a + 7b.
   (a) $6a^2 + 31ab + 9b^2$
   (b) $4a^2 + 26ab + 9b^2$
   (c) $21a^2 + 17ab + 49b^2$
   (d) $15a^2 + 31ab + 14b^2$

37. Which of the following would come in place of the question mark (?) in the following letter number series?

$\frac{1}{81}, \frac{1}{54}, \frac{1}{36}, \frac{1}{24}, ?$

   (a) $\frac{1}{52}$ (b) $\frac{1}{9}$
   (c) $\frac{1}{16}$ (d) $\frac{1}{18}$

38. A tile measures 10 cm × 10 cm. How many such tiles are required to cover a wall 4 m × 2.5 m?
   (a) 800 (b) 1000
   (c) 1120 (d) 1260

39. The perimeter of a circle is 44 cm. Find its area and diameter.
   (a) 17 cm^2 ; 7 cm
   (b) 154 cm^2 ; 14 cm
   (c) 117 cm^2 ; 22 cm
   (d) 17 cm^2 ; 24 cm

40. The area of the shaded face of the cuboid is 32 cm^2. Its height is 4 cm. What is its volume?

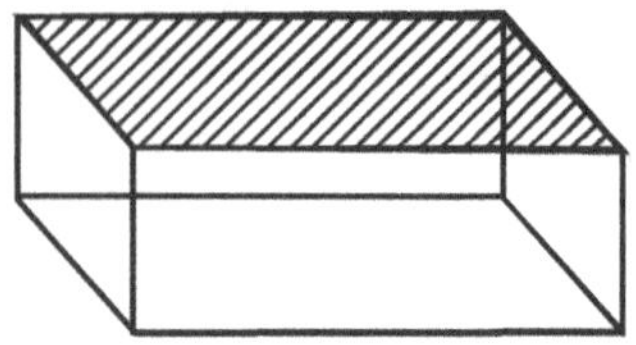

   (a) 28 cm^3 (b) 36 cm^3
   (c) 128 cm^3 (d) 136 cm^3

41. If A and B are different integers, both divisible by 5, then which of the following is not necessarily true?
   (a) (A + B) is divisible by 5.
   (b) (A + B) is divisible by 10.
   (c) (A – B) is divisible by 5.
   (d) $A^2 + B^2$ is divisible by 5.

42. A boy saves ₹4.65 daily. Find the least number of days in which he will be able to save an exact number of rupees
   (a) 20 (b) 22
   (c) 23 (d) 29

43. Denominator of a fraction is 6 greater than its numerator. If the sum of denominator and numerator is 16, find the fraction.
   (a) $\frac{5}{11}$ (b) $\frac{7}{13}$
   (c) $\frac{8}{14}$ (d) $\frac{2}{8}$

Space for Rough Work

44. First, second and third terms of a proportion are respectively 20, 18, 40. Find its fourth terms.
    (a) 72 (b) 36
    (c) 80 (d) 27

45. How many envelopes can be made out of a sheet of paper 125 cm by 85 cm supposing each envelope requires a piece of paper of size 17 cm by 5 cm?
    (a) 75 (b) 110
    (c) 125 (d) 206

46. Which of the following figure has 4 lines of symmetry?

(a) 

(b) 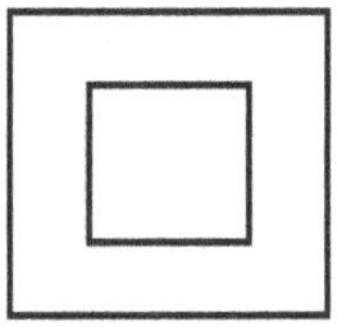

(c) 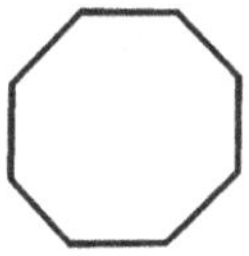

(d) 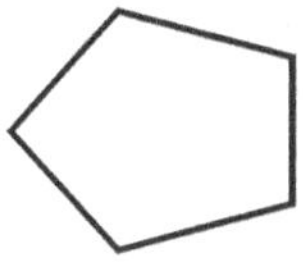

47. Average age of five children is 8 yrs. 4 months.
    If the average age of four children is 7 yrs. 10 months, the age of fifth child is__________.
    (a) 9 yrs. 8 months
    (b) 7 yrs. 5 months
    (c) 8 yrs. 6 months
    (d) 10 yrs. 4 months

DIRECTIONS (Qs. 48 to 50): The bar graph given below represents the circulation of newspaper in different languages in a city. Study bar graph and answer the following questions.

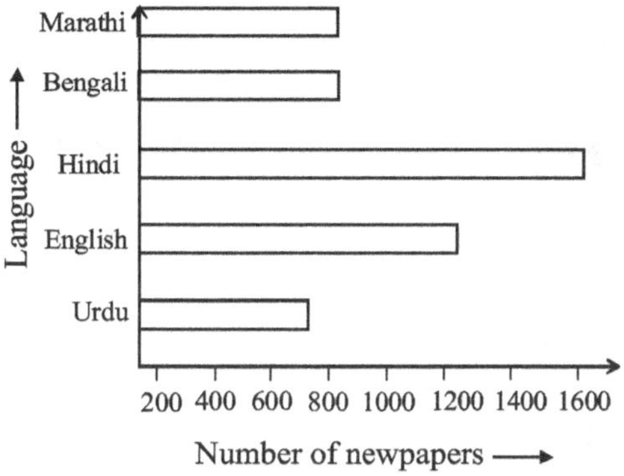

48. What is the circulation of English newspaper?
    (a) 5000 (b) 2000
    (c) 1200 (d) 4000

49. By how much is the circulation of newspaper in Hindi more than the newspaper in Bengali ?
    (a) 700 (b) 900
    (c) 1000 (d) 800

50. Name the two languages in which circulation of newspaper is the same
    (a) Marathi and Bengali
    (b) Marathi and Urdu
    (c) Hindi and English
    (d) Urdu and English

Space for Rough Work

OLYMPIAD

Mock Test 5

Name : _________ **Max. Marks : 50**

Number of Questions : 50 **Time : 2 Hours**

There is no negative marking in the test.

1. Subtract $4x^2y - 3xy + 5x$ from $10x^2y - 6xy + 15x - 25$?
   (a) $8x^3 + 2x^2 + 9x$
   (b) $6x^2y - 3xy + 10x - 25$
   (c) $5x - 3X^2 + 6$
   (d) All of these

2. Chinmay had ₹610000. He gave ₹87500 to Jyoti, ₹126380 to Javed and ₹350000 to John. How much money was left with him?
   (a) ₹56120 (b) ₹36120
   (c) ₹48120 (d) ₹46120

3. Solve $\left[\frac{3}{8}\right] \div \left[-\frac{24}{27}\right]$
   (a) $\frac{1}{3}$ (b) 1.33
   (c) $\frac{1}{9}$ (d) None of these

4. The number of students in three sections A, B and C of class VI in a school are 30, 35 and 40. Find the minimum number of books required for the class library for equal distribution in section A, B and C.
   (a) 720 (b) 840
   (c) 860 (d) 940

5. A vendor supplies 32 litres of milk to a hotel in the morning and 68 litres of milk in the evening. If the milk costs ₹15 per litre, how much money is due to the vendor per day?
   (a) ₹1900
   (b) ₹1750
   (c) ₹1500
   (d) ₹750

6. Ravi bought x cans of water at ₹1.50 each and y packets of biscuits at ₹2.70 each.

Space for Rough Work

Which of the following expressions shows the total amount Ravi paid, in ₹ ?

(a) $150x + 270y$
(b) $1.5x + 2.7y$
(c) $15x + 27y$
(d) $0.15x + 0.27y$

7. Subtract the sum of $\frac{5}{7}$ and $\frac{2}{3}$ from $2\frac{1}{2}$.

(a) $1\frac{5}{42}$ (b) $2\frac{2}{6}$
(c) $1\frac{3}{16}$ (d) $2\frac{5}{41}$

8. Two tankers contain 850 litres and 680 litres of petrol respectively. Find the minimum capacity of a container which can measure the petrol of either tanker in exact number of times.

(a) 170 litres (b) 210 litres
(c) 578 litres (d) 940 litres

9. Simplify $2\frac{1}{4}\times\frac{3}{14}\div1\frac{2}{7}$.

(a) $\frac{3}{8}$ (b) $\frac{4}{9}$
(c) $\frac{9}{7}$ (d) $\frac{3}{14}$

10. Two numbers are in the ratio 5 : 6. If the sum of the numbers is 132, find the numbers.

(a) 60, 72 (b) 32, 100
(c) 116, 16 (d) 87, 45

11. 23 thousandths more than four hundred ninety six is ____.

(a) 496.023
(b) 496.23
(c) 496.0023
(d) 496.00023

12. Which of the following is correct statement?

(a) Product of two negative numbers is negative.
(b) Sum of two positive numbers is negative.
(c) Division of a positive and negative number is negative.
(d) Subtraction of a negative and a positive number is definitely negative.

13. Decimal form of mixed fraction $7\frac{11}{13}$ is

(a) 7.2
(b) 7.84
(c) 6.2
(d) None of the above

Space for Rough Work

14. Fill the $\square$ with correct fraction :

$\square - \frac{3}{21} = \frac{5}{21}$.

(a) $\frac{7}{8}$ (b) $\frac{8}{21}$

(c) $\frac{8}{23}$ (d) $\frac{10}{41}$

15. The sum of the greatest and the least six digit numbers formed by the digits 2, 0, 4, 7, 6, 5 using each digit only once is :

(a) 1069987 (b) 969987

(c) 869987 (d) 769987

16. The greatest possible rate at which a man can walk 68 km, 102 km and 51 km in exact number of days is ________.

(a) 16 km (b) 15 km

(c) 14 km (d) 17 km

17. Raju bought a book for ₹46.50. He gave ₹100 to the shopkeeper. How much will he get back from the shopkeeper ?

(a) ₹67.75 (b) ₹53.50

(c) ₹41.25 (d) ₹26.75

18. The traffic lights at three different road crossings change after every 48 seconds, 72 seconds and 108 seconds respectively. If they change simultaneously at 7 a.m. after what time will they change again simultaneously?

(a) 9 min 14 sec (b) 5 min 23 sec

(c) 11 min 16 sec (d) 7 min 12 sec

19. The ratio of the income to the expenditure of a family is 7 : 6. Find the savings if the income is ₹21000.

(a) ₹3,000 (b) ₹7,000

(c) ₹18,000 (d) ₹20,000

20. Simplify $(-12a^3b + 18a^2b^2 - 24ab^3) \div (-6ab)$

(a) $4a^2 - 6ab + b^2$

(b) $2a^2 - 3ab + 4b^2$

(c) $-2a^2 + 6ab - 9b^2$

(d) $2a^2 - 4ab + b^2$

21. The ratio of male to female in a state is 6 : 5. Find the total number of males in the state if total number of females is 560000.

(a) 760000 (b) 680000

(c) 672000 (d) 4278969

22. Which of the following is incorrect ?

(a) line $\overleftrightarrow{AB}$ is same $\overleftrightarrow{BA}$

(b) line segment $\overline{AB}$ is same as line segment $\overline{BA}$

(c) Ray $\overrightarrow{AB}$ is same as ray $\overrightarrow{BA}$

(d) both (a) and (b) are correct.

23. In a school the ratio of number of boys to the girls is the same as ratio of number of girls to the number of teachers. If there are 180 girls and 90 teachers, find the number of boys in the school.

Space for Rough Work

(a) 540 (b) 180
(c) 720 (d) 360

24. In the ΔABC drawn here, find the measure of the angle marked with letter x.

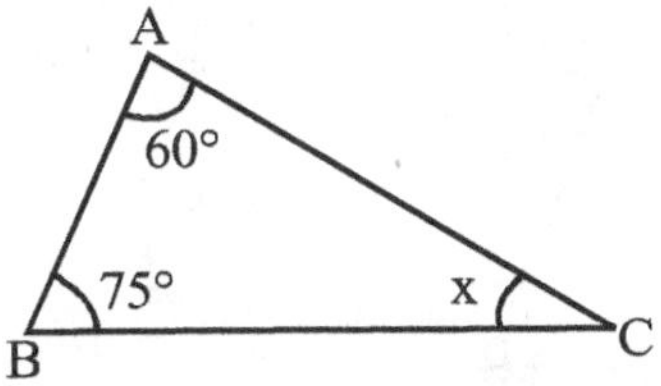

(a) 20° (b) 15°
(c) 30° (d) 45°

25. 15 envelopes cost ₹10.50. How many envelopes can be bought for ₹70. What will be the cost of 30 such envelopes?
(a) 100, ₹12 (b) 80, ₹18
(c) 100, ₹21 (d) 96, ₹24

26. The ratio equivalent to 18 : 12 is
(a) 2 : 3 (b) 3 : 2
(c) 5 : 1 (d) 1 : 5

27. Find the two consecutive integers between which the rational number $-7\frac{1}{2}$ lies ?
(a) 1 and – 7 (b) – 7 and – 8
(c) – 7 and 8 (d) 1 and 8

28. Simplify : $50 - 42 \div 3 \text{ of } 7 - (-11 + 5) \div 4 \times 2$.
(a) 51 (b) 64
(c) 72 (d) 81

29. The audience at a school function occupies $\frac{5}{7}$ of the seats in the auditorium. There are 540 people present. How many seats are there in the auditorium ?
(a) 576 (b) 657
(c) 756 (d) 856

30. Divide 403.0496 by 4.78.
(a) 56.26 (b) 84.32
(c) 21.42 (d) 44.16

31. Multiply 3a + 2b and 5a + 7b.
(a) $6a^2 + 31ab + 9b^2$
(b) $4a^2 +\_26ab + 9b^2$
(c) $21a^2 + 17ab + 49b^2$
(d) $15a^2 + 31ab + 14b^2$

32. Read the following statements carefully and choose the correct option.
(i) : In 3 years the sum of ₹900 will yield an interest of ₹324 at 12% per annum simple interest.
(ii) : In 5 years the sum of ₹750 will yield ₹220 interest at 6% p.a.
(a) (i) is true only
(b) (ii) is true only
(c) Both (i) and (ii) are true
(d) Neither (i) nor (ii) is true

Space for Rough Work

33. Find the value of m if 4, m and 6 are in continued proportion.

(a) $2\sqrt{3}$ (b) $2\sqrt{6}$

(c) 16 (d) 32

34. The length of a rectangular plot of land is twice its breadth. If the perimeter of the plot be 300 m, find its area.

(a) 15000 m^2 (b) 12000 m^2

(c) 900 m^2 (d) 5000 m^2

35. Given figure shows a semicircle in a quadrant. The perimeter of the shaded part is $\left(\text{use } \pi = \frac{22}{7}\right)$

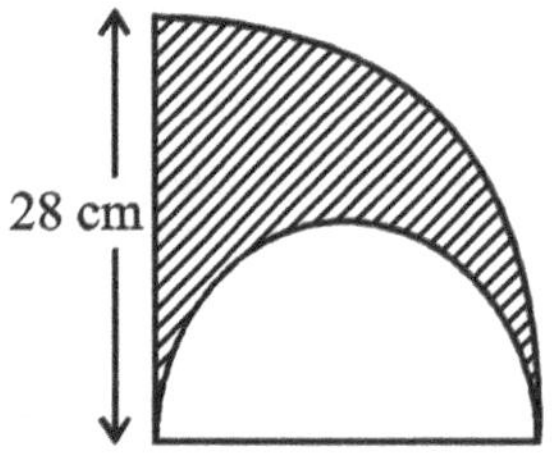

(a) 44 cm (b) 88 cm

(c) 116 cm (d) 72 cm

36. Thirty six vehicles are parked in a parking lot in a single row. After the first car, there is one scooter. After the second car, there are two scooters. After the third car, there are three scooters and so on. Work out the number of scooters in the second half of the row.

(a) 10 (b) 12

(c) 15 (d) 17

37. Which of the following statement is true about the given figure?

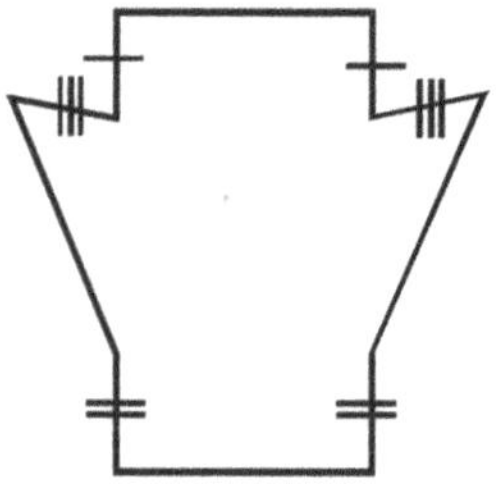

(a) It is an octagon.

(b) It is a regular polygon.

(c) It is a polygon.

(d) It is a quadrilateral.

DIRECTIONS (Qs. 38 to 40) : Read the passage(s) given below and answer the questions that follow.

Passage

Radha spends 40% of her salary on food and 20% on conveyance. If her savings at the end of a month are ₹ 4000.

38. What is her monthly salary?

(a) ₹9000 (b) ₹7000

(c) ₹12000 (d) ₹10,000

39. How much amount she spends on food ?

(a) ₹3000 (b) ₹2000

(c) ₹4000 (d) ₹2500

Space for Rough Work

40. How much amount she spends on conveyance ?
(a) ₹4500 (b)₹1500
(c) ₹2000 (d) ₹1500

41. The number 0.668 is represented in fraction as ___
(a) $\frac{267}{250}$ (b) $\frac{167}{500}$
(c) $\frac{257}{250}$ (d) $\frac{167}{250}$

42. Find the breadth of the rectangle whose length is 70 cm and perimeter 200 cm.
(a) 30 cm (b)34 cm
(c) 40 cm (d) 45 cm

43.

Column-I Measures of Triangle	Column-II Type of Triangles
A. Triangle which has three sides of equal length.	(i) Isosceles
B. Triangle which has two sides of equal length.	(ii) Scalene
C. Triangle which has one right angle with two sides of equal length.	(iii) Equilateral
D. Triangle which has all sides are of different length.	(iv) Isosceles right angled

(a) A → (iii); B → (i); C → (iv); D → (ii)
(b) A → (i); B → (iii); C → (ii); D → (iv)
(c) A → (iii); B → (iv); C → (ii); D → (i)
(d) A → (i); B → (ii); C → (iv); D → (iii)

44. Find the area of shaded region if the perimeter of the square is 56 cm.

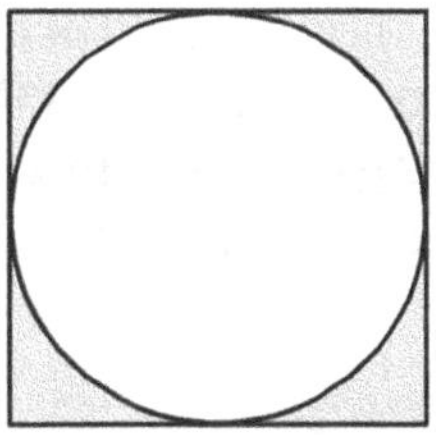

(a) 196 sq. cm (b)98 sq. cm
(c) 154 sq. cm (d) 42 sq. cm

45. A farmer has a rectangular field which measures 350 m by 240 m. He hopes that by sowing a variety of wheat, the yield will be 25 quintals per hectare, and it will sell in the market at ₹160 per quintal. What will be his expected income.
(a) ₹26,000
(b) ₹42,000
(c) ₹33,600
(d) ₹52,200

Space for Rough Work

46. In the figure given below, find the values of x + y + z.

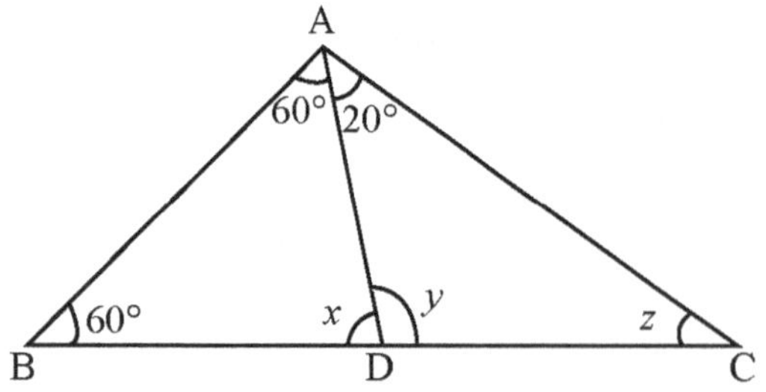

(a) 220° (b) 180°
(c) 270° (d) 140°

47. What would happen to the volume and surface area of cuboid if all its dimensions are doubled?
(a) New volume = 4 (original volume) New surface area = 4 (original surface area)
(b) New volume = 8 (original volume) New surface area = 4 (original surface area)
(c) New volume = 4 (original volume) New surface area = 8 (original surface area)
(d) New volume = 8 (original volume) New surface area = 8 (original surface area)

DIRECTIONS (Qs. 48 to 50): The following bar graph shows the number of houses (out of 100) in a town using different types of fuels for cooking.

Read the bar graph and answer the following questions:

Scale : 1unit length = 5 houses

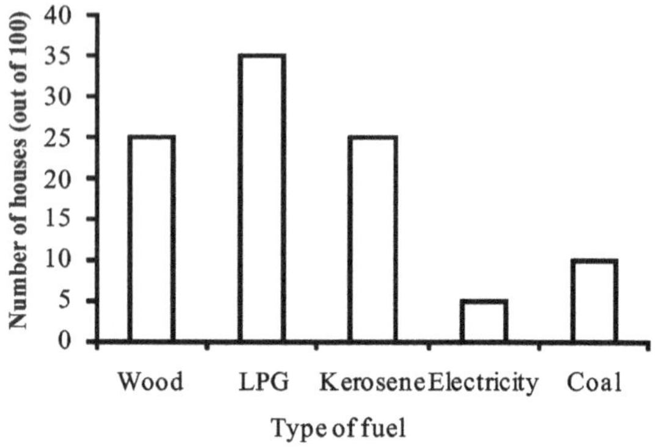

48. Which fuel is used in maximum number of houses ?
(a) Electricity (b) LPG
(c) Wood (d) Kerosene

49. How many houses are using coal as fuel ?
(a) 10 (b) 5
(c) 25 (d) 35

50. Suppose that the total number of houses in the town is 1 lakh. From the above graph estimate the number of houses using electricity.
(a) 500 (b) 50
(c) 5000 (d) 1000

Space for Rough Work

SCIENCE

OLYMPIAD Mock Test 1

Name : ________ **Max. Marks : 50**

Number of Questions : 50 **Time : 2 Hours**

There is no negative marking in the test.

PHYSICS

1. A light bulb is connected in series with a battery, a switch and some wires. However, the light bulb does not light up. What is/are the possible reason(s)?

   A. The battery is weak.

   B. The switch is closed.

   C. The bulb has blown.

   D. The wires are made of copper.

   (a) A only (b) A and C only

   (c) B and D only (d) B, C and D only

2. Study the classification chart below.

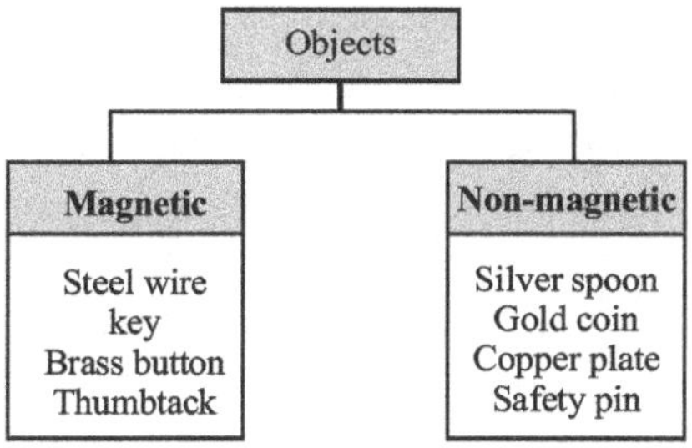

   Which of the above have been wrongly classified?

   (a) Key and copper plate

   (b) Thumbtack and safety pin

   (c) Steel wire and silver spoon

   (d) Brass button and safety pin

3. Study the circuit given.

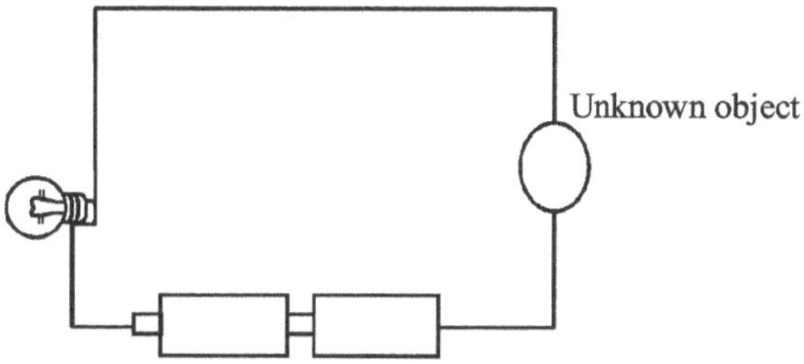

   Which of the following objects when placed in the circuit at the position shown would result in the bulb lighting up ?

A: Iron nail B: Toothpick

C: Metal ruler D: Birthday card

(a) B only

(b) A and C only

(c) C and D only

(d) A, B and D only

4. An ant moves as shown in the diagram. Which of the following can be used to determine the distance covered by that ant?

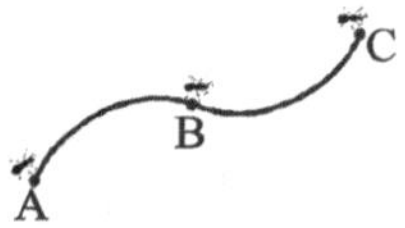

(a) A 15 cm scale and a meter scale

(b) A meter scale

(c) Hand span and a meter scale

(d) Thread and a meter scale

DIRECTION (Q. 5) : Match Column-I with Column-II and select the correct answer using the code given below the columns.

5.

Column-I	Column-II
(A) Bullock cart	(p) Modern means of transport
(B) Space craft	(q) Ancient unit of length
(C) Width of finger	(r) Ancient means of transport
(D) Metric system	(s) Developed in 1790 by the French

(a) A→(p); B→(q); C→(r); D→(s)

(b) A→(r); B→(p); C→(q); D→(s)

(c) A→(r); B→(p); C→(s); D→(q)

(d) A→(q); B→(r); C→(p); D→(s)

6. Which of the following is an example of contact force?
(a) Magnetic force
(b) Gravitational force
(c) Electric force
(d) Muscular force

7. Which of the following best describes the reason that the shadow of an apple is formed on a screen?
(a) The apple reflects the light.
(b) The apple absorbs the light.
(c) The light from the light source is too bright.
(d) The light from the light source is blocked by the apple.

8. Why do we always see a lightning before we hear thunder?
(a) Because lightning occurs first.
(b) Because light travels faster than sound.
(c) Because thunder occurs first.
(d) Because sound travels faster than light.

Space for Rough Work

9. Which of the following objects having more than one type of motion?
   (a) A swinging pendulum of a wall clock
   (b) A train approaching towards a station
   (c) A race car speeding on a race track
   (d) The earth revolving around the sun

10. The results of some observations about the number of iron pins attracted by a bar magnet are shown below. In your opinion which of the given reading are correct?

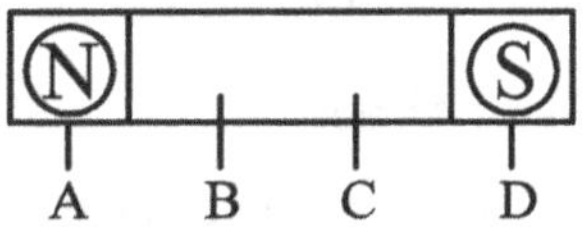

Number of pins attracted

Observation	A	B	C	D
(i)	10	2	2	10
(ii)	10	5	5	4
(iii)	6	6	6	6
(iv)	2	10	10	2

   (a) (i)
   (b) (ii)
   (c) (iii)
   (d) (iv)

11. Lisa carried out an experiment to test the electrical conductivity of some liquids. Her set-up and results are shown below.

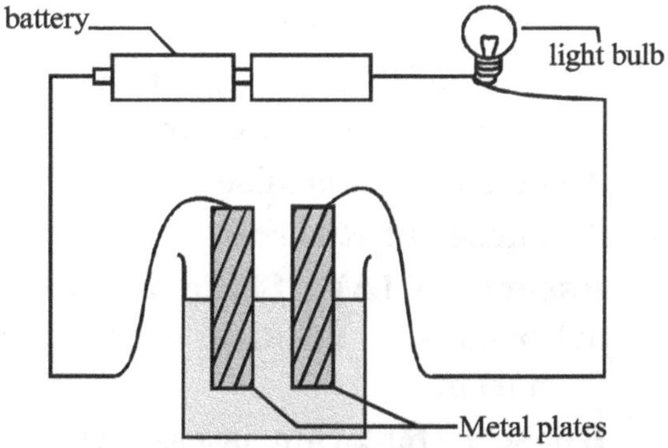

Liquid	Light bulb
Distilll water	Did not light up
Mercury	Bright light
Lemon Juice	Dim light
Tap water	Bright light

Which of the liquids is an insulator of electricity?
(a) Distill water (b) Mercury
(c) Lemon juice (d) Tap water

DIRECTION (Q. 12) : *The questions in this segment consists of two statements, one labelled as "Assertion A" and the other labelled as "Reason R". You are to examine these two statements carefully and decide if the Assertion A and Reason R are individually true and if so, whether the reason is a correct explanation of the assertion. Select your answers to these questions using codes given below.*

Space for Rough Work

(a) Both A and R are true and R is the correct explanation of A.
(b) Both A and R are true but R is not the correct explanation of A.
(c) A is true but R is false.
(d) A is false but R is true.

12. **Assertion (A) :** Solar and lunar eclipses are results of shadow formation.
Reason (R) : Sun is essential for shadow formation.

13. Choose the incorrect statement.
(a) A switch is the source of electric current in a circuit.
(b) A switch help to complete or break the circuit.
(c) A switch helps us to use electricity as per our requirement.
(d) When the switch is open there is an air gap between its terminals.

14. A bar magnet is immersed in a heap of iron filings and pulled out. The amount of iron filling clinging to the
(a) North pole is almost equal to the south pole.
(b) North pole is much more than the south pole.
(c) North pole is much less than the south pole.
(d) Magnet will be same all along its length.

CHEMISTRY

15. Select the fibre that is obtained from a plant source.
(a) Wool (b) Silk
(c) Cotton (d) Nylon

16. What name has been given to the solution in which no more substance can be dissolved at the given temperature?
(a) Saturated solution
(b) Unsaturated solution
(c) Diluted solution
(d) All of these

17. Pliers used by electrician usually have plastic cover on the handle. Why?
(a) Plastic is a bad conductor of heat
(b) Plastic is a water resistant
(c) Plastic is a bad conductor of electricity
(d) All of these

18. Melting of coal tar on heating is an example of :
(a) Reversible change
(b) Irreversible change
(c) Chemical change
(d) Periodic change

Space for Rough Work

19. Observe the picture of objects given below carefully. Which one of the following objects will float in water?

(a) 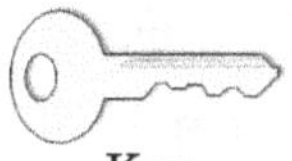
Key

(b) 
Coin

(c) 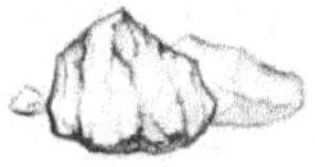
Stone

(d) 
Disposable cups

20. In which one of the following kind of changes, new molecule is formed?

(a) Physical changes

(b) Chemical changes

(c) Reversible changes

(d) All of these

21. Three substances given below were kept in the open for a few days and some changes were observed.

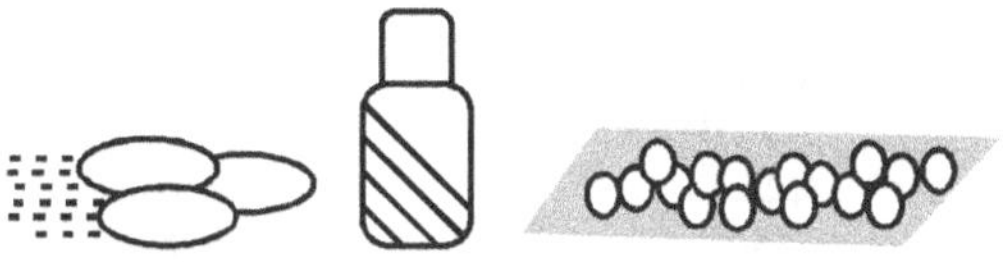

Eggs (P) Bottle (Q) Moth balls (S)

Which of the substances will show chemical changes?

(a) Eggs.

(b) Plastic bottle.

(c) Both eggs & moth balls.

(d) All eggs, plastic bottle and moth balls.

22. In a pressure-kerosene stove–

(i) We pump kerosene and convert it into vapours.

(ii) The vapours are then ignited.

Which of the following option is correct about the above statements?

(a) (i) is a chemical change; (ii) is a physical change.

(b) (i) is a physical change; (ii) is a chemical change.

(c) (i) and (ii) both are physical changes.

(d) (i) and (ii) both are chemical changes.

23. Which of the following statement is correct for nitrogen gas?

(a) It supports combustion.

(b) It burns itself.

(c) It regulates burning in atmosphere.

(d) It is harmful.

24. What happens as one goes up in the atmosphere?

(a) The amount of nitrogen in air increases.

(b) The amount of oxygen in air decreases.

(c) Air becomes denser.

(d) One feels lighter.

Space for Rough Work

25. Which of the following statements is correct for aquatic plants and animals?
    (a) They use the oxygen dissolved in water to breathe.
    (b) They have to come out of water to breathe.
    (c) They breathe through the water.
    (d) They use carbon dioxide dissolved in water to breathe.

26. Study the diagram below.

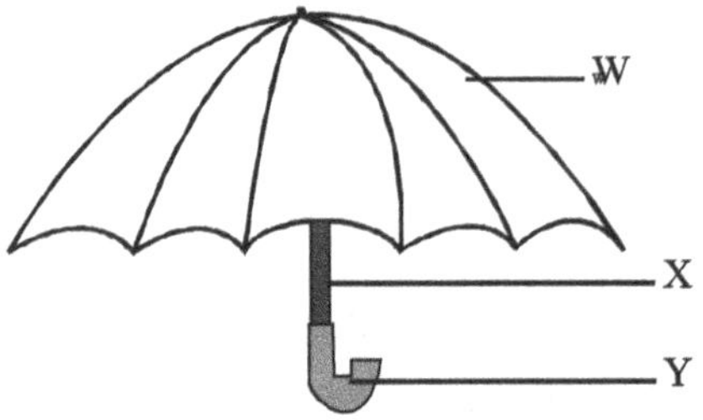

Which of the following combinations is the best choice for making the object above?

	W	X	Y
(a)	Cloth	Rubber	Metal
(b)	Paper	Rubber	Metal
(c)	Plastics	Metal	Wood
(d)	Plastics	Wood	Cloth

27. Divya accidentally dropped a glass plate on the floor and it broke into many smaller pieces. She replaced the glass plate with a plastic plate which does not break when dropped. Which of the following properties is shown by the glass?
    (a) Flexibility
    (b) Brittleness
    (c) Hardness
    (d) Degree of transparency

28. The properties of different types of materials were tested and the results are shown in the table below.

Property	Material P	Material Q	Material R	Material S
Strong	✓	✓	×	×
Flexible	×	×	✓	×
Lightweight	×	✓	✓	×
Waterproof	×	✓	✓	✓

Ravi needs to choose a suitable material to make a container that can hold 10*L* of water. Which material should he choose?
    (a) Material P (b) Material Q
    (c) Material R (d) Material S

29. Study the classification chart below.

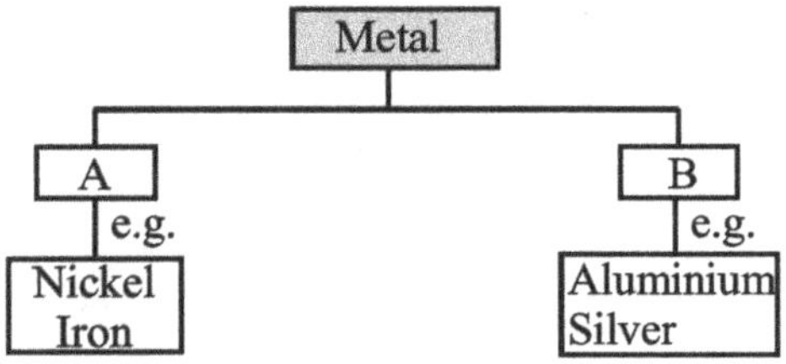

Which of the following shows the property by which the metals are classified in the above chart?
    (a) Heat conductivity
    (b) Magnetic property
    (c) Electrical conductivity
    (d) Ability to float or sink in water

Space for Rough Work

30. The separation of substances is done to
    (a) remove the non-useful or harmful component.
    (b) obtain the useful component.
    (c) improve the quality of the substance.
    (d) all of these.
31. Elephants spray muddy water on their bodies to keep cool. Which of the following statements explains how this happens?
    (a) The muddy water allows water vapour to condense on the elephant's skin.
    (b) When the water evaporates, it removes heat from the elephant's body.
    (c) The mud forms dry layer on the body of elephant and protects them from the heat of sun.
    (d) None of these

BIOLOGY

32. Study the diagram below.

Which of the following processes does the insect help to carry out?
    (a) Seed dispersal
    (b) Pollination
    (c) Fertilisation
    (d) Germination
33. Objects made from plastics are commonly used. How does the use of plastics add to environmental pollution?
    A: They take a very long time to decompose.
    B: They are produced from natural resources.
    C: They produce harmful gases when burnt.
    D: They are waterproof.
    (a) A and B only
    (b) A and C only
    (c) B and C only
    (d) B and D only
34. Study the diagram below.

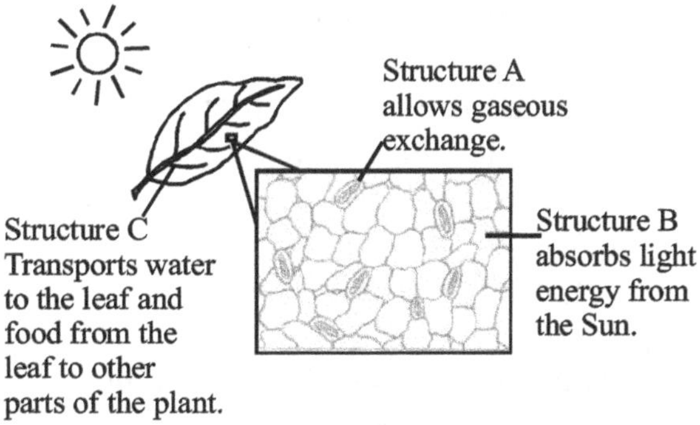

Space for Rough Work

Which of the following represents the structures, A, B and C correctly?

	A	B	C
(a)	Stomata	Leaf stalk	Chlorophyll
(b)	Vein	Stomata	Leaf stalk
(c)	Chlorophyll	Carotenoids	Stomata
(d)	Stomata	Chlorophyll	Vein

35. Which of the following reasons explain why the bird shown below cannot fly?

(a) It does not have wings.
(b) It does not have feathers.
(c) It is too heavy for its flight muscles.
(d) It is so light that the wind can blow it away easily.

36. When lemon/vinegar is added to warm milk, it results in
(a) setting of milk.
(b) curdling of milk.
(c) pasteurization.
(d) creaming.

37. Which one of the following is a parasitic plant?
(a) Rose plant
(b) Jasmine plant
(c) Mango tree
(d) Cuscuta

38. The microscopic animals which live in water are called:
(a) Zooplanktons
(b) Phytoplanktons
(c) Hydrophytes
(d) All of these

39. Iron, a biological nutrient, is found in human body in
(a) bones. (b) blood.
(c) hair. (d) All of these.

40. Which one of the following is an annual plant?
(a) Paddy (b) Rose
(c) Lemon (d) Neem

41. Which one of the following statements is correct about the soil?
Statement A: It provides a medium for the growth of plants.
Statement B: It provides sunlight to the root of the plant.
(a) Both the statement A and B are correct
(b) Statement A is correct and B is incorrect
(c) Statement B is correct and A is incorrect
(d) Both the statement A and B are incorrect

Space for Rough Work

42. The process of respiration is the reverse of:
    (a) Photosynthesis
    (b) Transpiration
    (c) Diffusion
    (d) All of these
43. Which one of the following statement is true?
    Statement A: Ozone layer is not necessary for the living organisms.
    Statement B: In the food chain plants are called producers and animals are called consumers.
    (a) Only Statement A is correct
    (b) Only Statement B is correct
    (c) Both Statement A and Statement B are correct
    (d) Both Statement A and Statement B are incorrect
44. Based on the following statements, which one of the following options is correct?
    Statement A: Fenugreek is a seed.
    Statement B: Coconut is a leaf.
    (a) Statement A is false and Statement B is true
    (b) Both, Statement A and Statement B are true
    (c) Both, Statement A and Statement B are false
    (d) Statement B is false and Statement A is true
45. Given below the two Statements:
    Statement A: Matter and energy flows between organisms and physical environment.
    Statement B: Living organisms, such as producers and consumers are abiotic factors present in the environment.
    Which one of the following is correct with regard to above statements?
    (a) Only Statement A is correct
    (b) Only Statement B is correct
    (c) Both Statement A and Statement B are correct
    (d) Both Statement A and Statement B are incorrect
46. Underwater divers wear fin-like flippers on their feet to
    (a) swim easily in water.
    (b) look like a fish.
    (c) walk on water surface.
    (d) walk over the bottom of the sea (sea bed).
47. Which of the following is an incorrect statement about excretion?
    (a) Excretion takes place in plants.
    (b) Excretion takes place both in plants and animals.
    (c) Excretion is the process of getting rid of excess water only.
    (d) Secretion is one method of excretion.

Space for Rough Work

48. A camel is a desert animal. It shows many adaptations. Which of the following statements (P, Q, R & S) is incorrect?

P - It has a hump where fat is stored.

Q - It can stay without water for long time.

R - It sweats a lot.

S - It excretes large amount of urine.

(a) P only (b) Q only
(c) P & Q (d) R & S

49. Read the following sentences about photosynthesis:

(i) Sunlight, carbon dioxide, chlorophyll and water are necessary.

(ii) Oxygen is absorbed.

(iii) Leaves carry out photosynthesis.

(iv) Proteins are made during photosynthesis.

Choose the correct pair of sentences that are true to photosynthesis

(a) (iii) and (iv) (b) (ii) and (iii)
(c) (ii) and (iv) (d) (i) and (iv)

50. Ritu gave the following ill effects of the practice of burning dried leaves and other plant parts:

(i) Burning degrades the soil.
(ii) Burning produces harmful gases/fumes.
(iii) Precious raw materials to obtain manure at low cost is lost.
(iv) Lot of heat is generated unnecessarily.

According to you the correct reasons why we should not burn leaves are:

(a) i, ii and iv only
(b) i, ii, iii, and iv
(c) ii and iii only
(d) ii, iii, and iv only

Space for Rough Work

OLYMPIAD

Mock Test 2

Name : ________ **Max. Marks : 50**

Number of Questions : 50 **Time : 2 Hours**

There is no negative marking in the test.

PHYSICS

1. In an electric circuit, the two terminals of the electric cell are
   (a) connected directly to each other
   (b) connected to the filament of the bulb
   (c) connected to the two terminals of the bulb
   (d) All the above are correct
2. The brightness of a bulb does not depend on ________ .
   (a) the arrangement of the batteries in a circuit.
   (b) the number of batteries used in a circuit.
   (c) the length of the wire used in a circuit.
   (d) the number of bulbs used in a circuit.
3. William places Magnet R on a stand and then slowly places Object Q on top of it. He notices that Object Q does not stick to Magnet R but instead floats above it.

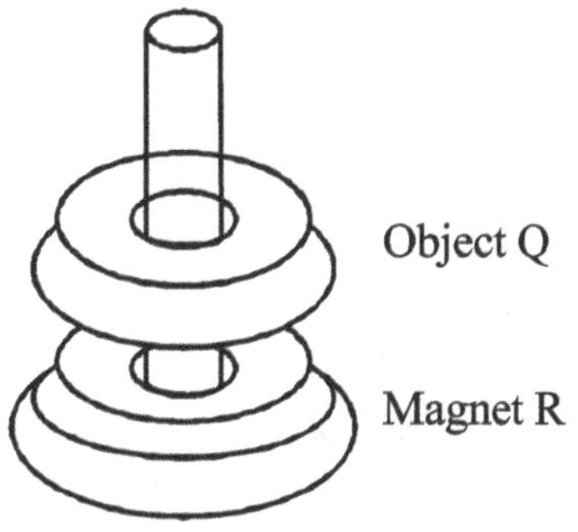

Which of the following statements best explains why Object Q does not stick to Magnet R ?

Space for Rough Work

(a) Object Q is an electromagnet.
(b) Object Q is made of steel and Magnet R exerts a repulsive force on magnetic materials like steel and iron.
(c) Object Q is a magnet. The unlike poles of Object Q and Magnet R are facing each other, thereby exerting a repulsive force between them.
(d) Object Q is a magnet. The like poles of Object Q and Magnet R are facing each other, thereby exerting a repulsive force between them.

4. How much distance a car travels in 10 minutes if the speed of the car is 40 kmph?
(a) 6.67 km (b) 7.80 km
(c) 10.50 km (d) 5.25 km

5. What kind of eclipse do we see when the moon is entirely within the Earth's umbral shadow?
(a) Partial lunar
(b) Partial solar
(c) Total lunar
(d) Total solar

6. Select the correct statement :
(a) Electrical sockets are made up of conductors, while plug tops are made up of insulators
(b) Electrical sockets are made up of insulators, also plug tops are made up of insulator
(c) Wire coverings are made up of insulators, also fuse wires are made up of insulators.
(d) Fuse wires are made up of conductors, while bulb filament is made up of insulators

7. A nail is magnetized as shown in the figure. Which polarity will develop at A and B?

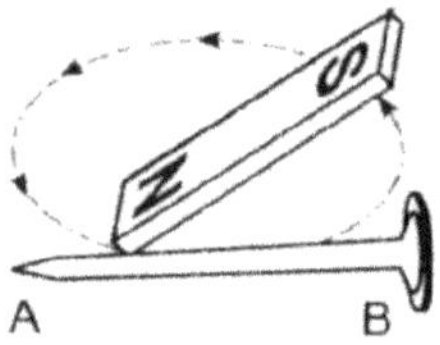

(a) A – North, B – North
(b) A – North, B – South
(c) A – South, B – South
(d) A – South, B – North

8. If no force acts on a body, it will :
(a) get deshaped
(b) move with increasing speed
(c) either remain at rest or move in a straight line
(d) break

9. An instrument in a vehicle which is used to measure the distance travelled by the vechicle from zero is called–
(a) Speedometer
(b) Ohmmetre
(c) Odometre
(d) Amperemetre

Space for Rough Work

10. Study the circuit below.

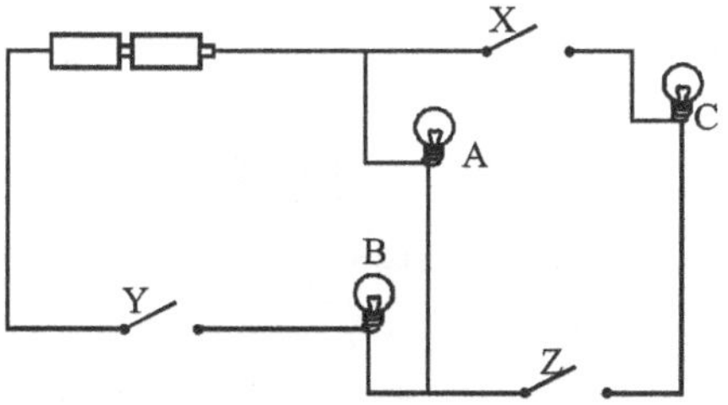

If switches X and Y are closed, which bulbs will light up?
(a) A and B only
(b) A and C only
(c) B and C only
(d) A, B and C

11. Sunlight shining through the windows of a public library makes the place too bright and glaring. A decision was made to substitute the windows with another material so as to cut down on the glare and brightness. Which of the following materials would be a suitable substitute?
(a) Soft wood
(b) Clear plastic
(c) Frosted glass
(d) Wired clear glass

12. Which of the following does not express a time interval?
(a) A day
(b) A second
(c) A school period
(d) Time of the first bell in the school

13. Ram observed the shadow of a tree at 8:00 a.m., 12:00 noon and 3:00 p.m. Which of the following statements is closest to his observation about the shape and size of the shadow?
(a) The shape of the shadow of the tree changes but the size remains the same.
(b) The size of the shadow of the tree changes but the shape remains the same.
(c) Both the size and shape of the shadow of the tree change.
(d) Neither the shape nor the size of the shadow changes.

14. In the following circuit the flow of current is in which route?

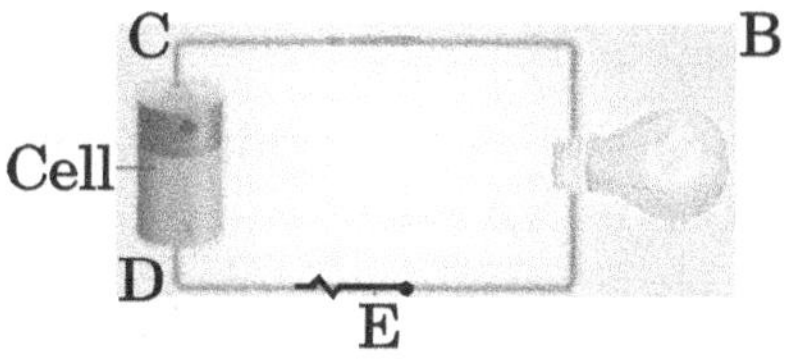

(a) CBED
(b) DEBC
(c) Either of the above two
(d) None of these

CHEMISTRY

15. 250 mL of water was poured into each of the three containers, P, Q and R.

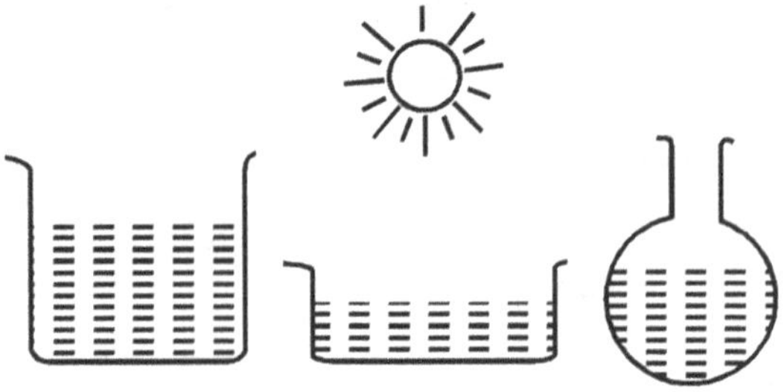

The containers were placed under direct sunlight for two hours. Which of the following shows the correct arrangement of the containers according to the amount of water left in each container after two hours? Begin with the container with the most amount of water left.

(a) P, R, Q (b) P, Q, R
(c) Q, P, R (d) R, P, Q

16. Which of the following is correct for the term 'Lustre'?
(a) Hardness
(b) Softness
(c) Dull appearance
(d) Shiny appearance

17. Jyoti wants to buy a cooking pot for her mother. The pot she is looking for must satisfy the following criteria.

- It is a good conductor of heat.
- It does not rust easily.
- The handles are good insulators of heat.
- While cooking, she is able to see the contents in the pot through the lid without lifting it.

The various parts of the pot are most likely to be made of _______ .

(a) rubber, iron and wood
(b) aluminium, glass, copper
(c) clay, ceramics and rubber
(d) stainless steel, glass and plastic

18. Rahul conducted several tests on four different materials. The results were recorded in the table below.

Material	Is it waterproof?	Is it flexible?
P	✓	×
Q	✓	✓
R	×	✓
S	×	×

Which of the following materials is most suitable for making a garden hose?

(a) P (b) Q
(c) R (d) S

Space for Rough Work

19. Study the diagram below.

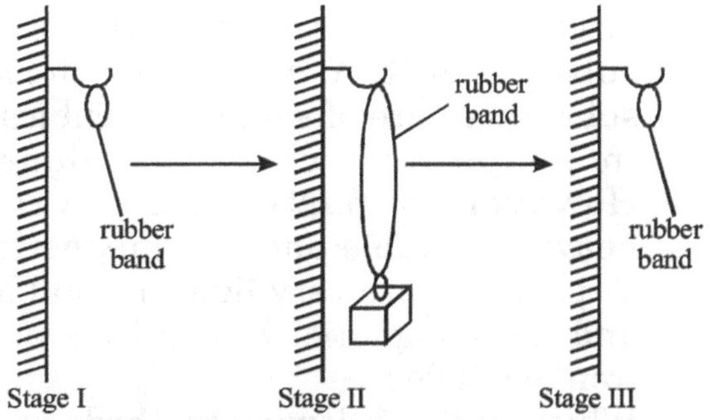

The above experiment shows that a rubber band is ________ .
(a) elastic (b) ductile
(c) durable (d) malleable

20. Which method is used to separate the mixtures whose component are of different sizes?
(a) Sieving (b) Winnowing
(c) Threshing (d) Filtration

21. Any change in which the original substance can be obtained by reversing conditions is known as a
(a) reversible change.
(b) periodic change.
(c) physical change
(d) Both (a) and (c)

22. Which of the following gases comprises major fraction of Earth's atmosphere?
(a) Nitrogen
(b) Carbon monoxide
(c) Hydrogen
(d) Oxygen

23. Medium sized weaving machine run on power, used to produce cotton clothes on large scale is called ____________.
(a) handloom
(b) powerloom
(c) weaving machine
(d) stitching machine

24. Choose the correct option on the basis of statements (i) and (ii)
(i) Hydrogen gas reacts with oxygen gas to form liquid water.
(ii) Liquid water on evaporation changes to water vapour.
(a) (i) is a chemical change, (ii) is a physical change.
(b) (i) is a physical change, (ii) is a chemical change.
(c) Both (i) and (ii) are physical changes.
(d) Both (i) and (ii) are chemical changes.

25. Anaerobic bacteria digest animal waste and produce biogas (Change *A*). The biogas is then burnt as fuel (Change *B*). The following statements are related to these changes. Choose the correct one.
(a) *A* is a chemical change whereas *B* is a physical change.
(b) *B* is a chemical change whereas *A* is a physical change.
(c) Both *A* and *B* are physical changes.
(d) Both *A* and *B* are chemical changes.

Space for Rough Work

26. The cotton is separated from the seeds in machines called
    (a) gins (b) bins
    (c) bales (d) tins.

27. The process of separating gummy skin from jute fibres is called:
    (a) Carding (b) Ginning
    (c) Bailing (d) Retting.

28. Study the diagram of the water cycle below.

Which of the following do X, Y and Z represent?

	X	Y	Z
(a)	Condensation	Evaporation	Precipitation
(b)	Condensation	Precipitation	Evaporation
(c)	Precipitation	Evaporation	Condensation
(d)	Evaporation	Condensation	Precipitation

29. Bleaching or dyeing are usually done
    (a) just before the fabrics are made.
    (b) after the fabrics are made.
    (c) before the yarns are made.
    (d) after the yarns are made.

30. In an activity, Shyam took large quantity of mixture containing tiny particles of three different substances X, Y and Z. All these substances are of same size, cubical in shape and white in colour. However, X particles are very heavy, insoluble and non-magnetic. Y- particles are very light, insoluble and non-magnetic. Z- particles are iron particles.
    Which of the following methods will Shyam use to separate X, Y and Z in the fastest manner?
    (a) Filtration followed by sublimation.
    (b) Winnowing followed by sublimation.
    (c) Winnowing followed by magnetic separation.
    (d) Filtration followed by magnetic separation.

31. The given figure illustrates a bicycle. Which of the following combinations of materials is suitable for making the marked area in bicycle? Give reasons.

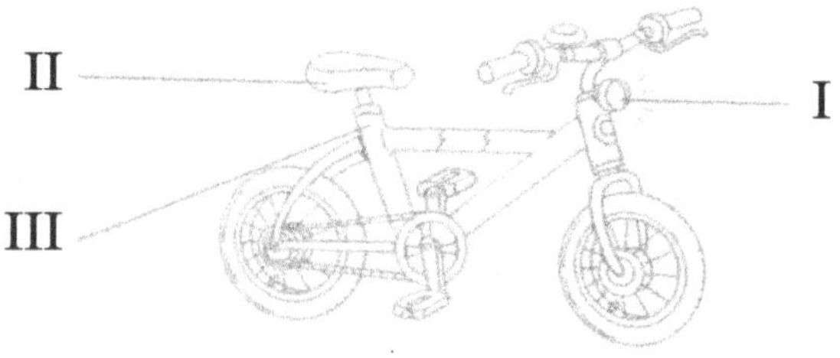

Space for Rough Work

(a) I-Metal; II-Plastic; III-Glass
(b) I-Glass; II-Leather; III-Metal
(c) I-Rubber; II-Nylon; III-Metal
(d) I-Leather; II-Wood; III-Metal

BIOLOGY

32. Which of the following is the most suitable method of reproducing an African violet plant?
(a) From a seed
(b) From a root
(c) From a leaf
(d) From an underground stem

33. Which of the following measures can help to reduce air pollution?
A: Use of windmills
B: Use of solar cells
C: Use of insecticides and pesticides
D: Use of hydroelectric power station
(a) A and C only
(b) B and D only
(c) A, B and D only
(d) A, B C, and D

34. The polar bear and the arctic fox have white fur during winter. Which of the following is their white fur useful for?
A. To attract prey
B. To help them to lose heat quickly
C. To keep them warm
D. To help them camouflage
(a) A and B only
(b) C and D only
(c) A, B and C only
(d) B, C and D only

35. Some human activities have negative effects on our environment. Which of the following is such an example?
(a) Using bacteria to ferment cheese.
(b) Cultivating plants that are resistant to pesticides.
(c) Burying a large amount of rubbish underground.
(d) Recycling paper to reduce the cutting down of trees.

36. When Joan was cooking, she was mostly using her ___________

A. skeletal system
B. muscular system
C. digestive system
D. Circulatory system
(a) A and B only
(b) A and D only
(c) B and C only
(d) A, C and D only

Space for Rough Work

37. Select the one that is incorrect about cartilage.
    (a) It is a firm but flexible skeletal material.
    (b) It is as hard as bones.
    (c) It can be bent.
    (d) It is found in the joints of our body.

38. Which one of the following statements is correct?

    Statement A: Stomata is present in leaves.

    Statement B: Stomata is present in root.
    (a) Statement A is correct
    (b) Statement B is correct
    (c) Both statements are correct
    (d) Both statements are incorrect

39. Which one of the following is correct for the term 'Xerocoles'?
    (a) Animals which live in fresh water
    (b) Animals which live in mountains
    (c) Animals which live in forest
    (d) Animals which live in desert

40. It is a low-lying open area of ground where city's garbage is normally dumped. Name it
    (a) Landfill
    (b) Disposal field
    (c) Open field
    (d) Both (b) and (c)

41. *Amoeba*, *Paramecium*, *Entamoeba*, *Plasmodium* are the example of:
    (a) Bacteria
    (b) Virus
    (c) Protozoa
    (d) Algae

42. Which of the following statement is correct about obesity?

    Statement A: It is due to undernutrition

    Statement B: It occurs because of eating too much junk food.
    (a) Both the statement A and B are correct
    (b) Statement A is correct and B is incorrect
    (c) Statement A is incorrect and B is correct
    (d) Both the statement A and B are incorrect

43. Snakes
    (a) move with the help of ribs and scales
    (b) slither on the ground by looping side ways
    (c) Both the above
    (d) None of these

Space for Rough Work

44. The rest period which many seeds undergo before they begin to grow is called
   (a) Viability (b) Germination
   (c) Pollination (d) Dormancy
45. Which of the following statement is true about the formation of soil?
   Statement A: The rock particles which are larger than silt particles form sand.
   Statement B: The largest size rock particles which are present in soil are called gravel.
   (a) Statement A and B both are correct
   (b) Statement A is correct and B is incorrect
   (c) Statement B is incorrect and B is correct
   (d) Statement A and B both are incorrect
46. Which one of the following parts of flower contains male sex cell?
   (a) Stigma (b) Pollen grains
   (c) Filament (d) All of these
47. Based on the following statements, which one of the following options is correct?
   Statement A: Fats are stored under the skin.
   Statement B: Ghee provides fat.
   (a) Statement A is False and Statement B is True
   (b) Both, Statement A and Statement B are True
   (c) Both, Statement A and Statement B are False
   (d) Statement B is False and Statement A is True
48. If you happen to go to a desert, what changes do you expect to observe in the urine you excrete? You would
   (i) excrete small amount of urine.
   (ii) excrete large amount of urine.
   (iii) excrete concentrated urine.
   (iv) excrete very dilute urine.
   Which of the above would hold true?
   (a) (i) and (iii) (b) (ii) and (iv)
   (c) (i) and (iv) (d) (i) and (ii)
49. Find the odd one out
   (a) Ovary, style, stigma
   (b) Filament, anther, pollen
   (c) Beetroot, potato, onion
   (d) Beetroot, carrot, radish
50. Which of the following are characteristics of living beings ?
   (i) Respiration
   (ii) Reproduction
   (iii) Adaptation
   (iv) Excretion
   Choose the correct answer from the options below:
   (a) (i), (ii) and (iv) only
   (b) (i) and (ii) only
   (c) (ii) and (iv) only
   (d) (i), (ii), (iii) and (iv)

Space for Rough Work

OLYMPIAD Mock Test 3

Name : ________ **Max. Marks : 50**

Number of Questions : 50 **Time : 2 Hours**

There is no negative marking in the test.

PHYSICS

1. Container (A) and (B), contain pure water but in different quantity. If both of the containers have same shape, same size and kept at same surface but height from the ground $h_1 > h_2$.

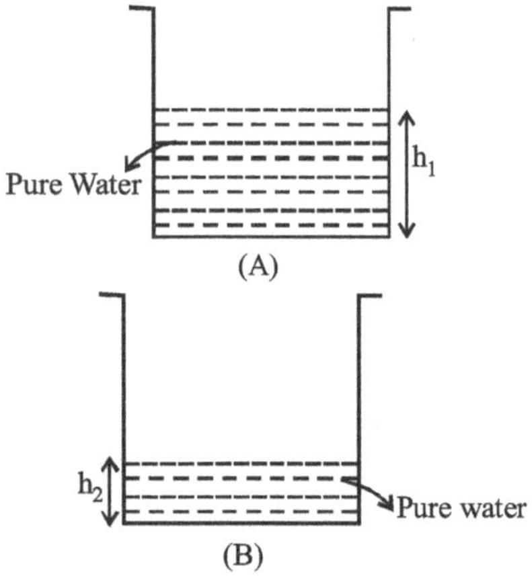

Which container will have more pressure?

(a) Same in A and B
(b) Container B
(c) Container A
(d) None of these

2. Study the arrangements of three magnets below.

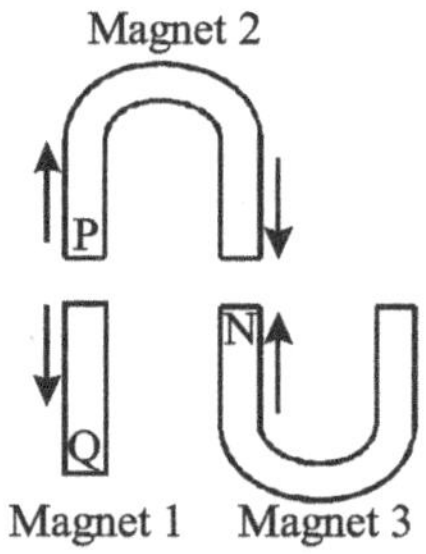

What could the poles at P and Q be?

	P	Q
(a)	N	N
(b)	N	S
(c)	S	N
(d)	S	S

Space for Rough Work

3. If an object placed in the path of light allowed almost the whole of the light falling on it to pass through it, then the object is classified as (a) transparent (b) transluscent (c) opaque (d) none of these

4. Study the circuits below.

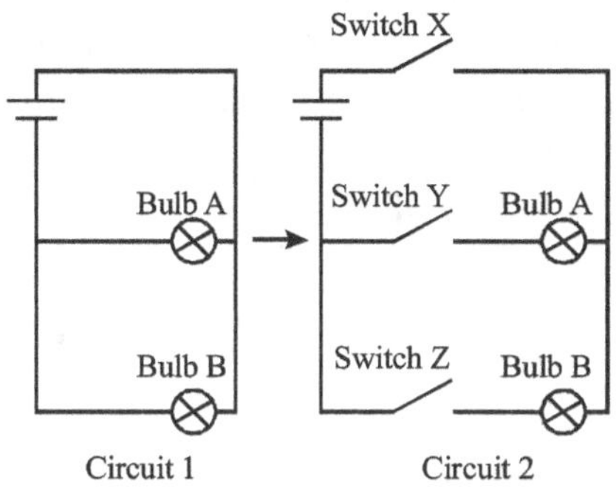

Amar set up Circuit 1 and then made some changes to it to obtain Circuit 2.

Which of the following statements explain(s) how the changes affect the circuit?

A. We can use Switch Y to control Bulb A.
B. We can use Switch Z to control Bulb B.
C. We can use Switch X to control Bulb A and Bulb B.
D. Bulb A and Bulb B can now be lit independently of each other.

(a) A only
(b) C only
(c) A and B only
(d) A, B, C and D

5. An object has moved from one position to another position then (a) its distance is zero
(b) its displacement is zero
(c) neither its distance nor displacement is zero
(d) none of these

6. What will be the angle of reflection if more than one beam of light is falls on the rough surface ?
(a) Beam of light will reflect at the same angle of reflection
(b) Beam of light will diffuse
(c) Beam of light will not reflect
(d) All of these

DIRECTION (Q. 7): The questions in this segment consists of two statements, one labelled as "Assertion A" and the other labelled as "Reason R". You are to examine these two statements carefully and decide if the Assertion A and Reason R are individually true and if so, whether the reason is a correct explanation of the assertion. Select your answers to these items using codes given below.

Space for Rough Work

(a) Both A and R are true and R is the correct explanation of A.
(b) Both A and R are true but R is not the correct explanation of A.
(c) A is true but R is false.
(d) A is false but R is true.

7. **Assertion (A) :** Silver is not used to make electric wires.
Reason (R) : Silver is a bad conductor.

8. On which one of the following factors speed of a running car depends?
(a) Distance travelled by the car
(b) Time taken to travel that distance
(c) Weight of the car
(d) Both (a) and (b)

9. Which parts of the magnet below can attract the most number of pins?

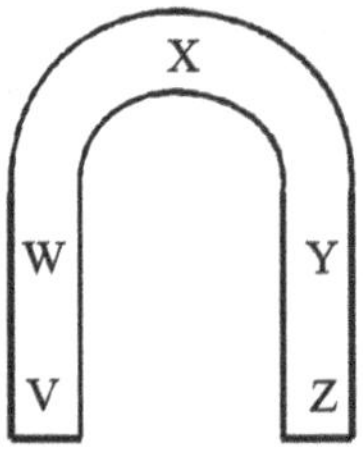

(a) V and Z only
(b) W and Y only
(c) V, W and X only
(d) W, X and Y only

10. A force F_1 acting on a body of 2 kg produces an acceleration of 2.5 m/sec². Another force F_2 acting on the body of mass 5 kg produces an acceleration of 2 m/sec². Find the ratio of F_2/F_1.
(a) 2 (b) 4
(c) 6 (d) 8

11. Our body is:
(a) Good conductor of electricity.
(b) Bad conductor of electricity.
(c) Sometimes good and sometimes bad conductor.
(d) None of these

12. Kamlesh moves on a straight road from point A to point C. She takes 20 minutes to cover a certain distance AB and 30 minutes to cover the rest of distance BC. She then turns back and takes 30 minutes to cover the distance CB and 20 minutes to cover the rest of the distance to her starting point. She makes 5 rounds on the road the same way. Kamlesh concludes that her motion is
(a) only rectilinear motion.
(b) only periodic motion.
(c) rectilinear and periodic both.
(d) neither rectilinear nor periodic.

13. Which of the following can never form a circular shadow?
(a) A ball
(b) A flat disc
(c) A shoe box
(d) An ice cream cone

Space for Rough Work

14. The diagram below shows a bar magnet resting on top of a piece of white paper. The north and south poles of the magnet are labeled N and S. Points A, B, C, and D represent four locations around the magnet.

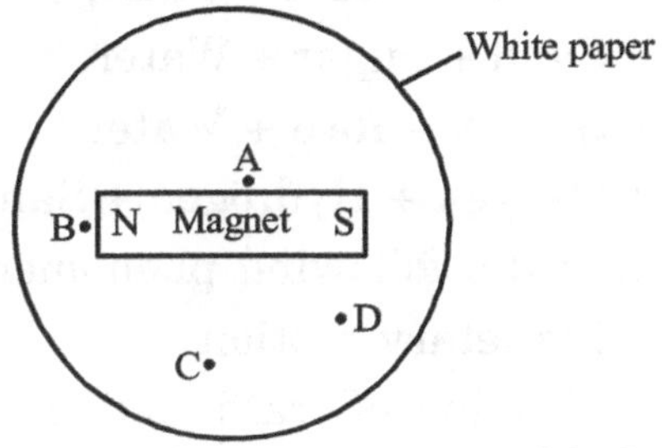

If iron filings were sprinkled evenly across the entire paper circle, at which location would the greatest concentration of iron filings be found after 30 seconds?

(a) A (b) B
(c) C (d) D

CHEMISTRY

15. The two objects given below belong to the same group because they

Iron nail

Needle

(a) are poor conductors of heat.
(b) are made of flexible materials.
(c) float in water.
(d) are hard and magnetic.

16. Washing powder on stirring disappear in water due to:
(a) Solubility
(b) Transparency
(c) Conduction
(d) Magnetic property

17. New materials that are formed during burning of a candle are
(a) oxygen
(b) wax
(c) water and carbon dioxide
(d) no new material is formed

18. The given figure illustrates burning of a matchstick.

It is an example of :
(a) Exothermic reaction
(b) Chemical and irreversible change
(c) Fast change
(d) All of the above

19. Halley's comet appear after every 76 years. It is a .... change.
(a) permanent
(b) chemical
(c) reversible
(d) periodic

Space for Rough Work

20. We group the materials for our convenience and also for some other reasons. Materials are grouped together on the basis of
    (a) similarities in their properties
    (b) differences in their properties
    (c) both on similarities and difference in their properties
    (d) None of the above is correct

21. Which of the following materials would not be a suitable choice for making the part labelled Q?

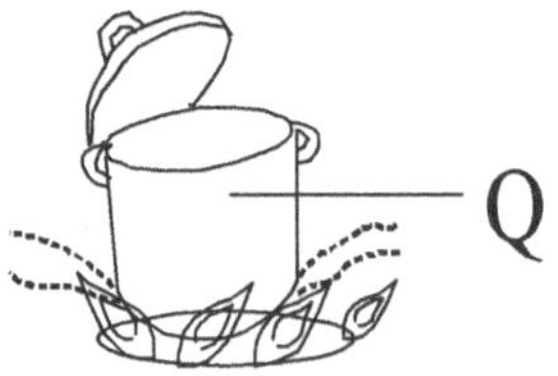

(a) Steel (b) Glass
(c) Wood (d) Ceramics

22. In a classroom, a student did the following activity to separate the constituents of a mixture.
What according to you are the constituents of mixture?

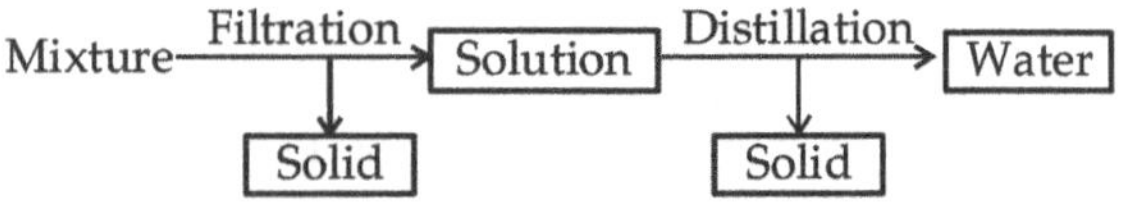

(a) Water + Sand + Glass
(b) Sand + Sugar + Water
(c) Stones + Rice + Water
(d) Oxygen + Hydrogen + Salt

23. Study the following phenomena.
I. Planetary motion
II. Blinking of traffic lights
III. Motion of fan blades rotating
IV. Swinging of a pendulum
What is common among the above given phenomena?
(a) They are all chemical changes.
(b) They are all physical changes.
(c) They are all periodic changes.
(d) They are all undesirable changes.

24. Match column I and column II and choose the correct option from codes given below the columns.

Column-I		Column-II
(A) Change of water to ice	(i)	Chemical change
(B) Ripening of fruits	(ii)	Physical change
(C) Bursting of crackers	(iii)	Periodic change
(D) Phases of moon	(iv)	Fast chemical change
(E) Volcanic eruptions	(v)	Non-periodic change

(a) A-(ii), B-(i), C-(iv), D-(iii), E-(v) (b) A-(i), B-(iv), C-(ii), D-(iii), E-(v)
(c) A-(ii), B-(i), C-(iv), D-(v), E-(iii) (d) A-(iv), B-(i), C-(v), D-(iii), E-(ii)

Space for Rough Work

25. Study the classification chart below. Which of the following materials has been classified wrongly?

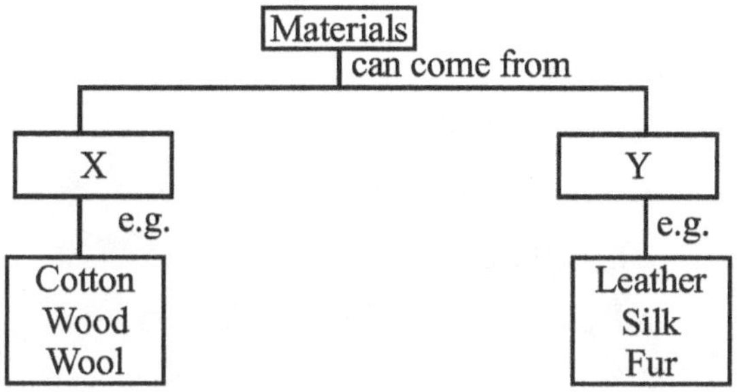

(a) Fur(b) Silk
(c) Wool (d) Cotton

26. Which of the following part of cotton plant is used to obtain cotton fibre?
(a) Fruit (b) Flower
(c) Seed (d) Stem

27. While doing an experiment Reena took an empty plastic bottle, turned it upside down and dipped its open mouth into a bucket filled with water. She then tilted the bottle slightly and made the following observations.
(i) Bubbles of air came out from the bottle.
(ii) Some water entered the bottle.
(iii) Nitrogen gas came out in the form of bubbles and oxygen got dissolved in water.
(iv) No bubbles formed, only water entered the bottle.
Which observations is/are correct?
(a) (i) and (ii) (b) (iv) only
(c) (iii) and (iv) (d) (i) only

28. Following changes were observed during lighting of a candle
(i) Wax was melting.
(ii) Candle was burning.
(iii) Size of the candle was reducing.
Of the above, the changes that can be reversed are
(a) (i) and (ii)
(b) (ii) and (iii)
(c) (iii) only
(d) (i) only

29. Rihana always carries water in a transparent plastic bottle to her school,during summer. One day she left her bottle in the school. The bottle still had some water left in it. The following day, she observed some water droplets on the inner surface of the empty portion of the bottle. These droplets of water were formed due to
(a) boiling and condensation.
(b) evaporation and saturation.
(c) evaporation and condensation.
(d) condensation and saturation.

Space for Rough Work

30. Which of the following materials are transparent?
    (i) Magnifying glass
    (ii) Mirror
    (iii) Stainless steel plate
    (iv) Glass tumbler
    (a) (i) and (ii) (b) (i) and (iii)
    (c) (i) and (iv) (d) (iii) and (iv)

31. Divya was feeling thirsty but there was only a pot of water at home which was muddy and unfit for drinking. Which of the following is the correct sequence of methods that can be used to make this water fit for drinking .
    (a) Loading, boiling, filtration
    (b) Filtration, loading, decantation, boiling
    (c) Sedimentation, decantation, filtration
    (d) Sedimentaion, decantation, filtration, loading

BIOLOGY

32. Study the diagram shown:
    In order for the seed to reach the stage shown, which of the following conditions are necessary?

A Correct temperature
B Sunlight
C Oxygen
D Water
(a) A and B only
(b) A and C only
(c) A, C and D only
(d) A, B C and D

33. Which of the following ways help to control and maintain the daily production of rubbish at a minimum?
    A: Reusing products.
    B: Recyling materials.
    C: Incineration of rubbish.
    D: Burying rubbish in landfills.
    E: Reducing the use of materials.
    (a) A and C only
    (b) B and E only
    (c) A, B and E only
    (d) A, C, D and E only

34. Ritu often complains of dry skin and is unable to see properly in dim light. She is suffering from
    (a) anaemia.
    (b) night-blindness.
    (c) beri- beri.
    (d) None of these.

35. The figure given below has flowers that are pollinated by ________.

(a) water (b) animal
(c) wind (d) insect

36. The diagram below shows a platypus.

In which location are you likely to find the platypus?

	Temperature	Amount of water	Amount of light
(a)	low	High	Low
(b)	Moderate	High	High
(c)	High	Low	High
(d)	Moderate	Low	Low

37. The lines on the broad green part of the leaf are called
(a) lamina (b) veins
(c) venation (d) None of these

38. Tommy studies the following organisms.
- Grass
- Giraffe
- Goldfish

Which one of the following statements is true of all three organisms?
(a) They live on land.
(b) They make their own food.
(c) They indirectly depend on the Sun for energy.
(d) They grow when provided with the essential living conditions.

39. Which of the following statements is true ?
(a) Bone has a soft substance called bone marrow inside it.
(b) The only movable bone in skull is the upper jaw bone.
(c) Longest bone in human body is humerus.
(d) Floating ribs are joined to the breastbone.

40. In which one of the following process oxidation of food occurs?
(a) Reproduction
(b) Photosynthesis
(c) Respiration
(d) Transportation

Space for Rough Work

41. Consider the following statements:
Statement A: Green plants prepare their own food.
Statements B: Plants also respire.
Which one of the following is correct about the above statements?
(a) Statement A is true and B is false
(b) Statement B is true and A is false
(c) Both A and B are true
(d) Both A and B are false

42. Which one of the following statements is correct:
Statement A: Coastal habitats are the aquatic habitats
Statement B: Pond habitats are the terrestrial habitats.
(a) Statement A
(b) Statement B
(c) Both statements are correct
(d) Both statements are incorrect

43. Presence of huge quantity of water vapour, methane, nitrous oxide and carbon dioxide in the atmosphere that reflect back heat on to the earth surface produces which one of the following?
(a) Reflection of light
(b) Green house effect
(c) Holes in the ozone layer
(d) All of these

44. Which one of the following microorganisms has the ability to perform photosynthesis?
(a) Virus (b) Fungi
(c) Algae (d) Protozoa

45. Which one of the following statements is correct about rainforest habitat?
(a) Rainforest habitat are hot and wet.
(b) Rainforest habitat are very cold and covered with snow.
(c) Rainforest habitat get plenty of rain.
(d) Both (a) and (c)

46. Which one of the following plants is a hydrophyte?
(a) Babool (b) Ber
(c) Lily (d) Wheat

47. Nitrogen is one of the essential component for all life form on the earth. Plant use nitrogen from atmosphere to make an important nutrient which is essential for the growth of plant. Which one of the following essential nutrients it makes by using nitrogen?
(a) Vitamin (b) Fats
(c) Protein (d) Starch

Space for Rough Work

48. Which one of the following statements is correct?
Statement A: Clayey soil is more fertile than sandy soil
Statement B: Clayey soil is less fertile than sandy soil
(a) Statement A
(b) Statement B
(c) Both statements are correct
(d) Both statements are incorrect

49. A science teacher takes the students out for practical activity to know more about the aquatic plants. She shows the students an underwater. She says that underwater leaves do not have waxy waterproof coating and asks them the reason for the same. Here is the reply from the students.
Student A: This is because the whole leaf surface can be used for other purposes.
Student B: This is because the whole leaf surface is required for exchanging gases between the plant and water.
Student C: This is because the whole leaf surface is required for transporting food.
Student D: This is because the whole leaf surface is required for transporting food.
Who has given the correct answer?
(a) Student A
(b) Student B
(c) Student C
(d) Student D

50. Following are some features of desert plants:
(i) They lose a lot of water through transpiration.
(ii) Their leaves are always broad and flat.
(iii) They lose very little water through transpiration.
(iv) Their roots grow very deep into the soil.
Which of the combination of above features are typical of desert plants?
(a) (i) and (ii)
(b) (ii) and (iv)
(c) (ii) and (iii)
(d) (iii) and (iv)

Space for Rough Work

OLYMPIAD

Mock Test 4

Name : ________ **Max. Marks : 50**

Number of Questions : 50 **Time : 2 Hours**

There is no negative marking in the test.

PHYSICS

1. Steve shone a torch into a hole on the left side of a box as shown below.

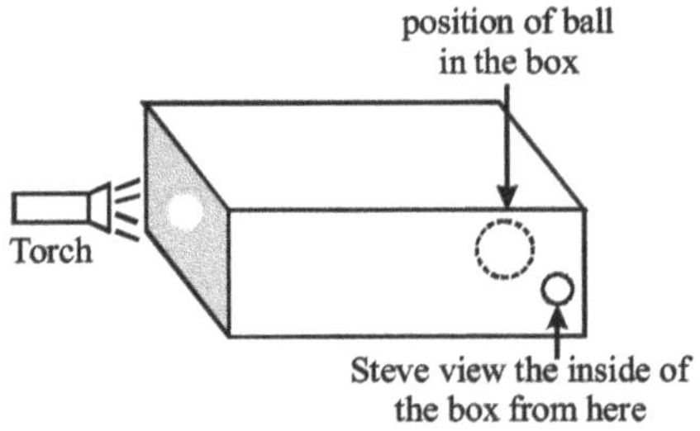

A ball was placed in the position shown in the above diagram. What would Steve see when he looked into the box through the hole indicated on the diagram?

(a) He would be able to see the whole ball.

(b) He would be able to see the left half of the ball.

(c) He would be able to see the right half of the ball.

(d) He would not see anything because the inside of the box was too dark.

2. Joseph used four different brands of batteries to light up four identical torches. The table below shows the amount of time the torches stayed lit using the four different brands of batteries.

Brand	Time (minutes)
W	450
X	550
Y	520
Z	500

What can he conclude from his experiment?

Space for Rough Work

(a) Brand X is the most lasting brand.
(b) Brand Z has the shortest lifespan.
(c) Brand W is the most expensive brand of battery.
(d) Brand Y enables the torch to shine brighter than brand Z.

3. Betty sets up the experiment as shown below to find out whether the surface of an inclined plane affects the amount of force needed to move an object up the inclined plane.

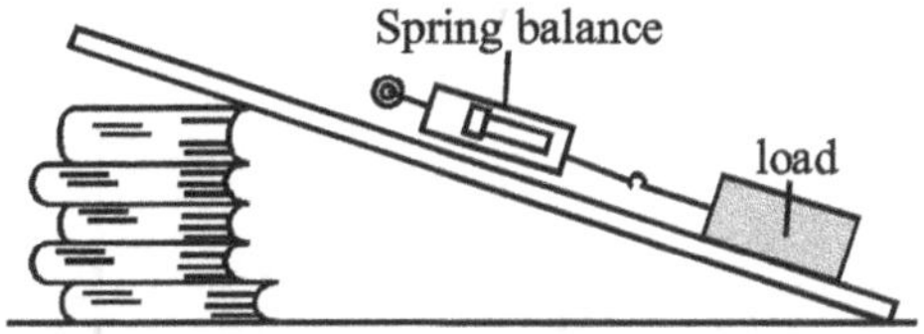

To ensure that the test is fair, which of the following variable(s) must she keep the same?

A. Mass of the wooden block
B. Material of the ramp used
C. Length of the ramp used
D. Number of books used

(a) C only
(b) B and C only
(c) A, B and D only
(d) A, C and D only

DIRECTION (Q. 4): *Match Column-I with Column-II and select the correct answer using the codes given below the columns.*

4.

Column I	Column II
A. Lunar eclipse	(p) Has colour of the object
B. Solar eclipse	(q) Always black
C. Image	(r) Moon between sun and earth
D. Shadow	(s) Earth between sun and moon.

(a) A → (s); B → (p); C → (r); D → (q)
(b) A → (p); B → (q); C → (r); D → (s)
(c) A → (s); B → (r); C → (q); D → (p)
(d) A → (s); B → (r); C → (p); D → (q)

5. The pole of a freely suspended magnet which points toward north direction is called:

(a) North pole
(b) South pole
(c) East pole
(d) West pole

Space for Rough Work

6. Richard brought a bar magnet near Object X.

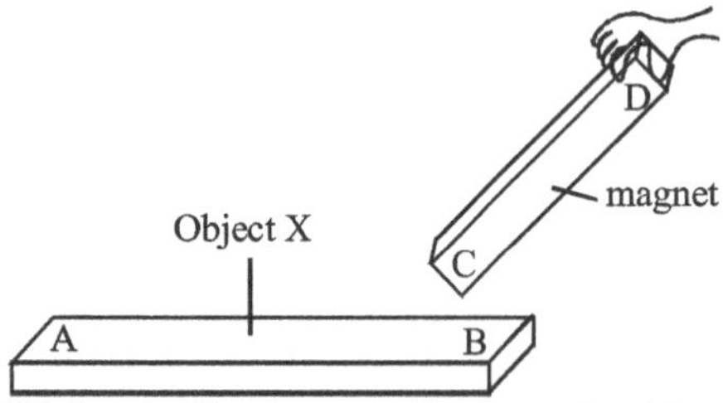

Object X moves towards the bar magnet in Richard's hand. Which of the following statements could be true?

A. B and C are like poles.
B. Object X is an iron bar.
C. B and C are unlike poles.
D. Object X is an aluminium bar.

(a) A only
(b) B and C only
(c) B and D only
(d) A, C and D only

7. The pressure exerted by a column of liquid is independent of the ____.
(a) density of the liquid
(b) weight of the liquid
(c) depth of the liquid
(d) shape of the container

8. Which one of the following substances allow the electricity to pass through it?
(a) Air
(b) Water
(c) Glass
(d) All of these

9. In the circuit below, which switches should be left open and which switches should be closed so that only bulb Y lights up?

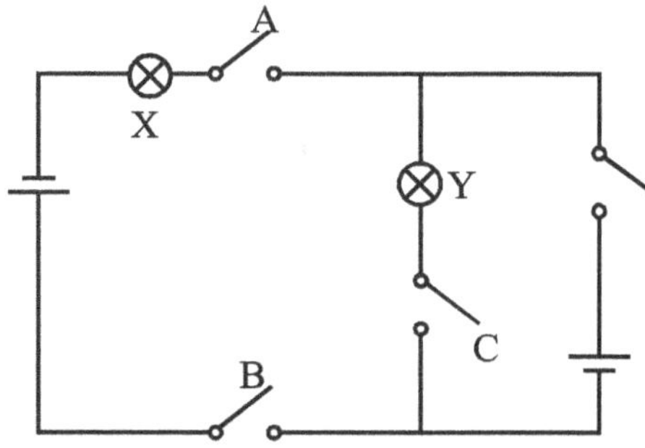

	Switch A	Switch B	Switch C	Switch D
(a)	Closed	Closed	Open	Open
(b)	Closed	Open	Open	Closed
(c)	Open	Open	Closed	Closed
(d)	Open	Closed	Closed	Open

10. Which one of the following was not used for the measurement of time in ancient world?
(a) Sand watch
(b) Electronic watch
(c) Sundial
(d) Water watch

Space for Rough Work

11. For the formation of shadow, essential condition is
    (a) There should be a source of light
    (b) There should be a screen
    (c) An opaque substance should be placed between the source of light and screen
    (d) All of the above
12. Rubber is a / an:
    (a) Conductor
    (b) Insulator
    (c) Semiconductor
    (d) None of these
13. A fly is moving on a paper and the movement of the fly shown on it. The distance travelled by fly from A to F is ________.

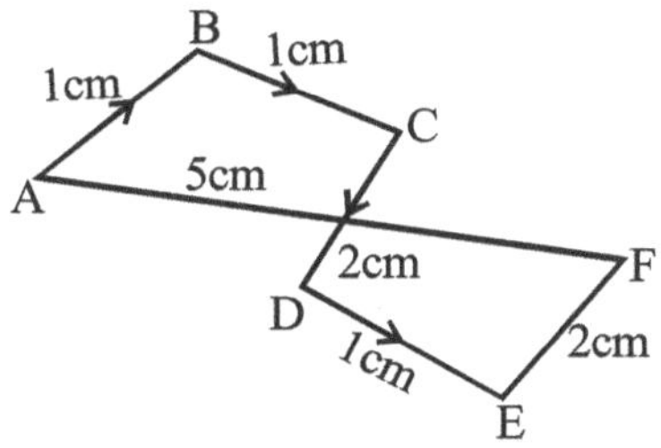

[Distances AB = 1 cm, BC = 1 cm, CD = 2 cm, DE = 1 cm, EF = 2 cm, AF = 5 cm]
    (a) 3 cm
    (b) 5 cm
    (c) 7 cm
    (d) 2 cm
14. Ajay is running short of connecting wires. To complete an electric circuit, she may use a
    (a) glass bangle.
    (b) thick thread.
    (c) rubber pipe.
    (d) steel spoon.

CHEMISTRY

15. Sohan wants to make a hammock. Which of the following properties of material he would choose?

    (a) Hard and strong
    (b) Strong and flexible
    (c) Insulator, flexible and opaque
    (d) Flexible, transparent and waterproof
16. It is a material that floats on the surface of water and is opaque. It is used to make chair, table etc.
    What material is it?
    (a) Paper (b) Wood
    (c) Aluminium (d) None of these

Space for Rough Work

17. Car windscreens are made of glass because it is __________.
    (a) shiny and waterproof
    (b) strong and transparent
    (c) flexible and waterproof
    (d) flexible and transparent
18. Rama's grandmother wants to make yarn from fibre at home. Which of the following will she use to carry out the task?
    (a) Powerloom
    (b) Handloom
    (c) Charkha
    (d) Knitting needles
19. Given below are two columns – column I and column II. Match the two columns and choose the correct option from the codes given below the column.

	Column-I		Column-II
A.	An odourless gas, needed by green plants to make food.	(i)	Oxygen
B.	Vital gas needed by all living beings	(ii)	Carbon dioxide
C.	Most abundant constituent of air	(iii)	Smoke
D.	It rises into the air when the sun heats the oceans and rivers	(iv)	Nitrogen
E.	Produced by burning of fuel	(v)	Water vapour

    (a) A-(ii), B-(i), C-(v), D-(iii), E-(iv)
    (b) A-(ii), B-(i), C-(iv), D-(v), E-(iii)
    (c) A-(i), B-(iv), C-(v), D-(iii), E-(ii)
    (d) A-(iv), B-(i), C-(ii), D-(v), E-(iii)

20. Artificial ripening of fruit is a /an
    (a) reversible change
    (b) periodic change
    (c) irreversible change
    (d) fast change
21. Choose correct option on the basis of statements (i) and (ii).
    (i) When hydrogen burns in oxygen, water is formed.
    (ii) When water is electrolysed, hydrogen and oxygen are formed.
    (a) (i) is a physical change and (ii) is a chemical change.
    (b) (i) is a chemical change and (ii) is a physical change.
    (c) Both (i) and (ii) are physical changes.
    (d) Both (i) and (ii) are chemical changes.

Space for Rough Work

22. Raju is a farmer. His field has black soil and the climate is warm. Which fibre yielding plant should he grow in his field?
    (a) Jute (b) Cotton
    (c) Coconut (d) Wool
23. The components of air which are harmful to living beings are
    (a) nitrogen and carbon dioxide.
    (b) dust and water vapour.
    (c) dust and smoke.
    (d) smoke and water vapour.
24. Consider the following phenomena.
    I. Boiling of water
    II. Melting of ice.
    III. Freezing of water.
    Which of the above take place with the evolution of energy?
    (a) I and II (b) II and III
    (c) I and III (d) Only III
25. Four mixtures are given below
    (i) Kidney beans and chick peas
    (ii) Pulses and rice
    (iii) Rice flakes and corn
    (iv) Potato wafers and biscuits
    Which of these can be separated by the method of winnowing?
    (a) (i) and (ii)
    (b) (ii) and (iii)
    (c) (i) and (iii)
    (d) (iii) and (iv)
26. Which of the following is an example of solubility of gas in water?
    (a) Oxygen in air
    (b) Oxygen in ocean
    (c) Cold drink
    (d) Both (b) and (c)
27. In an activity, a teacher dissolved a small amount of solid copper sulphate in a tumbler half filled with water. Which method would you use to get back solid copper sulphate from the solution?
    (a) Decantation
    (b) Evaporation
    (c) Sedimentation
    (d) Condensation
28. Match column I and column II and choose the correct option given below the columns.

Column-I (Objects)	**Column-II (Materials)**
(A) Window pane	(i) Glass
(B) Book	(ii) Metal
(C) Water bottle	(iii) Plastic
(D) Nail	(iv) Paper

    (a) A-(i), B-(iv), C-(iii), D-(ii)
    (b) A-(iii), B-(iv), C-(i), D-(ii)
    (c) A-(ii), B-(iv), C-(iii), D-(i)
    (d) A-(ii), B-(iii), C-(i), D-(iv)

Space for Rough Work

29. Iron rim is made slightly smaller than the wooden wheel. The rim is usually heated before fixing into the wooden wheel, because on heating the iron rim
    (a) expands and fits onto the wooden wheel.
    (b) contracts and fits onto the wooden wheel.
    (c) no change in the size takes place.
    (d) expands first, then on cooling contracts and fits onto the wooden wheel.
30. ....i....... is preferred to be worn in a hot and humid place like India because they ......ii....... .
    Complete the given statement.
    (a) i-Cotton; ii-have more air space inside them
    (b) i-Cotton; ii-have less air space inside them
    (c) i-Wool; ii-have no air space inside them
    (d) i-Wool; ii-have lot of air space inside them
31. Study the table.

	Object	Properties of object	Materials used for making object
I	Shirt	Hard and flexible	Plastic
II	Brick	Strong and can float	Clay
III	Iron	Flexible and strong	Rubber
IV	Frying pan	Strong and hard	Metal

Which of the following is correctly matched?
(a) I (b) II
(c) III (d) IV

BIOLOGY

32. Which type of leaves are present in submerged plants?
    (a) Spinous
    (b) Narrow, long and thin
    (c) Thick
    (d) Having layer of wax like substance
33. Which of the following is not an example of response to stimulus?
    (a) Watering in mouth when we see delicious food items.
    (b) Closing of leaves of *Mimosa* plant when touched.
    (c) Shutting our eyes when an object is suddenly thrown in our direction.
    (d) A chick hatching out of an egg.
34. Below are names of some animals:
    (i) Cow (ii) Sheep
    (iii) Horse (iv) Ox
    Which of the above are sources of milk for human beings?
    (a) (i) and (iii)
    (b) (i) and (ii)
    (c) (ii) and (iii)
    (d) (iii) and (iv)

Space for Rough Work

35. Which of the following combination of features would you observe in grass?
    (a) Parallel venation and fibrous root
    (b) Parallel venation and tap root
    (c) Reticulate venation and fibrous root
    (d) Reticulate venation and tap root
36. Read the following statements about diseases.
    (i) They are caused by germs.
    (ii) They are caused due to lack of nutrients in our diet.
    (iii) They can be passed on to another person through contact.
    (iv) They can be prevented by taking a balanced diet.

    Which pair of statements best describe a deficiency disease?
    (a) (i) and (ii)
    (b) (ii) and (iii)
    (c) (ii) and (iv)
    (d) (i) and (iii)
37. How many muscles work together to move a bone?
    (a) One
    (b) Two
    (c) Three
    (d) Four
38. The plant given below shows sensitivity to the touch of human finger or any other animal. The name of the plant is:

    (a) *Mimosa* (b) Tuber
    (c) Cotton (d) Climber
39. Based on the following statements, which one of the following options is correct?

    Statement A: The top part of a pistil is called stigma

    Statement B: The bottom part of a pistil is called stigma
    (a) Statement A is False and Statement B is True
    (b) Both, Statement A and Statement B are True
    (c) Both, Statement A and Statement B are false
    (d) Statement B is False and Statement A is True

Space for Rough Work

40. The plant given in the figure below can survive in the areas with scarcity of water and has root system that penetrate deep in the soil in search of water. Name the plant.

(a) Cactus (b) Plum
(c) Strawberry (d) Rose

41. An animal that live in grasslands, has strong teeth for chewing hard plant stems and has long ears to hear movement of predators is
(a) Lion
(b) Tiger
(c) Deer
(d) All of these

42. Which of the following is correct:
Rahul: Living things are biotic components of environment.
Rajesh: Non-living things are abiotic components of environment.
(a) Rahul
(b) Rajesh
(c) Both are correct
(d) Both are incorrect

43. Incidences of disease like skin cancer increases if ____________
(a) oxygen in air decreases
(b) nitrogen in air decreases
(c) carbondioxide in air increases
(d) ozone layer decreases

44. The child in the given figure is suffering from a deficiency disease. This disease is caused due to deficiency of

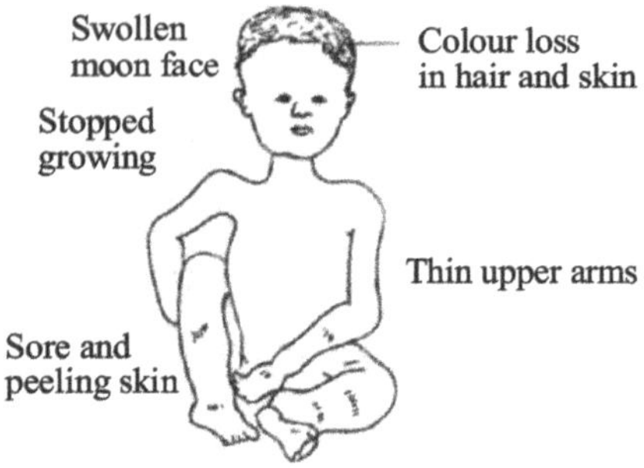

(a) carbohydrates
(b) proteins
(c) fats
(d) vitamins

45. Fruit A is dispersed by animals. Which of the following are possible characteristics of fruit A?
A. It is sweet and fleshy.
B. It splits open when ripe.
C. It has a wing-like structure.
D. It has brightly coloured skin.
(a) A and D only
(b) B and C only
(c) A, B and C only
(d) A, C and D only

Space for Rough Work

46. Study the diagram given below.

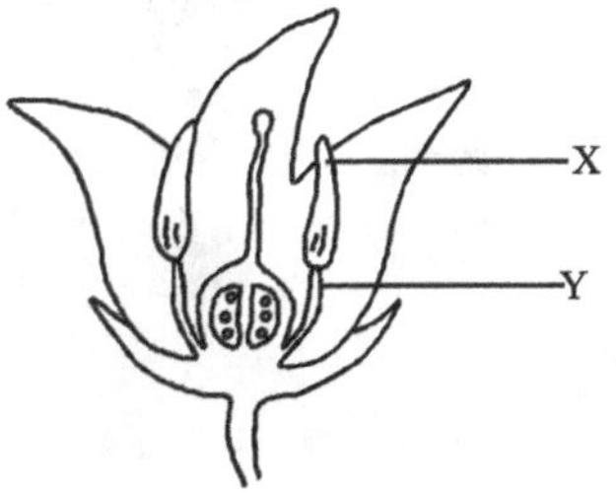

Which of the following statements about the flower above is true?
(a) The flower would be able to develop into a fruit.
(b) Structure Y holds the petals together.
(c) Structure labelled X receives pollen.
(d) It is a female flower.

47. The table below shows the descriptions of four pupils.

Pupil	Description
Jack	has attached earlobes
Kenny	has dark skin
Lisa	has black hair
Meg	has blue eyes

Whose descriptions refer to inherited characteristics?
(a) Jack and Lisa only
(b) kenny and Meg only
(c) Jack, Kenny and Meg only
(d) Jack, Kenny, Lisa and Meg

48. Which one of the following food item does not provide dietary fibre?
(a) Whole grains
(b) Whole pulses
(c) Fruits and vegetables
(d) Milk

49. Which of the following terms constitute the female part of the flower.
(a) Sepals, petal and stamen
(b) Stigma, style and ovary
(c) Ovary, stamen and stigma
(d) Ovary, style and stamen

50. The steps required for conversion of kitchen garbage into manure are given below in a jumbled form.
(i) Put garbage in a pit
(ii) Cover the bottom of the pit with sand
(iii) Cover the pit loosely with a gunny bag or grass
(iv) Add worms

Which of the following shows the correct sequence of the above steps?
(a) (ii); (i); (iii); (iv)
(b) (i); (ii); (iii); (iv)
(c) (ii); (iv); (i); (iii)
(d) (iv); (i); (ii); (iii)

Space for Rough Work

OLYMPIAD

Mock Test 5

Name : ________ **Max. Marks : 50**

Number of Questions : 50 **Time : 2 Hours**

There is no negative marking in the test.

PHYSICS

1. When we break a magnet into pieces, each piece having
   (a) North Pole only
   (b) South Pole only
   (c) both North and South Poles
   (d) None of these

2. A body moves along the path PQR. What is the distance travelled by the body?

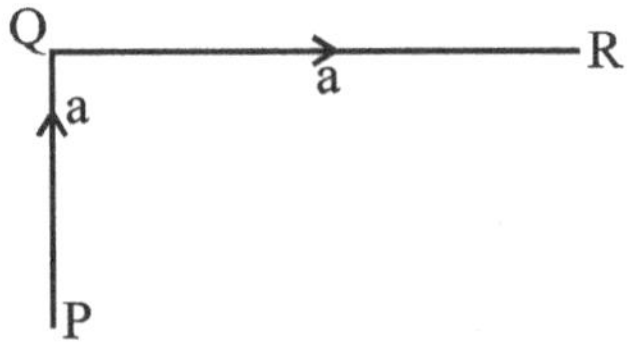

   (a) a (b) a – 2
   (c) 2a (d) a + 2

3. A car of mass 1000 kg can produce an acceleration of 8 m/s^2.Calculate the force produced by the engine ignoring friction.
   (a) 10,000 N (b) 100,000 N
   (c) 8000 N (d) 18000 N

4. Which of the following cannot work without making use of magnetism ?

A. 

B. 

C. 

D. 

   (a) A only
   (b) A and B only
   (c) B and D only
   (d) B, C and D only

Space for Rough Work

5. A stone of mass 4 kg is dropped from a height. Find the force exerted by it on ground if acceleration due to gravity is 10 m/s^2.
   (a) 20 N (b) 2.5 N
   (c) 40 N (d) 0.4 N
6. The blades of a moving fan show
   (a) circular motion.
   (b) rotatory motion.
   (c) translatory motion.
   (d) oscillatory motion.
7. What is a substance called which does not conduct electricity?
   (a) Conductor
   (b) Insulator
   (c) Semiconductor
   (d) Semi insulator
8. North pole of a magnet can be identified by
   (a) another magnet having its poles marked as North pole and South pole.
   (b) another magnet no matter whether the poles are marked or not.
   (c) using an iron bar.
   (d) using iron filings.
9. Non-magnetic materials are:
   (a) Plastic, wood, iron, paper
   (b) Iron, nickle and cobalt
   (c) Leather, iron, nickle and clothes
   (d) Plastic, leather, clothes and paper
10. The diagrams below show three closed circuits in which all the bulbs light up. The bulbs and batteries used in each circuit are the same.

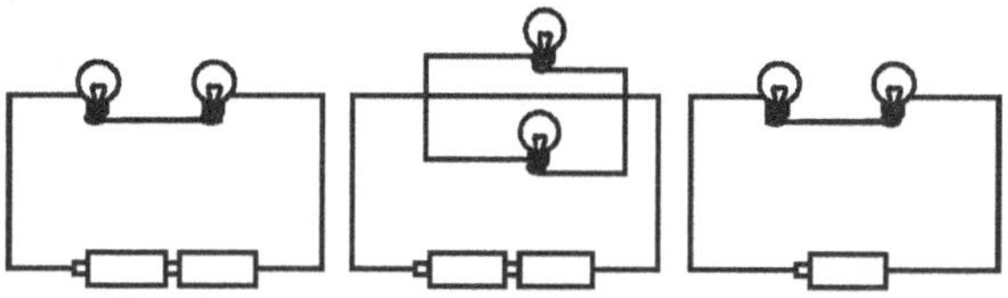

Circuit A Circuit B Circuit C

Arrange the circuits according to the brightness of the bulbs, beginning with the brightest.
   (a) A, B, C (b) B, A, C
   (c) C, A, B (d) C, B, A

DIRECTION (Q. 11) : Match column-I with column-II and select the correct answer using the codes given below the columns.

11.

Column I	**Column II**
A. Lightning	(p) Collection of tiny water droplets
B. Thunder	(q) Falling of water from the sky
C. Clouds	(r) Loud sound with lightning
D. Rain	(s) Flash of light

(a) A $\rightarrow$ (p); B $\rightarrow$ (r); C $\rightarrow$ (s); D $\rightarrow$ (q) (b) A $\rightarrow$ (s); B $\rightarrow$ (r); C $\rightarrow$ (p); D $\rightarrow$ (q)
(c) A $\rightarrow$ (p); B $\rightarrow$ (s); C $\rightarrow$ (r); D $\rightarrow$ (q) (d) A $\rightarrow$ (s); B $\rightarrow$ (p); C $\rightarrow$ (r); D $\rightarrow$ (q)

Space for Rough Work

12. A solar cell converts ________
    (a) chemical energy to light energy.
    (b) light energy to electrical energy.
    (c) electrical energy to light energy.
    (d) light energy to chemical energy
13. Which one of the following metals can be used to make the needle of a compass?
    (a) Gold (b) Silver
    (c) Iron (d) Copper
14. Parul arranged a magnet and a piece of cardboard as shown in the diagram. He then introduced a paper clip into the set-up.

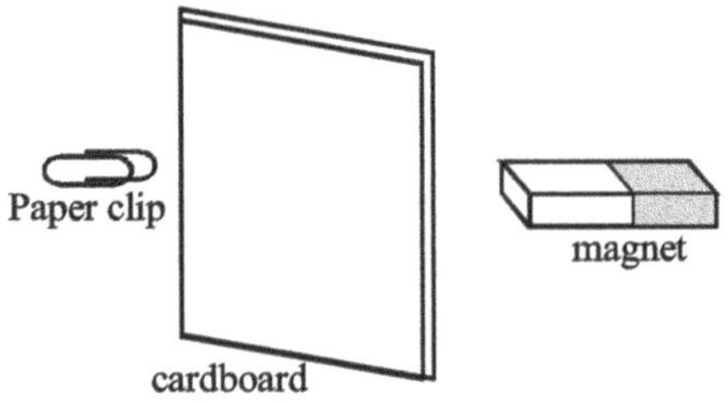

The paper clip moved towards the magnet. Paul removed the paper clip and the cardboard. He placed an iron sheet in the same position previously occupied by the cardboard. He introduced the paper clip again. The paper clip did not move towards the magnet. Which of the following statements explains the above observations?
A. The paper clip became magnetised.
B. The iron sheet was covered with rust.
C. A magnetic force can pass through the cardboard.
D. A magnetic force cannot pass through the iron sheet.
    (a) B only
    (b) C only
    (c) C and D only
    (d) A, B and D only

CHEMISTRY

15. Match column I with column II and choose the correct option.

Column-I	Column-II
(A) Cotton	(p) Highly porous
(B) Wool	(q) Elastic
(C) Rayon	(r) Absorbent
(D) Nylon	(s) Artificial silk

    (a) A-(p); B-(q); C-(r); D-(s) (b) A-(q), B-(s), C-(p), D-(r)
    (c) A-(r); B-(p); C-(s); D-(q) (d) A-(q), B-(p), C-(s), D-(r)

Space for Rough Work

16. Silk
    (a) is a natural fibre obtained from an adult silk worm.
    (b) is a natural fibre obtained from cocoon of silk worm.
    (c) is an artificial fibre.
    (d) None of the above is correct.
17. Select a reversible change.
    (a) Milk to paneer
    (b) Growth of a tree
    (c) Cow-dung to biogas
    (d) Ice-cream to molten ice cream
18. **Assertion (A) :** Those changes in which a new substance is formed is known as a chemical change.
    Reason (R) : Physical changes can be reversed easily.
    (a) Both A and R are true and R is the correct explanation of A.
    (b) Both A and R are true but R is not the correct explanation of A.
    (c) A is true but R is false.
    (d) A is false but R is true.
19. Read the following statements carefully and choose the correct option.
    (i) Cotton fibre is obtained from root of cotton plant.
    (ii) Jute fibre is hard and silky.
    (iii) Rayon is obtained from glucose obtained from wood pulp.
    (a) Statement (i) and (iii) are incorrect while statement (ii) is correct.
    (b) Statement (i) and (ii) are incorrect while (iii) is correct.
    (c) All the statements are correct.
    (d) All the statements are incorrect.
20. Fractional distillation is used to obtain the components of which of the following?
    I. Seawater
    II. Muddy water III. Crude oil
    (a) I, II (b) II, III
    (c) III only (d) I only
21. Priya observed bubbles coming out of soil while watering the plants. The bubbles contain
    (a) water vapour.
    (b) only oxygen gas.
    (c) air.
    (d) hydrogen gas.
22. Study the following classification chart and answer the question.

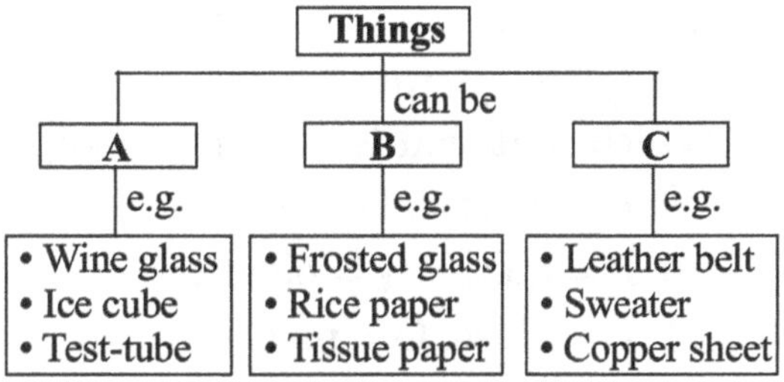

Space for Rough Work

A ceramic vase can be grouped under ______ .
(a) B only
(b) C only
(c) A and B only
(d) A and C only

23. What should be the property of the material that is used for making swimming board.
(a) waterproof
(b) low density
(c) flexible
(d) both (a) and (b)

24. Which of the following objects is/are made of material(s) that do(es) not absorb water?
A. Boots
B. Bottles
C. Raincoats
D. Newspapers
(a) D only
(b) A and C only
(c) A and D only
(d) A, B and C only

25. Swati classified a few changes occurring around us as shown in the table.

S.No.	Changes	Type
1.	Sharpening of pencil	Physical, reversible
2.	Evaporation of water	Physical, irreversible
3.	Opening of a bud	Chemical, irreversible
4.	Rusting of iron	Chemical, reversible

Which of the changes is/are classified correctly?
(a) 2 and 3 only (b) 3 and 4 only
(c) 1 and 4 only (d) 3 only

26. Which of the following fabric is smooth to touch, had vibrant colour and shine
(a) Cotton (b) Wool (c) Silk (d) Jute

27. Study the picture below.
Which material is used to make P and Q in above figure
(a) P = plastic, Q = metal
(b) P = metal, Q = plastic
(c) P = glass, Q = metal
(d) P = metal, Q = wood

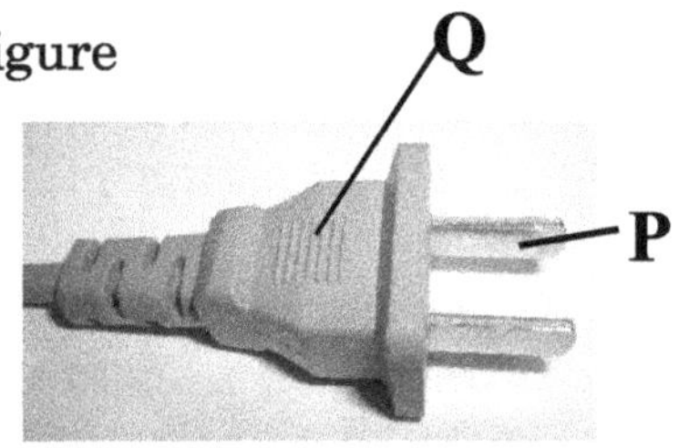

Space for Rough Work

28. Study the conept map below.
Which of the following can Gas A be?

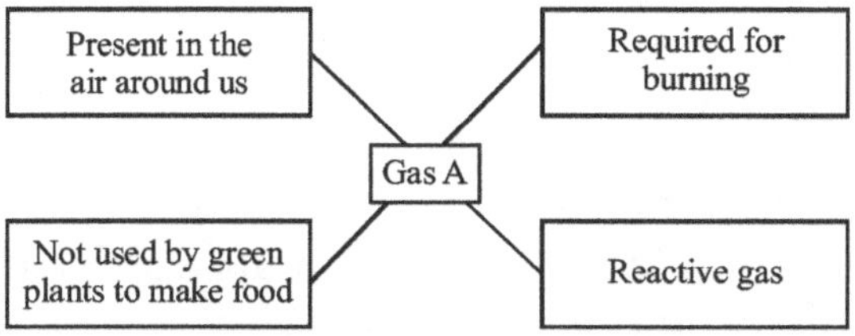

(a) Nitrogen (b) Oxygen
(c) Carbon dioxide (d) Argon

29. The burning of magnesium in air is accompanied by production of heat and light. This can be classified as
(a) physical and exothermic change.
(b) chemical and exothermic change.
(c) physical and endothermic change.
(d) chemical and endothermic change.

30. Sedimentation process can be speeded up by loading. Which of the following is used in loading?
(a) Common salt (b) Oxygen
(c) Alum (d) Sugar

31. Yarn is woven to get fabric using
(a) charkha.
(b) spinning machines.
(c) looms.
(d) knitting needles.

BIOLOGY

Study the diagram below and answer Questions (32 and 33).

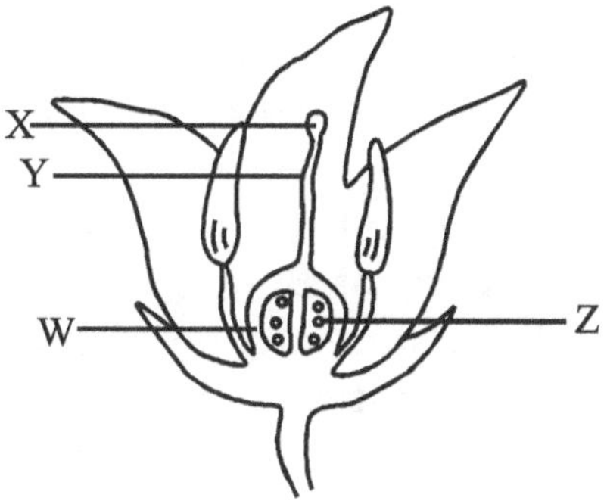

32. Pollen grains land on the part labelled ________.
(a) W (b) X
(c) Y (d) Z

33. Which of the following changes will take place after fertilisation?

	(Before fertilisation)	(After fertilisation)
A:	Structure W	Fruit
B:	Structure X	Seed
C:	Structure Y	Fruit stalk
D:	Structure Z	Seed

(a) B only
(b) A and D only
(c) B and C only
(d) A, C and D only

Space for Rough Work

34. Which one of the following statements is correct?
Statement A: Upper Jaw is movable as it is connected to skull by fixed joint.
Statement B: Lower jaw is movable as it is connected to skull by hinge joint.
(a) Statement A
(b) Statement B
(c) Both statements are correct
(d) Both statements are incorrect

35. Study the food web shown below.

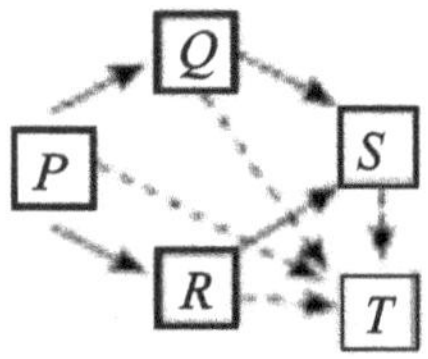

How is organism P in the food web different from the organisms Q, R, S and T?
(a) It causes decomposition.
(b) It feeds on plants.
(c) It feeds on animals.
(d) It can photosynthesize.

36. Which of the following structures help the redworms to grind their food?
(a) Mouth (b) Teeth
(c) Tongue (d) Gizzard

37. Which of the following is a tissue building nutrient ?
(a) Fat
(b) Protein
(c) Vitamin
(d) Carbohydrate

38. There is a group of animals which eat the dead and decayed organic substance. Which of the following animals belongs to this group?
(a) Leopard
(b) Hen
(c) Jackals
(d) Deer

39. Which one of the following adaptations is found in fish?
(a) Streamlined body
(b) Flexible backbone
(c) Flight feathers
(d) Both (a) and (b)

40. Name the vitamin that gets destroyed because of heat during cooking–
(a) Vitamin A
(b) Vitamin B
(c) Vitamin C
(d) Vitamin D

Space for Rough Work

41. Refer to the given figure and select the correct option.

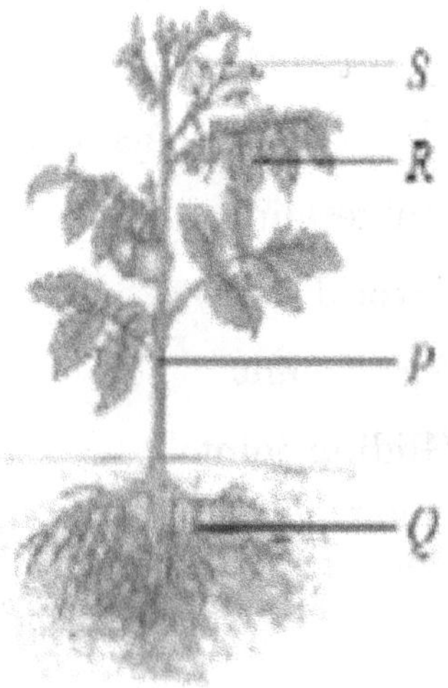

(a) The parts labelled R and Q are edible parts in spinach and turnip respectively.
(b) The part labelled R is edible in lettuce, tumeric and moringa.
(c) The part labelled S is edible in brocoli, clove and cabbage.
(d) All of these

42. Name the joint which is present between thigh bone and hip bone.
(a) Hinge joint
(b) Fixed joint
(c) Pivot joint
(d) Ball and socket joint

43. 'A habitat provides everything to the organisms, which they need to live in'. The given statement is ______ .
(a) true (b) false
(c) partly true (d) partly false

44. Farmers plough their fields before they plant seeds because
(a) it loosens the soil and allows the air to enter into the spaces between soil particles.
(b) the sprouting seed will be able to use the trapped air.
(c) plants will absorb some air through their roots and also take in water and minerals from the soil.
(d) All of the above

45. Which of the following statements about the importance of seed dispersal is true?
(a) It is to encourage overcrowding.
(b) It is to ensure that a new type of plant will grow.
(c) It is to stop the adult plant from reproducing.
(d) It is to reduce competition for space, nutrients and sunlight.

46. The plants whose life cycle requires one season for completion are called ....i...... plants. They are generally ....ii...... . The information in which row completes the given statements?

Space for Rough Work

(a) i-annual; ii-shrubs

(b) i-perennial; ii-shrubs

(c) i-annual; ii-herbs

(d) i-perennial; ii-herbs

47. A liquid used to test the presence of starch in food is–

(a) Copper sulphate (b) Iodine

(c) Caustic soda (d) Glycerine

48. Plants with ....i......... system bear leaves that are generally broad and have a criss cross network of veins called ....ii........ venation. The information in which row completes the given statement?

(a) i-tap root; ii-parallel

(b) i-fibrous root; ii-parallel

(c) i-tap root; ii-reticulate

(d) i-fibrous root; ii-reticulate

49. The joint in between the adjacent vertebrae in the backbone is:

(a) Hinge joint

(b) Pivotal joint

(c) Fixed joint

(d) Gliding joint

50. The diagram shows germination of a seedling. Which part is the plumule?

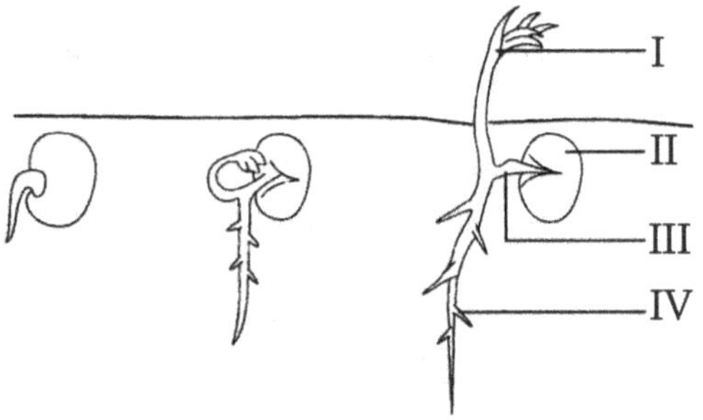

(a) I (b) II

(c) III (d) IV

Space for Rough Work

GENERAL KNOWLEDGE

OLYMPIAD

Mock Test 1

Name : __________

Number of Questions : 25

Max. Marks : 25

Time : 1 Hour

There is no negative marking in the test.

1. This is the largest flightless bird native to Africa. Its skin is used for leather products and its meat is marketed commercially. Name this bird.
   (a) Emu (b) Ostrich
   (c) Albatross (d) Siberian Crane
2. Dinosaurs are a diverse group of reptiles of the clade Dinosauria that first appeared during the Triassic period. They became the dominant terrestrial vertebrates after the Triassic–Jurassic extinction event 201 million years ago. Dinosaurs are
   (a) Carnivores (b) Herbivores
   (c) Omnivores (d) None of these
3. Darwin's finches were first collected by Charles Darwin on the Galápagos Islands during the second voyage of the Beagle. These finches refer to
   (a) Fishes (b) Birds
   (c) Amphibians (d) Fishes
4. This group of animals is the largest mammal on the Earth. It is the largest toothed predator on earth. Several species exhibit sexual dimorphism and the females are larger than males. Identify the animal.
   (a) Elephant (b) Whale
   (c) Dinosaur (d) Rhinoceros
5. Some plants with soft stems attain height up to five feet. These plants are
   (a) Herbs
   (b) Shrubs
   (c) Trees
   (d) None of the above
6. Trees shed their leaves in a particular season. Trees are leafless for a shorter or longer season of the year in
   (a) Evergreen forest
   (b) Mangrove forest
   (c) Scrub Jungle forest
   (d) Deciduous forest

Space for Rough Work

7. Photosynthesis is a process in which plants prepare food from water and carbon dioxide. Oxygen liberated during photosynthesis comes from
   (a) Carbon dioxid
   (b) Water
   (c) Break down of chlorophyll
   (d) Atmosphere
8. Stilt roots are aerial adventitious roots which grow obliquely down wards from basal nodes of the main stem and fix firmly to the soil. Which of the following plants has stilt roots?
   (a) Banyan (b) Maize
   (c) Mango (d) China rose
9. Below figure shows an insectivorous plant that has poorly developed root systems. They obtain the missing nutrients by trapping, 'digesting' and absorbing insects. Which one of the following parts of the pitcher plant becomes modified into a pitcher?

   (a) Leaf (b) Flower
   (c) Fruit (d) Flower bud
10. Global warming, which is a gradual rising of Earth's temperature, affects living and non-living organisms around us. As the Earth becomes warmer, due to global warming, which of the following areas will be affected most?
   (a) Weather conditions
   (b) Plate movement
   (c) Mountain formation
   (d) Earthquake frequency
11. Increase in human population impacts which of Earth's spheres?
   (a) Biosphere only
   (b) Biosphere and hydrosphere only
   (c) Biosphere, hydrosphere, and atmosphere only
   (d) Biosphere, hydrosphere, atmosphere, and geosphere
12. Match column I with column II and select the correct option from the given codes.

   Column I
   Column II
   A. World Forest Day
   (A) 21 March
   B. World Environment Day
   (B) 22 April
   C. Earth Day
   (C) 5 June
   D. International Tiger Day
   (D) 29 July
   (a) 1-(B), 2-(A), 3-(D), 4-(C)
   (b) 1-(B), 2-(A), 3-(C), 4-(D)
   (c) 1-(A), 2-(C), 3-(B), 4-(D)
   (d) 1-(A), 2-(B), 3-(C), 4-(D)
13. This organisation is a scientific body formed under the guidance of the United Nations. It aims to stabilize greenhouse gas concentrations in the atmosphere at a level that would

Space for Rough Work

prevent anthropogenic interference with the climate system. Which organization is this?

(a) Intergovernmental Panel on Climate Change
(b) United Nations Environment Programme
(c) Both A and B
(d) None of the above

14. Silent Valley Movement aimed to protect the Silent Valley from being destroyed by a hydroelectric project. In which state the Silent Valley is located?

(a) Kerala
(b) Tamil Nadu
(c) Madhya Pradesh
(d) Odisha

15. World Environment Day is the United Nation's main initiative for encouraging worldwide awareness and action for the protection of our environment. It is celebrated on

(a) 5 June
(b) 3 April
(c) 5 September
(d) 2 December

16. Read the following statements:

I. Protocol on Environmental Protection to the Antarctic Treaty was implemented on January 14, 1998.

II. Tourism has been excluded from environmental assessment.

Choose the correct option.

(a) I only
(b) II only
(c) Both (I) and (II)
(d) None of these

17. White tiger is rarely found in India. A spotted 'white tiger' with a pale skin colour for the first time has been seen in India. In which region was it seen?

(a) Nilgiris
(b) Aravalli
(c) Vindhya Range
(d) Hindu Kush

18. Halley's Comet is a short-period comet which is the only known short-period comet that is regularly visible to the naked eye from Earth. Halley's Comet can be seen with the naked eye

(a) 76 times a year.
(b) every 78 years.
(c) every 76 years.
(d) never.

19. Who was the only Indian woman Prime Minister?

(a) 

Pratibha Patil

Space for Rough Work

(b)

Indira Gandhi

(c)

Sonia Gandhi

(d) None of the above

20. He was the king of South India Thanjavur and founded the imperial Chola Empire. He ruled over the region to the north of the river Kaveri. Who was he?
    (a) Vijayalaya (b) Rajaraja
    (c) Rajendra (d) Virarajendra
21. Who won the Nobel Prize in literature 2022?
    (a) Annie Ernaux
    (b) Ales Bialiatski
    (c) Bob Dylan
    (d) Alice Munro
22. Dadasaheb Phalke Award is India's highest award in cinema. Who won the Dadasaheb Phalke award in 2022?
    (a) Ranbir Kapoor
    (b) Manoj Kumar
    (c) Gulzar
    (d) Vinod Khanna
23. Where was first cricket match held in India?
    (a) Bangalore (b) Chennai
    (c) Mumbai (d) Delhi
24. Composite numbers are those numbers which have:
    (a) More than two factors
    (b) Infinite factors
    (c) One factor
    (d) Two factors
25. Who is the Chief Election Commissioner of India?
    (a) Nasim Zaidi
    (b) Rajiv kumar
    (c) S.Y. Quraishi
    (d) Om Prakash Rawat

Space for Rough Work

OLYMPIAD

Mock Test 2

Name : __________
Number of Questions : 25

Max. Marks : 25
Time : 1 Hour

There is no negative marking in the test.

1. Maize, jowar, and pulses belong to this category of cereal grain. It is also called as 'coarse grain' and has been attributed to its resistance to drought. Identify this crop.
   (a) Rice (b) Millet
   (c) Barley (d) Maize

2. This animal is an extinct small hopping marsupial found in desert regions of central Australia. It has forelimb and hindlimb of different size. Which animal is this?
   (a) Desert rat-kangaroo
   (b) Kangaroo
   (c) Desert Wolf
   (d) Desert Rabbit

3. 'X' is the molten rock expelled by a volcano during an eruption. When it has stopped moving, it solidifies to form igneous rock. It is a liquid usually at temperatures from 700 to 1,200°C. Identify 'X'.
   (a) Lava (b) Magma
   (c) Andesite (d) Pyroclasts

4. Select the option which on rearrangement will give the term used for the accumulation of toxic substances in organisms at successively higher levels in a food chain.
   (a) MIICATION AGONBFI
   (b) AKIAHDGSONSI
   (c) LOIANSGHYT
   (d) GREEYROYFA

5. Which of the following if buried in the earth is expected to remain for a long time in the environment?
   (a) Paper (b) Plastic
   (c) Wood (d) None of these

6. The sum total of the populations of the same type of organisms constitute
   (a) Colony (b) Genus
   (c) Species (d) Community

7. In the 1770's, a Scottish physician and chemist Daniel Rutherford performed a simple experiment with which he discovered a gas. The gas is the lightest member of group 15

Space for Rough Work

of the periodic table, often called the pnictogens. Identify the gas.

(a) Helium (b) Carbon Dioxide
(c) Nitrogen (d) Oxygen

8. A container has a liquid which tastes sour. Another liquid is added to the container and the pH of the resulting solution is found to be neutral. Identify the liquid with sour taste.
(a) Acid (b) Base
(c) Water (d) Salt solution

9. Venera 9 was an unmanned space mission launched by Soviet Union. It consisted of an orbiter and a lander. It was sent in space to record surface conditions of
(a) Moon (b) Venus
(c) Jupiter (d) Sun

10. India launched a mission to Mars called MOM (Mangalyaan) on 5th November, 2013. Which space agency was responsible for the this mission?
(a) NASA
(b) ISRO
(c) BARC
(d) European Space Agency

11. Who among the following has been elected as the President of India?
(a) Meira Kumar
(b) Ram Nath Kovind
(c) Droupadi Murmu
(d) Venkaiah Naidu

12. What is Pradhan Mantri Suraksha Bima Yojana (PMSBY)?
(a) Accidental insurance cover
(b) Life insurance cover
(c) Overdraft up to Rs. 5,000
(d) None of above

13. The Arya Samaj was founded in 1875 to oppose polytheism, image worship, caste-based restrictions, and child marriage. It supported female education and widow remarriage. Who was the founder of the Arya Samaj?
(a) Swami Dayananda Saraswati
(b) Rabindranath Tagore
(c) Swami Vivekananda
(d) Sanjay Sangvi

14. Give one word for 'to accuse falsely'.
(a) Conjuncture (b) Detest
(c) Admonish (d) Calumniate

15. Read the few lines of a poem and identify the poet.
I wandered lonely as a cloud
That floats on high o'er vales and hills, A host, of golden daffodils;
Besides the lake, beneath the trees,
Fluttering and dancing in the breeze.
(a) Henry Abbey
(b) William Wordsworth
(c) Ryan Adams
(d) Robert Frost

16. "The Age of 1000 Entertainments" is also known as
(a) Tang Dynasty
(b) Ming Dynasty
(c) Shang Dynasty
(d) Qin Dynasty

Space for Rough Work

17. Which creative art form is Sonal Mansingh associated with?
   (a) Dance
   (b) Vocal music (Hindustani)
   (c) Painting
   (d) Instrumental music
18. World Athletics Championships, 2022 was held in __________.
   (a) New York (b) Oregon, US
   (c) London (d) Tokyo
19. Wimbledon Championship is an annual tennis tournament first contested in 1877 and played on outdoor grass courts. Who has won the 2022 Women's Singles Wimbledon Championship?
   (a) Simona Halep
   (b) Serena Williams
   (c) Elena Rybakina
   (d) Garbine Muguruza
20. Stan Wawrinka represents and belongs to which country?
   (a) Russia
   (b) Switzerland
   (c) USA
   (d) France
21. Where is the largest India's EV Charging station has been launched?
   (a) Delhi (b) Mumbai
   (c) Gurugram (d) Chennai
22. Where is the 'Infinity Bridge' in world?
   (a) Singapore
   (b) London
   (c) Dubai
   (d) Jakarta
23. The concept that describes the beliefs of an individual or culture is called
   (a) Values
   (b) Attitude
   (c) Behavior
   (d) Personality
24. What does this sign mean?

   (a) Slow down and prepare to stop if necessary
   (b) Come to a complete stop at the intersection
   (c) Proceed ahead and maintain a constant speed
   (d) Stop for emergency vehicles
25. World TB Day is celebrated on
   (a) 24th February
   (b) 24th March
   (c) 2th December
   (d) 27th June

Space for Rough Work

OLYMPIAD

Mock Test 3

Name : __________

Number of Questions : 25

Max. Marks : 25

Time : 1 Hour

There is no negative marking in the test.

1. An earthworm is a tube-shaped, segmented worm found in the phylum Annelida. Earthworms are commonly found living in soil, feeding on live and dead organic matter. Earthworms breath through :
   (a) Skin (b) Gills
   (c) Lungs (d) Stomata
2. A pneumatic bone is a bone that is hollow or contains many air cells, such as the mastoid process of the temporal bone. It is also called hollow bone. Pneumatic bone is found in
   (a) Lizard (b) Pigeon
   (c) Shark (d) Whale
3. Fibrous root system is usually formed by thin, moderately branching roots growing from the stem. Which of the following has fibrous root?

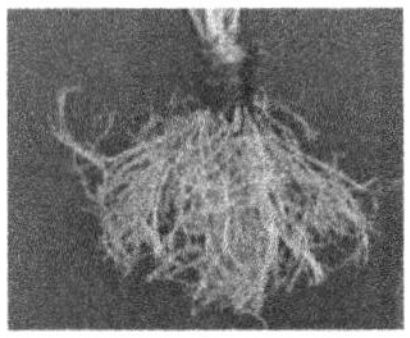

   (a) Mango (b) Peas
   (c) Neem (d) Wheat
4. Match column I and column II and select the correct option from the given codes.

	Column I		**Column II**
A.	Wet evergreen forests	(p)	Madhya Pradesh
B.	Semi-evergreen forests	(q)	Eastern Himalayas
C.	Moist deciduous forest	(r)	Western Ghats
D.	Broad-leaved forests	(s)	Andaman and Nicobar Islands

Space for Rough Work

(a) A-r, B-s, C-p, D-q
(b) A-q, B-s, C-p, D-r
(c) A-r, B-p, C-s, D-q
(d) A-p, B-s, C-r, D-q

5. Read the following statements.
   I. Air pollution can be controlled by planting trees.
   II. Acid rain contains sulphuric acid and nitric acid.

   Choose the correct option.
   (a) I is true
   (b) II is true
   (c) Both I and II are true
   (d) Both I and II are false

6. World Environment Day is the United Nation's principal initiative for encouraging worldwide awareness and action for the protection of our environment. On which day it is celebrated?
   (a) 5th June (b) 1st December
   (c) 22nd March (d) 4th October

7. In 1772, Daniel Rutherford discovered a gas which he called "noxious air." The gas plays an important role in the life of plants and animals on Earth. It is an important component of amino acids. Identify the gas.

   (a) Nitrogen (b) Neon
   (c) Carbon dioxide (d) Oxygen

8. Where would you find the smallest atoms of elements in the periodic table?
   (a) Top and left-hand side
   (b) Top and right-hand side
   (c) Bottom and right-hand side
   (d) Bottom and left-hand side

9. A family of eight planets and moons, including asteroids, comets and other objects, all circling the Sun is known as a :

   (a) Galaxy (b) Solar system
   (c) Cluster (d) Milky way

10. The first person known to have built a reflector of telescope to see the planets is
   (a) Kepler (b) Galileo
   (c) Newton (d) Tycho

11. Who is the current Chief Justice of India?
   (a) D. Y. Chandrachud
   (b) T. S. Thakur
   (c) H. L. Dattu
   (d) Sharad Arvind Bobde

Space for Rough Work

12. Baffin Island is located in which country?

(a) Belarus (b) Bulgaria
(c) United States (d) Canada

13. Arya Samaj is an Indian Hindu reform movement that promotes values and practices based on the belief in the infallible authority of the Vedas. Who was the founder of the Arya Samaj?

(a) Dayanand Saraswati

(b) Rabindranath Tagore

(c) Swami Vivekananda

(d) Raja Ram Mohan Roy

14. President of India is the head of which of these government bodies?
(a) Executive (b) Judiciary
(c) Parliament (d) Legislature

15. Read the following statements given with codes.

P-Meet your friends at the corner to walk to school

Q-Roll over, sleepy eyed, and turn off the alarm clock

R-Get dressed for school and hurry downstairs for breakfast

Which of the following shows correct sequence of events?
(a) P, Q, R (b) P, R, Q
(c) R, Q, P (d) Q, R, P

16. Which of the following authors has not received the Nobel Prize in Literature?
(a) Bob Dylan (b) Mo Yan
(c) Alice Munro (d) Neil Gaiman

17. Which of the following films received the Best Film Award at the 68th National Film Awards ceremony?
(a) Hellaro
(b) Newton
(c) Sorari Pottru
(d) Mahayodha Rama

18. Which dance form is shown the figure below?

Space for Rough Work

(a) Kathakali
(b) Odissi
(c) Kuchipudi
(d) Bharatanatyam

19. Who won the 2022 US Open Women's Single tennis tournament title?
(a) Bianca Andresscu
(b) Saina Nehwal
(c) P.V. Sindhu
(d) Iga Swiatek

20. What is the national game of Spain?
(a) Volleyball (b) Hockey
(c) Cricket (d) Football

21. What would you do if a stranger knocks at your door?
(a) Inform your parents
(b) Ask him to go back
(c) Immediately open the door
(d) Offer him a glass of water

22. What will you do to protect the environment?
(a) Burn waste in open fields.
(b) Plant trees.
(c) Use diesel cars instead of petrol cars.
(d) Switch on all the lights in your home even if not required.

23. Who among the following won the 2022 Nobel Prize in Medicine?
(a) Peter Handke
(b) Svante Paabo
(c) Svetlana Alexievich
(d) Bob Dylan

24. Which of the following countries will host the men's World Boxing Championship in 2023?
(a) Spain
(b) Russia
(c) Uzbekistan
(d) Japan

25. Which country will host the 18th edition of G20 summit?
(a) Germany
(b) France
(c) India
(d) Japan

Space for Rough Work

OLYMPIAD

Mock Test 4

Name : ___________
Number of Questions : 40
Max. Marks : 40
Time : 2 Hours

There is no negative marking in the test.

1. What is the common character of plants listed below?
   Rice, wheat, onion, garlic.
   (a) They are all herbs.
   (b) They are modified stems.
   (c) They are modified roots.
   (d) They are modified leaves.
2. This is large, flat teeth at the back of the mouth. It is more developed in mammals and is used primarily to grind food during chewing. Identify the teeth.
   (a) Molars (b) Incisors
   (c) Canines (d) Premolars
3. This is an endangered animal species in India. Since 2010, it is listed as Endangered on the IUCN Red List. It is the national animal of both India and Bangladesh. Which animal has been described here?
   (a) Lion (b) Bengal Tiger
   (c) Cheetah (d) Monkey
4. This animal is one of the four living mammal species commonly known for eating ants and termites. They capture their prey by inserting their tongue into insects' nests. What is the name of the animal?

   (a) Anteater (b) Bats
   (c) Hedgehogs (d) Tenrec
5. Evolution of organisms can be defined as
   (a) change in physical characters of living organisms
   (b) change in genetic characters of living organisms
   (c) both (a) and (b)
   (d) none of these
6. This breed of dog is a medium-sized, solidly-built, intelligent, short-haired dog whose early ancestors came from the British Isles. Originally bred to "bait" bulls, the breed evolved into all-round farm dogs, and later moved into the house to become "nanny dogs." Which breed of dog is this?

Space for Rough Work

(a) American Pit Bull Terrier
(b) American Water Spaniel
(c) American Foxhound
(d) Alaskan Malamute

7. This nut is a popular snack and food source which makes it more effective than other nuts in thickening water-based dishes such as soups, meat stews, and some Indian milk-based desserts. The shell of this nut is toxic. Name the nut.
(a) Almond (b) Cashew nut
(c) Groundnut (d) Pine nut

8. This crop is a tropical evergreen shrub and grows between the Tropics of Cancer and Capricorn. It grows in mountainous areas and does not require mechanical harvesters. Which crop is this?
(a) Wheat (b) Rice
(c) Maize (d) Coffee

9. Evergreen trees bear leaves in all the seasons. The term "evergreen" means that trees will keep growing leaves as other leaves fall off. Which of the following is an example of an evergreen tree?
(a) Pine (b) Oak
(c) Maple (d) Birch

10. The branch of which tree is a symbol of peace?

(a) Eucalyptus (b) Fig
(c) Olive (d) Neem

11. Match column I with column II and select the correct option from the given codes.

Column I	Column II
A. World Ozone Day	(p) 22 April
B. Earth Day	(q) 16 Sept.
C. World Water Day	(r) 5 June
D. World Environment Day	(s) 22 March

(a) A-p, B-q, C-r, D-s
(b) A-q, B-p, C-r, D-s
(c) A-p, B-r, C-q, D-s
(d) A-q, B-p, C-s, D-r

12. Read the following statements.
I. Chipko Movement was a water conservation campaign.
II. Antarctic Treaty was signed on 1 November 1959.
III. CNG is environment friendly gas.
IV. An area where plants and animals live is called an ecosystem.
Choose the true statements.
(a) I, II and III (b) III and IV
(c) II and IV (d) None of these

13. Greenhouse effect means
(a) release of heat from the plants during daytime
(b) release of heat into the environment
(c) slowing the release of heat into environment at night
(d) none of these

14. World Planting Day is celebrated on
(a) 21 March (b) 22 June
(c) 5 December (d) 22 September

Space for Rough Work

15. Which of the following jumbled words is used for a process that increases air pollution?
    (a) REDEFONOSTATI
    (b) ORAFFEIOSTATN
    (c) TIONPLANTA
    (d) IONCONSERVAT
16. The chemical name of baking soda is
    (a) Sodium carbonate
    (b) Sodium bicarbonate
    (c) Potassium Nitrate
    (d) Sodium Nitrate
17. Which of the following will be attracted by magnets?

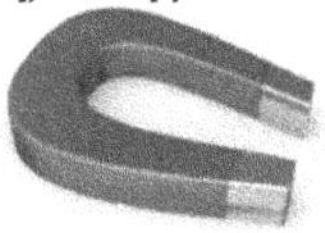

    (a) Plastic (b) Iron
    (c) Glass (d) Wood
18. Which of the following remains in its place when exposed to air for a long time?
    (a) Water (b) Camphor
    (c) Wood dust (d) Ether
19. Who among the following is known as the 'Father of Genetics'?

(a) William Harvey

(b) Gregor Mendel

(c) Robert Hook

(d) Charles Darwin

20. Which is the largest natural satellite of our solar system?

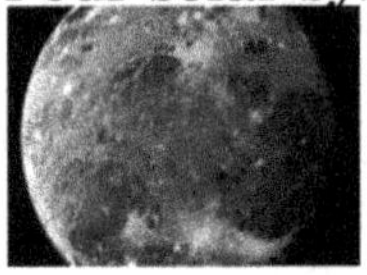

    (a) Callisto (b) Titan
    (c) Triton (d) Ganymede
21. Who among the following astronomers discovered the moon 'Titan' and found that Saturn's rings are made of rocks? He also invented pendulum clock?
    (a) Christiaan Huygens
    (b) Johannes Kepler
    (c) Edmund Halley
    (d) Galileo Galilei
22. The nearest large galaxy to the Milky Way is

    (a) The Whirpool Galaxy
    (b) Bob
    (c) Andromeda
    (d) Canis Major Dwarf

Space for Rough Work

23. Planet 'X' is named after the Roman God. It is nearest to the earth and its surface is thick with carbon dioxide. Identify the planet.

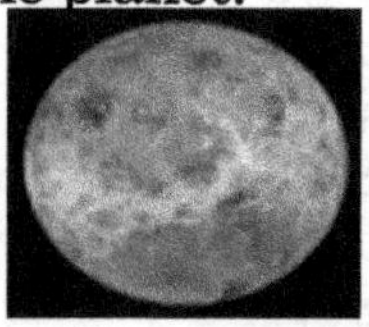

(a) Saturn (b) Venus
(c) Mars (d) Mercury

24. Who among the following is a Lieutenant Governor of a Union Territory (Punducherry) and former IPS officer?

(a) Kiran Bedi (b) Sheila Dixit

(c) Kamla Beniwal(d) Draupadi Murmu

25. Which of the following is not a gallantry award?
(a) Ashok Chakra
(b) Bharat Ratna
(c) Kirti Chakra
(d) Mahavir Chakra

26. Swachh Bharat Abhiyaan is a campaign by the Government of India to clean the streets, roads and infrastructure of India's 4,041 statutory cities and towns. In which year was the campaign launched in India?
(a) 2015 (b) 2014
(c) 2017 (d) 2016

27. Which of the following is the world's smallest island?
(a) Bishop Rock
(b) Isola Tiberina
(c) Tristan da Cunha
(d) Dunbar Rock

28. Who among the following was not a member of the Constituent Assembly of India?
(a) B.R. Ambedkar
(b) Rajendra Prasad
(c) H.C. Mukerjee
(d) Mahatma Gandhi

29. This is a national park of the United States and is regarded as the first national park in the world. This park is known for its wildlife and Old Faithful geyser. What is the name of the park?
(a) Yellowstone National Park
(b) Grand Canyon National Park
(c) Zion National Park
(d) Acadia National Park

30. Read the following statements given with codes.
P-Soon the cells grow into a swimming tadpole.
Q-The cells in the egg multiply and grow.
R-A mother frog lays her eggs in water.
Choose the correct sequence of events.
(a) P, R, Q (b) Q, R, P
(c) R, Q, P (d) P, Q, R

Space for Rough Work

31. Indian Ocean is a contemporary rock band from the capital city of Delhi, India. The rock band has compiled music from different genres. Who among the following is one of the members of the band?
    (a) Nikhil Rao
    (b) Mohit Chauhan
    (c) Zubeen Garg
    (d) Javed Ali
32. When was the film 'RRR' released?
    (a) 2017 (b) 2022
    (c) 2015 (d) 2018
33. Which of the following actors owns the film production company Red Chillies Entertainment?
    (a) Amitabh Bachchan
    (b) Amir Khan
    (c) Salman Khan
    (d) Shahrukh Khan
34. If you are unpleased with someone's behavior, then which of the following is the best option?
    (a) Never talk to that person
    (b) Hit that person
    (c) Stay calm
    (d) Complain to your parents
35. Who has been appointed as the brand ambassador for Swachh Bharat Mission in Uttar Pradesh?
    (a) Sachin Tendulkar
    (b) Amitabh Bachchan
    (c) Akshay Kumar
    (d) Aamir Khan
36. The Nal Sarovar Bird Sanctuary (NSBS) is located in which state?
    (a) Gujarat
    (b) Madhya Pradesh
    (c) Chhattisgarh
    (d) Uttarakhand
37. Which country hosted the 2022 North Atlantic Treaty Organization (NATO) Summit?
    (a) Romania (b) U.K.
    (c) Italy (d) Spain
38. BS-IV norms are related to
    (a) Automobile emission
    (b) Real estate development
    (c) Banking sector
    (d) Rural development
39. Who has become the world's highest wicket-taker in women ODI cricket?
    (a) Ekta Bisht
    (b) Jhulan Goswami
    (c) Mithali Raj
    (d) Harmanpreet Kaur
40. Who leads the toilet usage campaign "Darwaza Band" of the Union Government?

(a)  (b) 

(c)  (d) 

Space for Rough Work

OLYMPIAD
Mock Test 5

Name : __________ **Max. Marks : 40**
Number of Questions : 40 **Time : 2 Hours**

There is no negative marking in the test.

1. This animal species is largest of the true foxes, and are found in the Northern Hemisphere from the Arctic Circle to North Africa. It is listed as least concern by the IUCN. It is also included among the list of the "world's 100 worst invasive species". Identify the animal.
   (a) Kit Fox (b) Fennec Fox
   (c) Grey Fox (d) Red Fox
2. This disease causes swelling of the lung. Typical signs and symptoms include dry cough, chest pain, fever, and trouble breathing. It is caused by bacteria. What is the name of the disease?
   (a) Malaria (b) Pneumonia
   (c) Dengue (d) Diabetes
3. Which of the following is an incorrect statement?
   (a) Neem is a shrub.
   (b) Sweet potato is a root modification.
   (c) Stamens are reproductive organs of a plant.
   (d) Honey is produced by bees by collecting flower nectar.
4. Which of the following animals produces sound for locating insects they eat?
   (a) Crows (b) Owl
   (c) Bats (d) Ostrich
5. Whales are considered one of the largest animals on the earth. Which of the following are the characteristics of a whale?

   (a) They are not mammals.
   (b) They are warm-blooded.
   (c) They are very intelligent animals.
   (d) Both b and c

Space for Rough Work

6. Which of the following is associated with the change in characteristics of organisms with time?
   (a) Extinction (b) Gestation
   (c) Domestication (d) Evolution
7. This is an endangered species of an animal native to China. It eats bamboo and is a good climber. Which animal is this?
   (a) Giant panda (b) Giant otter
   (c) Raccoon (d) Monkey
8. The food prepared by plant leaves is stored as
   (a) Starch (b) Proteins
   (c) Sugars (d) Fats
9. Nocturnal animals sleep through the day, and remain active during the night. Which of the following is/are nocturnal animals?
   (a) Flying squirrel
   (b) Mink
   (c) Owl
   (d) All of these
10. Every year, 2nd February is celebrated across the world as:
    (a) World Wetlands Day
    (b) World Radio Day
    (c) World Environment Day
    (d) World Water Day
11. The Bishnoi Movement aims to save sacred trees from being cut down. In which of the following states the Bishnoi Movement took place?
    (a) Rajasthan
    (b) Madhya Pradesh
    (c) Odisha
    (d) Tamil Nadu
12. Match the Column I with Column II

Column I	Column II
A. Ozone depletion	(p) Non-renewable resource
B. Mercury	(q) Haemoglobin binding
C. Carbon monoxide	(r) Minamata
D. Fossil fuel	(s) Global warming

    Choose the correct option.
    (a) A-p, B-q, C-r, D-s
    (b) A-s, B-r, C-q, D-p
    (c) A-p, B-s, C-r, D-q
    (d) A-q, B-r, C-s, D-p
13. Read the following statements.
    I. Increase in sulphur dioxide concentration in the atmosphere lowers the population of lichens.
    II. Plastic bag is a biodegradable substance.

    Choose the correct option.
    (a) I is true
    (b) II is true
    (c) Both I and II are true
    (d) Both I and II are false

Space for Rough Work

14. Which is the biggest single structure made by living beings?

(a) Bora bora
(b) Uluru
(c) Great Barrier Reef
(d) Patagonian ice Fields

15. Which of the following cities has been put on UNESCO's list of World Heritage in danger?
(a) Ahmedabad
(b) Hebron
(c) Surat
(d) Mumbai

16. Ramsar Convention signed in 1971 is regarding
(a) Conservation of wetlands
(b) Conservation of Forest
(c) Conservation of wild animals
(d) Conservation of soil

17. Which of the following statements is correct?
(a) A gas expands on heating.
(b) A wood piece and an iron rod get heated at the same rate.
(c) Water turns into ice on heating.
(d) Ice when heated turns into water vapor.

18. An electric bell rings due to

(a) Electric effect of current
(b) Magnetic effect of current
(c) Both of these
(d) None of these

19. Which of the following scientists is associated with laws of floating bodies?

(a) Archimedes
(b) Newton
(c) Dalton
(d) Darwin

20. Why ball and bearings are used in machines?

(a) To reduce friction
(b) To produce less noise
(c) To increase productivity
(d) To look good

Space for Rough Work

21. Which of the following gases is used in beverages to produce fizz?

(a) Nitrogen dioxide
(b) Carbon dioxide
(c) Sulphur dioxide
(d) Carbon monoxide

22. On which of the following planets the length of each season is of about 7 years?

(a) Jupiter (b) Neptune
(c) Saturn (d) Venus

23. World's first artificial satellite was launched by

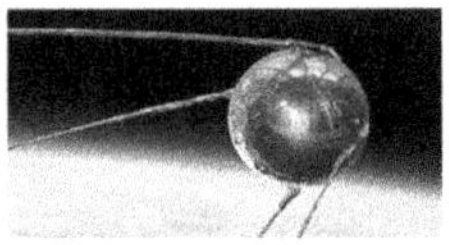

(a) United States
(b) Russia
(c) France
(d) United Kingdom

24. Which type of star is Proxima Centauri, the closest star to Earth after Sun?

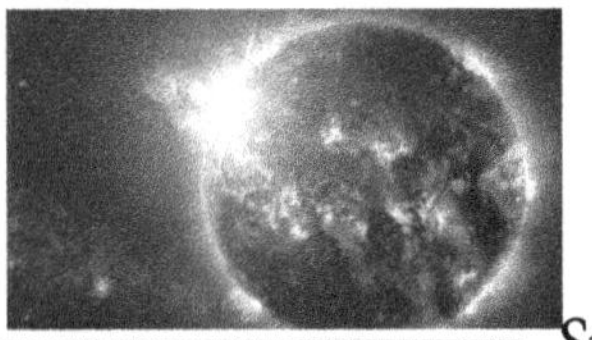

(a) Yellow dwarf star
(b) Blue giant star
(c) Brown dwarf star
(d) Red dwarf star

25. What is the currency of Argentina?

(a) Peso (b) Dollar
(c) Euro (d) Franc

26. Who among the following is not the recipient of the Padma Vibhushan award?

(a) K. J. Yesudas
(b) Jaggi Vasudev
(c) Sharad Pawar
(d) Virendra Shehwag

27. She is an Indian badminton player. She become the first Indian women to win an Olympic silver medal. She also won silver in Commonwealth Games 2018. Who is being about in this paragraph?

(a) Saina Nehwal
(b) Saina Mirza
(c) P.V. Sindhu
(d) Jwala Gutta

28. Who among the following is the CEO of Facebook?

(a) Sunder Pichai
(b) Mark Zuckerberg
(c) Satya Nadella
(d) Bill Gates

Space for Rough Work

29. Which of the following cities is/are situated along the river Ganges?
    (a) Kanpur
    (b) Allahabad
    (c) Haridwar
    (d) All of these
30. Which of the following is not declared an official language of the UN?
    (a) Hindi
    (b) Arabic
    (c) French
    (d) Spanish
31. Give one word for 'list of the business or subjects to be considered at a meeting'.
    (a) Timetable
    (b) Plan
    (c) Schedule
    (d) Agenda
32. When my uncle heard his neighbour bought a new car, he was "green with envy." What does 'green with envy' mean here?
    (a) He had lots of money.
    (b) He had a serious infection.
    (c) He was very jealous.
    (d) He had a mossy growth on him.
33. She is an activist and Indian classical dancer from Ahmedabad, Gujarat. She is the daughter of a classical dancer and is an accomplished Kuchipudi and Bharatanatyam dancer. Who is she?

    (a) Mallika Sarabhai
    (b) Sunanda Nair
    (c) Sonal Mansingh
    (d) Yamini Krishnamurthy
34. Which actress made her debut in the film 'Dhadak'?
    (a) Aalia Bhatt
    (b) Jhanvi Kapoor
    (c) Khushi Kapoor
    (d) Sonam Kapoor
35. Who became the first cricketer to frist 3000 runs in Twenty20 cricket match?

(a)  (b) 

(c)  (d) 

36. What names were given to the mascots of the 19th Asian Games 2022?
    (a) Krishnasar
    (b) Bhin Bhin
    (c) Lian lian
    (d) All of the above

Space for Rough Work

37. Which of the following is an example of verbal communication?
    (a) Interview
    (b) Email
    (c) Lianlian
    (d) Notice
38. Who is the current director of the Central Bureau of Investigation?
    (a) Subodh Kumar Jaiswal
    (b) Ranjit Sinha
    (c) Alok Verma
    (d) Rakesh Asthana
39. Who has written the book 'Indira Gandhi: A Life in Nature'?
    (a)  (b) 
    (c)  (d) 
40. Who has been sworn-in as the new chief minister of Nagaland?
    (a) TR Zeliang
    (b) Neiphiu Rio
    (c) Hokishe Sema
    (d) Vizol Angami

Space for Rough Work

OLYMPIAD

Mock Test 1

Name : ________ **Max. Marks : 25**

Number of Questions : 25 **Time : 1 Hour**

There is no negative marking in the test.

DIRECTIONS (Qs. 1 & 2): Out of the four choices given for each question, you have to select one that will maintain the relationship on the two sides of the sign :: the same if it is substituted for the question mark?

1. 12 : 30 : : 20 : ?
   (a) 25 (b) 32 (c) 35 (d) 42
2. CEG : EGC : : LNP : ?
   (a) LPN (b) UWY
   (c) NPL (d) MOP

DIRECTIONS (Qs. 3 & 4): In each of the following questions choose the missing number to complete the series.

3. 1, 3, 6, 10, ?
   (a) 12 (b) 21 (c) 18 (d) 15
4. 3, 9, 27, 81, ?
   (a) 162 (b) 210
   (c) 243 (d) 324
5. If the code of CORNER is GSVRIV, then what will be the code of CENTRAL?
   (a) GIRXVPE (b) DROUSBM
   (c) GJRYVEP (d) GIRXVEP
6. If 'LIGHT' is called 'MORNING', 'MORNING' is called 'DARK', 'DARK is called 'NIGHT', 'NIGHT' is called 'SUNSHINE' and 'SUNSHINE' is called 'DUSK', then when do we sleep?
   (a) DARK (b) DUSK
   (c) SUNSHINE (d) NIGHT
7. Pointing to a lady in the photograph, Neelam said, "Her son's father is the son-in-law of my mother". How is Neelam related to the lady?
   (a) Sister (b) Aunt
   (c) Cousin (d) Mother
8. X is the wife of Y and Y is the brother of Z, Z is the son of P. How is P related to X?
   (a) Aunt
   (b) Father-in-law
   (c) Sister
   (d) Brother-in-law

Space for Rough Work

9. If A is to the south of B and C is to the east of B, then in what direction is A with respect to C?
   (a) North-East (b) North-West
   (c) South-East (d) South-West

10. A, B, C and D are playing cards. A and B are partners. D faces towards North. If A faces towards West, then who faces towards South?
   (a) A (b) C
   (c) D (d) B

11. Which of the following diagram indicates the best relation amongst Travellers, Train and Bus?
   (a) 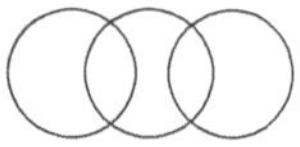 (b) 
   (c) 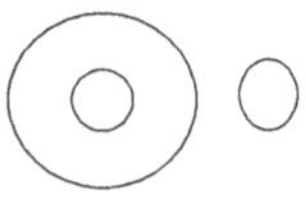 (d) 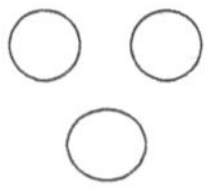

12. Which of the following elements satisfies the Venn diagram given here?

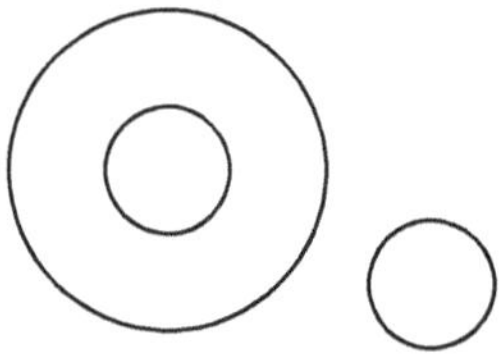

   (a) Judge, Thief, Criminal
   (b) Father, Mother, Parents
   (c) Teacher, College, Student
   (d) Polygons, Rectangles,Squares

13. How many C's are there in the following sequence, which are immediately preceded by D?
   A B D C D C C D C L C D D C I D C C D
   (a) Two (b) Three
   (c) Four (d) Five

14. Six persons Raj, Jiya, Rohit, Bani, Sonu and Mohit are standing in a circle. Jiya is between Mohit and Rohit, Raj is between Sonu and Bani, Mohit is to the left of Bani. Who is between Raj and Mohit?
   (a) Sonu (b) Rohit
   (c) Bani (d) Jiya

15. In the following question arrange the given words in a meaningful sequence.
   1. Key 2. Door 3. Lock
   4. Room 5. Switch On
   (a) 5,1,2,4,3 (b) 4,2,1,5,3
   (c) 1,3,2,4,5 (d) 1,2,3,5,4

16. If P denotes 'multiplied by', Q denotes 'subtracted from', M denotes 'added to' and L denotes 'divided by', then 28 L 7 P 8 Q 6 M 4 ?
   (a) 28 (b) 30
   (c) 32 (d) 34

17. Using the below table, identify the correct expression.

P	Q	R	S
+	−	÷	×

Space for Rough Work

(a) 17 Q 8 S 9 P 18 R 2 = 46
(b) 18 S 30 R 6 Q 5 P 0 = 85
(c) 27 Q 10 R 5 S 4 P 3 = - 32
(d) All of these

18. How many straight lines are there in the given figure?

(a) 14 (b) 16
(c) 18 (d) 20

19. Count the number of unit cubes in the given solid.

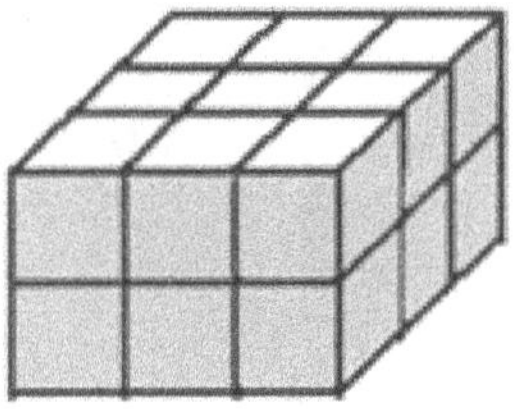

(a) 10 (b) 15
(c) 18 (d) 22

20. Two positions of a dice are shown below. Which digit will appear on the face opposite to the face with number 4?

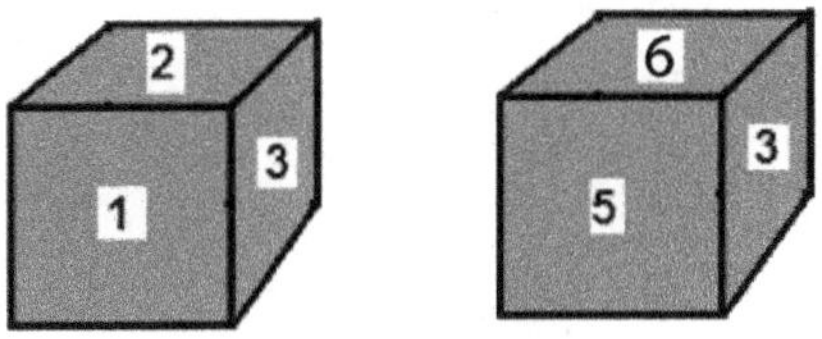

(a) 3 (b) 5
(c) 6 (d) 2

21. Find the correct water image of fig (X).

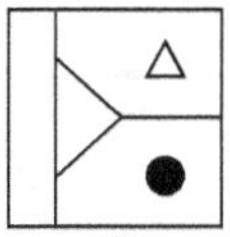

(X)

(a) 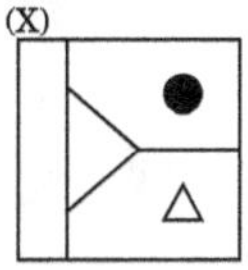 (b) 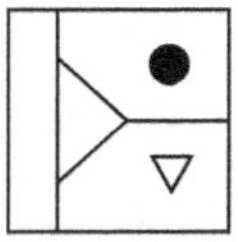

(c) 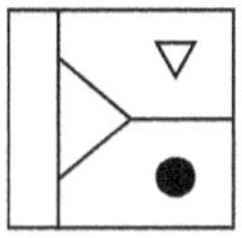 (d) 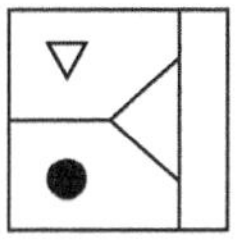

22. Select the correct mirror image of the fig. (X), if the mirror is placed along MN.

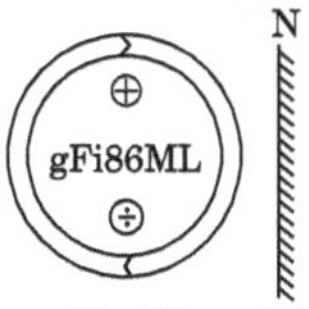

Fig. (X) M

(a)  (b) 

(c)  (d) 

Space for Rough Work

DIRECTION (Q. 23): In the following question, fig (X) is exactly embedded in any one of the four option figures (a), (b), (c) and (d). Find the option which contains fig. (X) as its part.

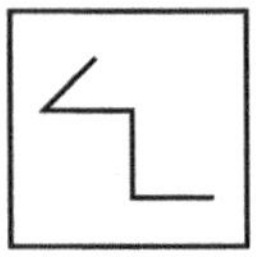

(X)

(a) 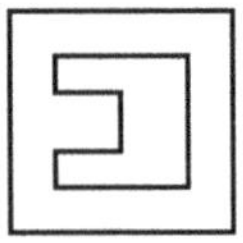 (b) 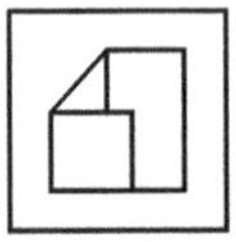

(c) 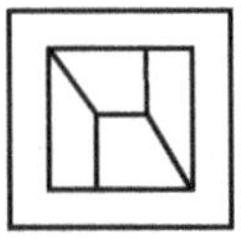 (d) 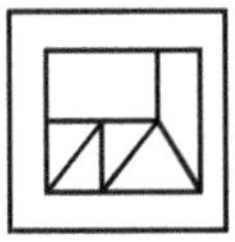

DIRECTION (Q. 24): In the following question, select the option in which all the components of the key figure (X) are available.

(X)

(a) 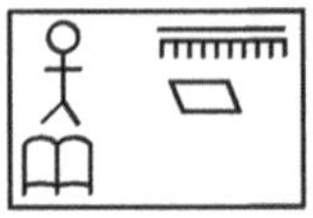 (b) 

(c) 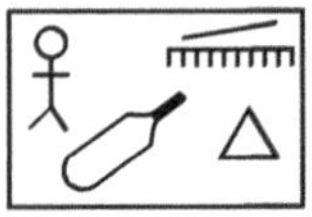 (d) 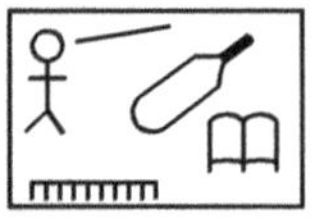

25. Select a figure form the options, which when placed in the blank space of fig. (X) would complete the pattern.

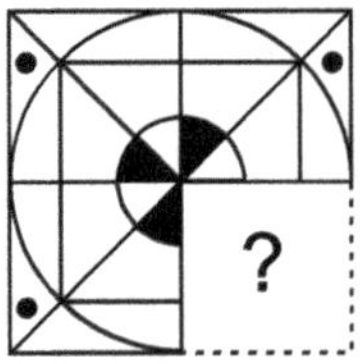

Fig. (X)

(a)  (b) 

(c)  (d) 

Space for Rough Work

OLYMPIAD

Mock Test 2

Name : ________ **Max. Marks : 25**
Number of Questions : 25 **Time : 1 Hour**

There is no negative marking in the test.

1. Identify the wrong series term in the series given below.
   Z A, D E, H I, O P, P Q
   (a) Z A (b) H I
   (c) D E (d) O P

2. Find the missing character in the given pattern.

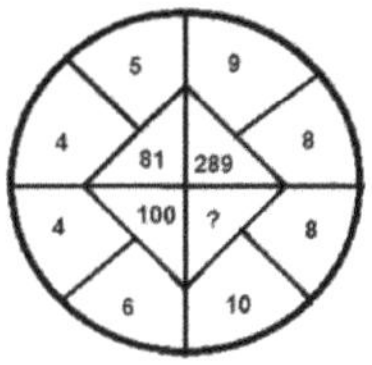

   (a) 164 (b) 324
   (c) 224 (d) 364

3. 7 is to 14 as 9 is to ________.
   (a) 14 (b) 20
   (c) 16 (d) 18

4. Choose the figure which is different from the rest of the three.

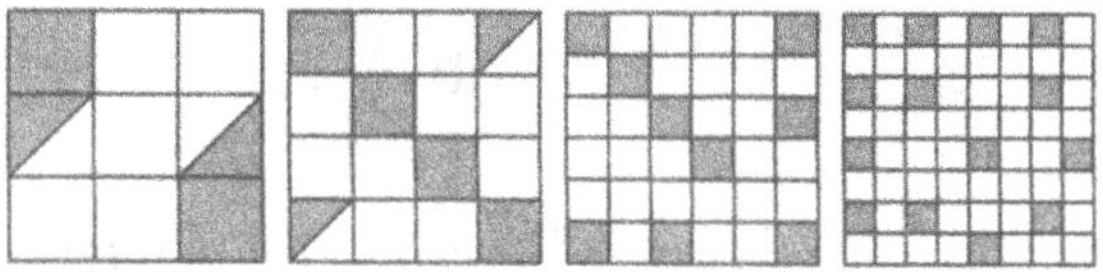

(P) (Q) (R) (S)

   (a) S (b) R
   (c) Q (d) P

5. In a certain code, 'BOY' is written as '$ * #' and 'HOUR' is written as '@ * £ +'. How is 'RUBY' written in that code?
   (a) + £ $ # (b) + $ £ #
   (c) # $ £ + (d) # £ $ +

6. If in a certain code, O is written as P, A as B, M as N, S as T and so on, then how will COMPANIES be written in that code?
   (a) DPNQBOJET
   (b) DPOQBPIES
   (c) DPNQBJOFT
   (d) DPNQBOJFT

Space for Rough Work

7. Select a figure from the options which will continue the series established by the Problem Figures.

Problem Figures

(a)  (b) 

(c)  (d) 

8. There is a definite relationship between fig. (i) & (ii). Establish the same relationship between fig. (iii) and (iv) by selecting a suitable figure from the options which will replace (?) in fig. (iv).

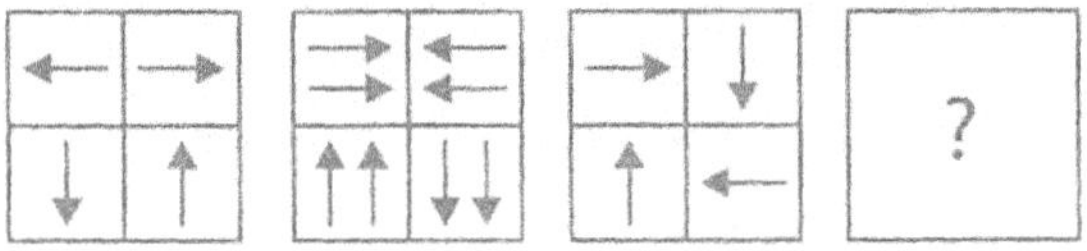

(i) (ii) (iii) (iv)

(a) 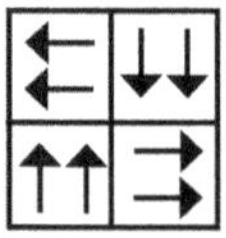 (b) 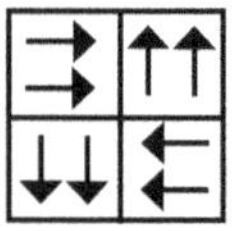

(c) 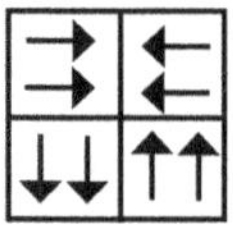 (d) 

9. Pointing to an old man, Amit said, "His son is my son's uncle." How is the old man related to Amit?

(a) Brother

(b) Uncle

(c) Father

(d) Grandfather

10. If S-T means S is the wife of T, S + T means S is the daughter of T and S ÷ T means S is the son of T. What will M + J ÷ K means?

(a) K is the father of M

(b) M is the grand daughter

(c) J is the wife of K

(d) K and M are brothers

11. Flights to Mumbai leave every 5 hours. At the information counter, I learnt that the flight took off 25 min before. If the time now is 10:45 a.m, what is the time for the next flight?

(a) 4:10 a.m.

(b) 2:20 a.m.

(c) 4:20 p.m.

(d) 3:20 p.m.

12. The calendar for the year 2005 is the same as for the year.

(a) 2010

(b) 2011

(c) 2012

(d) 2013

Space for Rough Work

13. Ayan walks 20m north from his house, turn right and walk 10m, turns left and walks 15m to reach his grandfather's house. In which direction is his grandfather's house from his house?
    (a) South-West
    (b) North-East
    (c) East
    (d) North

14. Veena is facing North-East. She turns 90° in the clockwise direction and then 135° in the anticlockwise direction. Which direction is she facing now?
    (a) East
    (b) South
    (c) North
    (d) West

15. In the given diagram, the triangle represents female graduates, square represents self-employed females and circle represents self-employed females with banks loan facility.

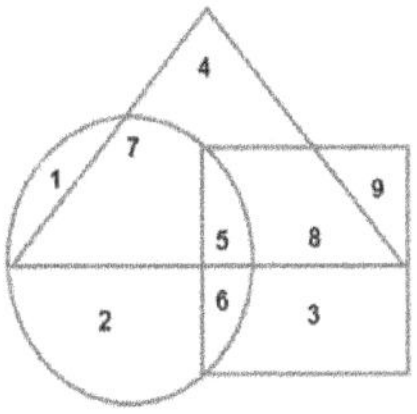

How many female graduates are there who are not self-employed?
(a) 4 (b) 10
(c) 12 (d) 15

16. Which of the following diagram indicates the best relation amongst Factory, Product and Machinery?

(a) 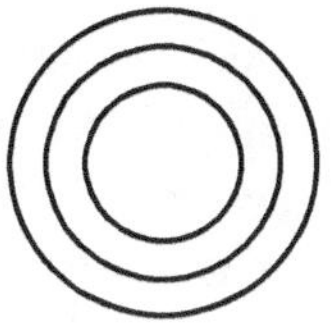 (b) 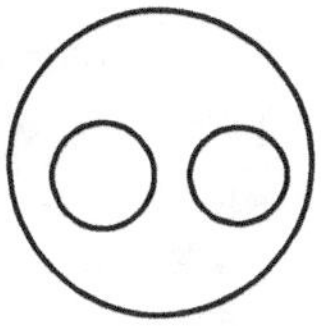

(c) 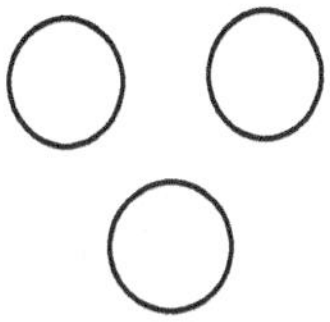 (d) 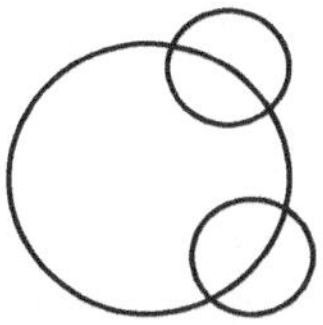

17. In a row of plants, one plant is sixth from either end of the row. How many plants are there in the row?
(a) 8 (b) 9
(c) 10 (d) 11

18. Study the set of numbers given below and answer the question which follows:

427 581 839 275 589

Which of the following numbers will be obtained if the second digit of the greatest number is subtracted from the second digit of the lowest number after adding two to each of the numbers?
(a) 1 (b) 2
(c) 3 (d) 4

Space for Rough Work

19. Arrange the following words in the sequence in which they occur in the dictionary.

1.	Select	2.	Seldom
3.	Send	4.	Selfish
5.	Seller		

(a) 1,2,4,5,3 (b) 2,1,5,4,3
(c) 2,1,4,5,3 (d) 2,5,4,1,3

20. If '+' is written as '×', '-' is written as '÷', '÷' is written as '+' and '×' is written as '-' then what is the value of 540 – 36 + 12 ÷ 75 × 55 ?

(a) 255 (b) 512
(c) 180 (d) 200

21. Count the number of triangles in the given figure.

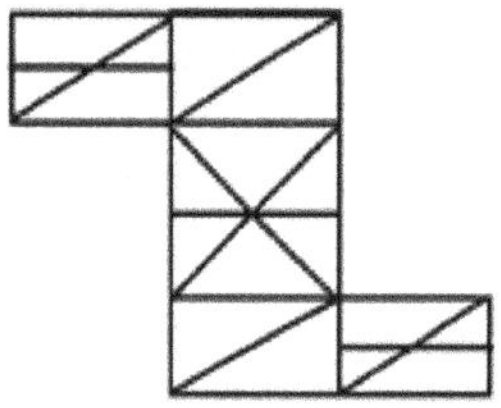

(a) 26 (b) 17
(c) 18 (d) None of these

22. Select the correct mirror image of below given combination, if the mirror is placed vertically to the left?

ScIeNcEOLYMPIAD

(a) ᗡAIꟼMY⅃OƎɔИɘIɔƧ
(b) ᗡAIPMY⅃OƎɔИɘIɔƧ
(c) ScIeNcEOLYMPIAD
(d) ᗡAIꟼMYLOƎɔИɘIɔƧ

23. Select a figure from the options in which Fig. (X) is exactly embedded as one of its part.

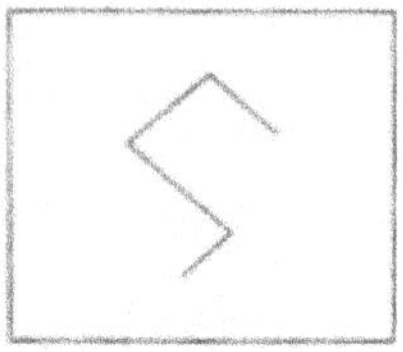

Fig. (X)

(a)  (b) 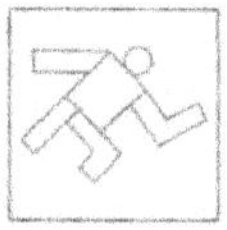

(c)  (d) 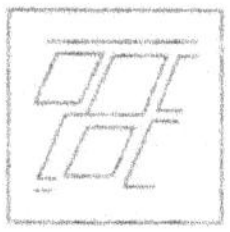

24. Select a figure from the options which will complete the pattern given in fig. (X).

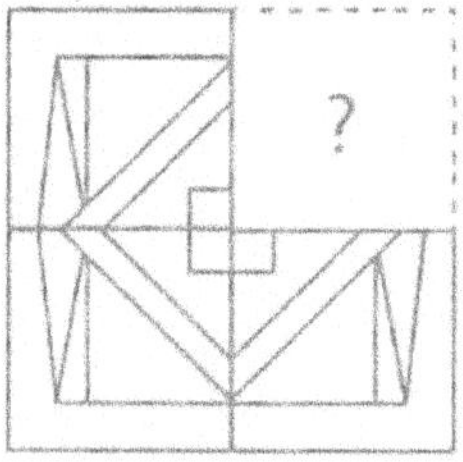

Fig. (X)

Space for Rough Work

(a)  (b) 

(c)  (d) 

25. A set of three figures X, Y and Z showing a sequence of folding of a piece of paper has been cut. Select a figure from the options which would closely resemble the unfolded form of paper.

X Y Z

(a) 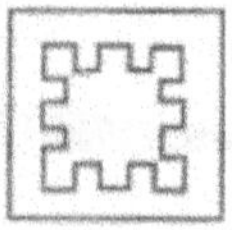 (b) 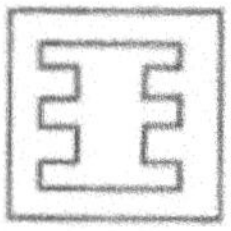

(c)  (d) 

Space for Rough Work

OLYMPIAD
Mock Test 3

Name : __________ **Max. Marks : 25**
Number of Questions : 25 **Time : 1 Hour**

There is no negative marking in the test.

1. A set of figures carrying certain characters is given. If the characters in each set follow a similar pattern, find the missing character.

15			18			21	
90	75		108	90		?	105

(a) 78 (b) 126
(c) 140 (d) 132

2. Select a figure from the given options which will continue the series as established by the four problem figures.

Problem Figures

(a)  (b) 

(c)  (d) 

DIRECTIONS (Qs. 3 & 4): In each of the following questions choose the missing number to complete the series.

3. 1,9,17,33,49,73,?
(a) 97 (b) 98
(c) 99 (d) 100
4. 1,2,3,5,8,?
(a) 9 (b) 10
(c) 12 (d) 13
5. There is a definite relationship between figures (i) and (ii). Establish a similar relationship between figures (iii) and (iv) by selecting a suitable figure from the options which would replace the (?) in fig (iii).

Space for Rough Work

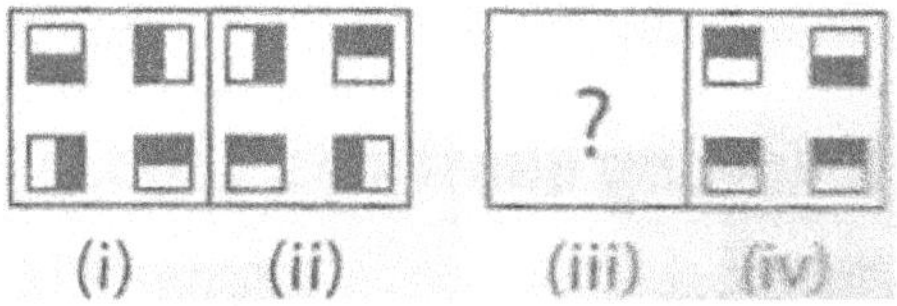

(a)  (b) 

(c)  (d) 

6. If  is related to , then  is related to ________.

(a) 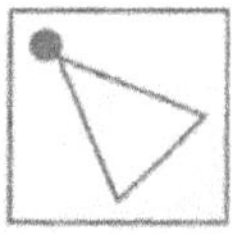 (b) 

(c)  (d) 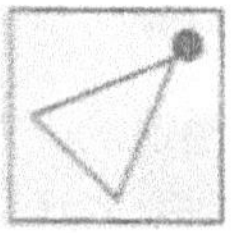

7. If SOFTWARE can be coded as TQIUYDSG, then TYPE is coded as____.
   (a) SZRG (b) VBRG
   (c) UASF (d) RXQH
8. While going to his office P meets a man Q who is related to P, because P has R, a son, who is married to T. T is the daughter of Q. T has a daughter A. How is P related to A?
   (a) Grandfather
   (b) Grandmother
   (c) Uncle
   (d) Father-in-law
9. Which of the following Venn diagrams best represents the relationship amongst "Mammals, Cows, Crows" ?

(a) 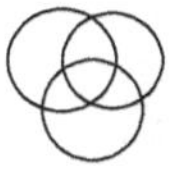 (b) 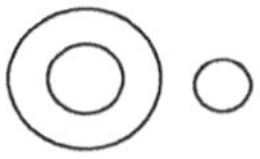

(c)  (d) 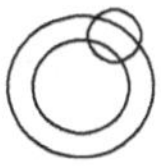

10. Count the number of cubes in the given figure.

   (a) 3 (b) 4
   (c) 5 (d) None of these
11. Select the correct mirror image of the given figure, if the mirror is placed along MN.

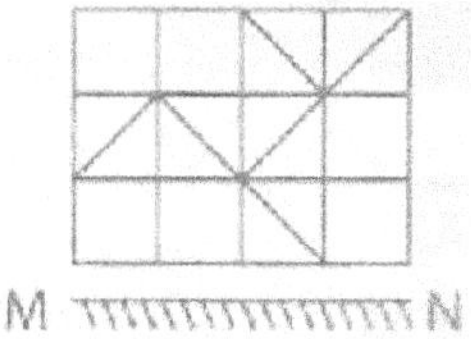

(a) 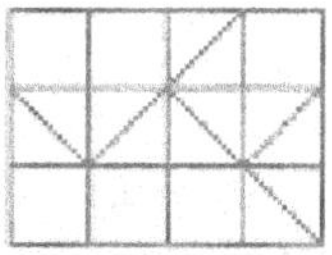 (b) 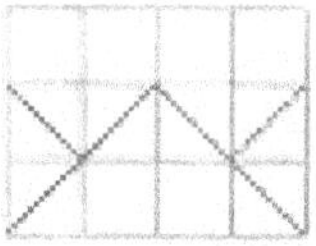

(c) 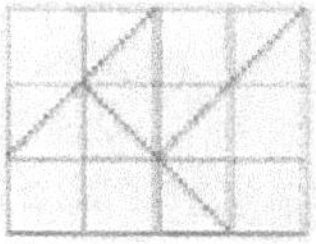 (d) 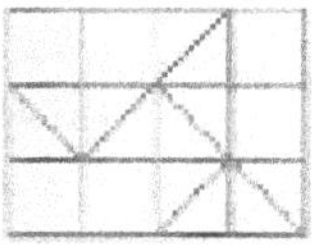

Space for Rough Work

12. Select the mirror image of Fig. (X) from the given options, if the mirror is placed along PQ.

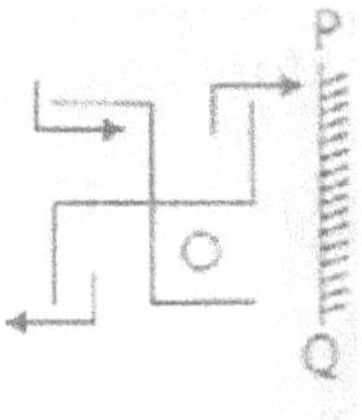

Fig. (X)

(a)  (b) 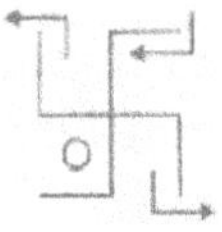

(c) 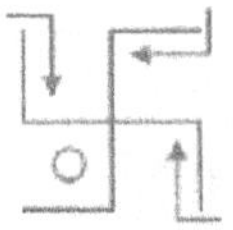 (d) 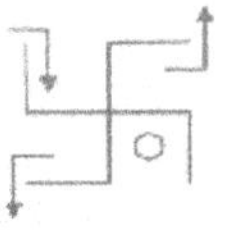

13. Pointing to woman in a photograph a man says, " She is the only daughter of my wife's mother-in-law". How is the woman related to the man?
(a) Daughter (b) Wife
(c) Sister (d) Sister-in-law

14. If SKY is called STAR, STAR is called CLOUD, CLOUD is called EARTH, EARTH is called TREE and TREE is called BOOK, then where do we live on?
(a) BOOK (b) SKY
(c) STAR (d) TREE

15. At my house I am facing east, then I turn left and go 10 m straight, then turn right and go 5 m straight, then I go 5 m straight towards the south and from there 5 m straight towards the west. In which direction am I from my house?
(a) East (b) West
(c) North (d) South

16. If the English alphabets are written in reverse order after interchanging alphabets from 'C to M' with those 'P to Z' respectively, which letter would be midway between F and T in the new order?
(a) Z (b) M
(c) N (d) X

17. Which number will be the smallest if the first and last digits are interchanged in all the given numbers?

389 476 635 847 568

(a) 389 (b) 476
(c) 635 (d) 568

18. if '+' denotes 'multiplication', '×' denotes 'subtraction', '÷' denotes 'addition', and '-' denotes 'division', then $175 - 25 \div 5 + 20 \times 3 + 10 = ?$
(a) 160 (b) 70
(c) 77 (d) 240

19. Find the number of triangles in the given figure.

(a) 12 (b) 16
(c) 18 (d) 20

Space for Rough Work

20. In the following question arrange the given words in a meaningful sequence.

1.	Word	2.	Paragraph
3.	Sentence	4.	Letters
5.	Phrase		

(a) 4,1,5,3,2 (b) 4,1,5,2,3
(c) 4,2,5,1,3 (d) 4,1,3,5,2

21. Select a figure from the options which completes the Fig. (X).

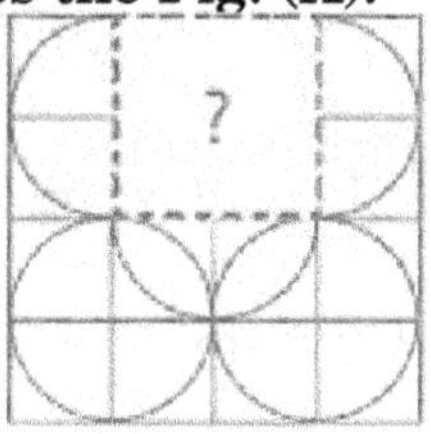

Fig. (X)

(a)  (b) 

(c)  (d) 

22. Select a figure from the options in which Fig. (X) is embedded as one of its part.

(a) 

(b) 

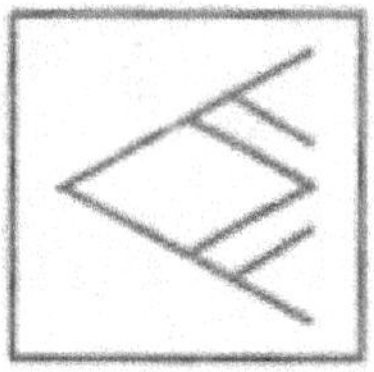

Fig. (X)

(c)  (d) 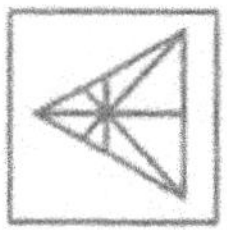

23. Group the given figures into three classes using each figure only once.

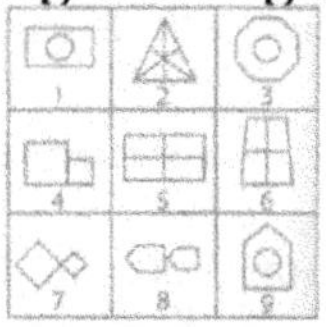

(a) 1, 3, 9; 2, 5, 6; 4, 7, 8
(b) 1, 3, 9; 2, 7, 8; 4, 5, 6
(c) 1, 2, 4; 3, 5, 7; 6, 8, 9
(d) 1, 3, 6; 2, 4, 8; 5, 7, 9

24. In a code language, if BANGED is coded as JJKQCC, then the word STRAY will be coded as
(a) DEUTV (b) DEUVT
(c) EFVWT (d) EFVVS

25. A sheet of paper is folded in a particular manner and a punch is made. Select a figure amongst the options that would closely resemble the unfolded form of given sheet.

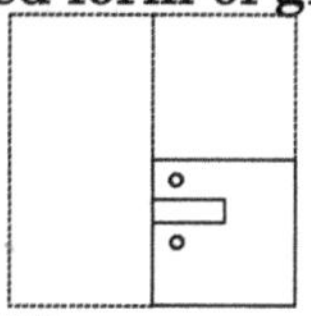

(a) 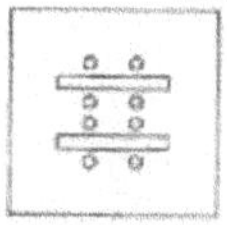 (b) 

(c)  (d) 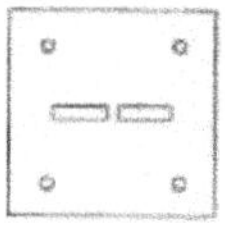

Space for Rough Work

OLYMPIAD

Mock Test 4

Name : __________ **Max. Marks : 40**

Number of Questions : 40 **Time : 2 Hours**

There is no negative marking in the test.

DIRECTIONS (Qs. 1 to 3): Each of the following questions is based on the following alphabet series.

A B C D E F G H I J K L M N O P Q R S T U V W X Y Z

1. In the English alphabet, which letter will be to the immediate left of M?
   (a) N (b) L
   (c) O (d) P

2. Which letter is sixth to the right of the letter which is fourth to the left of I?
   (a) K
   (b) T
   (c) C
   (d) V

3. Which letter is seventh to the right to the thirteenth letter from your left end?
   (a) S (b) T
   (c) U (d) V

4. Which of the following numbers will replace the question mark in the given below number pattern?

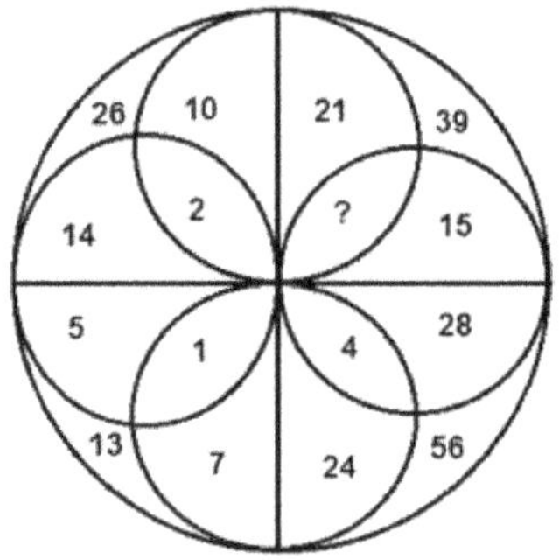

   (a) 2 (b) 3
   (c) 4 (d) 5

5. Find the missing figure so that the series formed by problem figures is continued.

Problem Figures

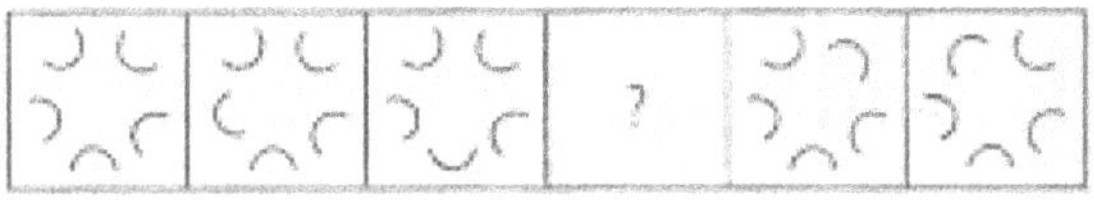

Space for Rough Work

(a)  (b) 

(c)  (d) 

6. Find the next term in the series given below.

   3F, 6G, 11I, 18L,?

   (a) 21 O (b) 25 N
   (c) 27 P (d) 27 Q

7. Pointing towards a boy, Namrata says, "He is the son of my grandfather's only child." How is the boy related to Namrata?

   (a) Brother
   (b) Cousin
   (c) Uncle
   (d) Data Inadequate

8. Find the missing number, if a certain rule is followed in all the three figures.

Top	Left	Centre	Right	Bottom
25	49	26	64	36
9	25	63	81	16
25	64	?	144	36

   (a) 91 (b) 23
   (c) 52 (d) 13

9. Select a figure from the options which will continue the same series as established by the Problem Figures.

Problem Figures

(a)  (b) 

(c)  (d) 

10. There is a certain relationship on either side of : :. Identify the relationship on the left of : : and find the missing term.

    M A D : J X A : : R U N : ?

    (a) ORK (b) OSQ
    (c) PRJ (d) UXQ

11. In the following question arrange the given words in a meaningful sequence.

    1. Police 2. Punishment
    3. Crime 4. Judge
    5. Judgement

    (a) 3,1,2,4,5 (b) 1,2,4,3,5
    (c) 5,4,3,2,1 (d) 3,1,4,5,2

Space for Rough Work

12. In the word MATHEMATICAL, if first and third letters, the fourth and the sixth letters, the seventh and the ninth letters & the tenth and the twelfth letters were interchanged, then which of the following would be the seventh letter from the left end?

(a) M (b) A
(c) H (d) I

13. P, Q, R, S, and T are five friends sitting around a pentagonal park facing O as shown below. If P and T interchange their positions & Q and R interchange their positions, then which of the following is true?

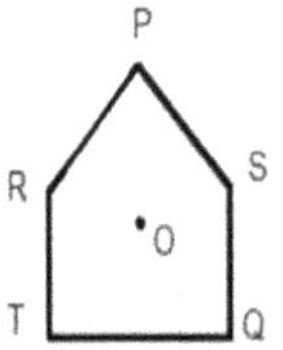

(a) R is to the left of P.
(b) Q is second to the right of R.
(c) T is second to the left of P.
(d) S is to the right of T.

14. Which of the following is the ninth to the right of the twentieth element from the right end in the given arrangement?

M % T A P 4 * E D 1 7 N I J 5 $ 3 F H 8 U B 6 @ W L 2 © K Q #

(a) T (b) 8
(c) U (d) N

15. How many cubes were removed from the solid on the left to obtain the solid on the right?

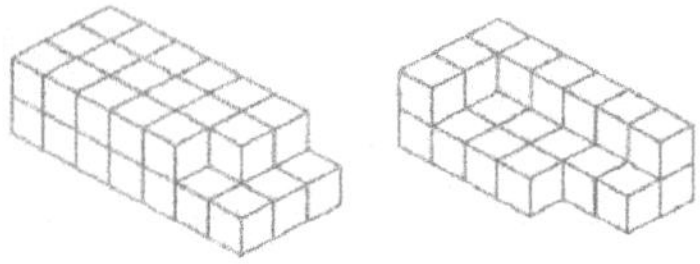

(a) 14 (b) 12
(c) 28 (d) 10

16. Select the correct mirror-image of Fig. (X), if the mirror is placed vertically to the left.

Fig. (X)

(a) 
(b) 
(c) 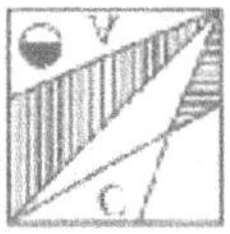
(d) 

17. Identify which number does not fit in the sequence?

2, 3, 7, 22, 155, ?

(a) 1706
(b) 1550
(c) 3411
(d) 3100

Space for Rough Work

18. A man walks northwards. After a while he turns towards his right and walks straight then he moves little further to his left. Finally, after walking a distance of one kilometer he turns to his left again. In which direction is he moving now?
   (a) North (b) South
   (c) East (d) West

19. X is to the south-west of Y, L is to the east of X and south-east of Y and M is to the north of L in a line with XY. In which direction of Y is M located?
   (a) South (b) South-West
   (c) North (d) North-East

20. If x stands for add, y stands for subtract, and z stands for multiply, then what is the value of (7 z 3) y 6 x 5?
   (a) 5 (b) 10
   (c) 15 (d) 20

DIRECTIONS (Qs. 21 to 23): In each question first two given words are related in some way. The same relation is in between third and fourth. Find out the one correct answer among the alternatives.

21. 211 : 333 : : 356 : ?
   (a) 358 (b) 359
   (c) 423 (d) 388

22. Wine : Grapes : : Vodka : ?
   (a) Apple (b) Potatoes
   (c) Oranges (d) Flour

23. TSR : FED : : WVU : ?
   (a) CAB (b) MLK
   (c) PQS (d) GFH

DIRECTIONS (Qs. 24 & 25): Study the following information and answer the questions given below.

S and R are brothers. T is daughter of S. U is the spouse of R and mother of Q. P is the daughter of V, who is the spouse of T.

24. Who is the grandfather of P?
   (a) U (b) S
   (c) R (d) V

25. Who is the cousin of Q?
   (a) T (b) V
   (c) R (d) P

DIRECTION (Qs. 26 to 27): In each of the following questions, a transparent sheet X with a design and a dotted line on it is given. Choose the correct figure from the four options that is the folded form of the sheet X.

26. 

(X)

(a) 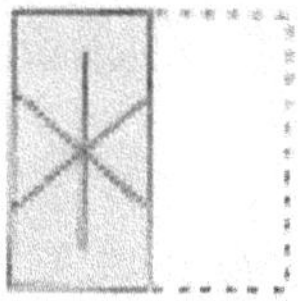 (b) 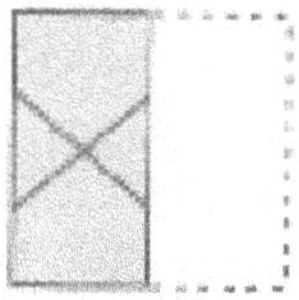

Space for Rough Work

(c) 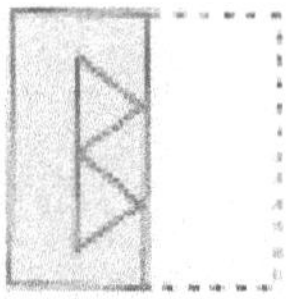 (d) 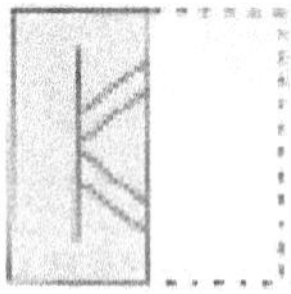

27. 

(X)

(a) 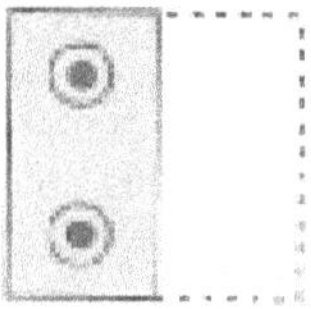 (b) 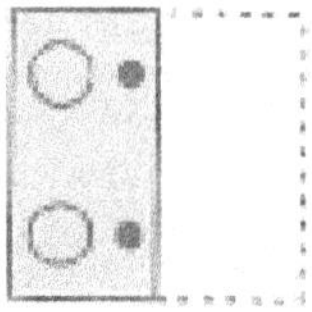

(c)  (d) 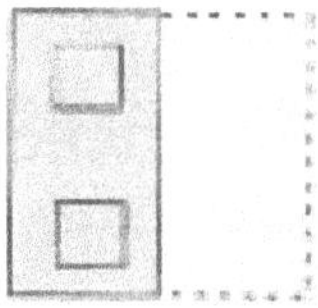

28. When the following sheet is folded to form a cube, how many dots lie opposite the face bearing five dots?

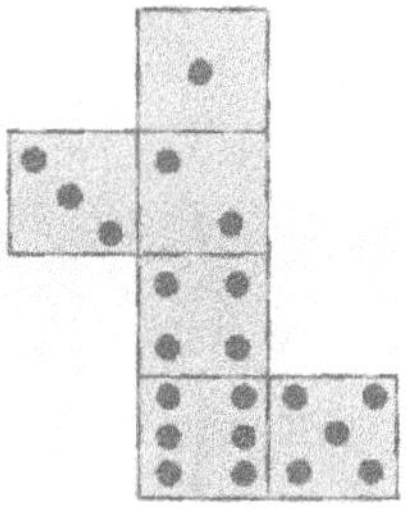

(a) 1
(b) 2
(c) 3
(d) 4

29. Choose the correct option

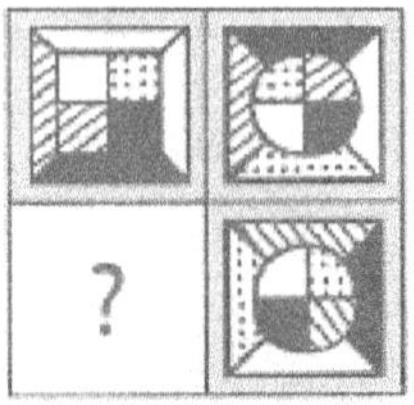

(a)  (b) 

(c)  (d) 

DIRECTION (Q. 30): In the following question, group the given figures into three classes using each figure only once. Hence choose the appropriate option.

30. 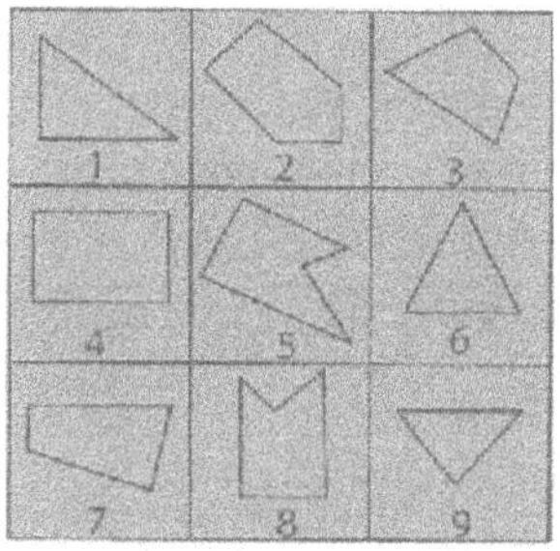

(a) 7, 8, 9; 2, 3, 4; 1, 5, 6
(b) 1, 2, 3; 4, 5, 7; 6, 8, 9
(c) 1, 6, 8; 3, 4, 7; 2, 5, 9
(d) 1, 6, 9; 3, 4, 7; 2, 5, 8

Space for Rough Work

31. From the following words, which word will come third if all of them are arranged alphabetically as in a dictionary?

Bishop, Bifocal, Bicycle, Bitter

(a) Bishop (b) Bifocal
(c) Bicycle (d) Bitter

32. If the day before yesterday was Thursday, when will Sunday be?

(a) Today
(b) Yesterday
(c) Tomorrow
(d) Day after tomorrow

33. Which of the following diagrams indicates the best relation amongst Writer, Player and Singer?

(a)
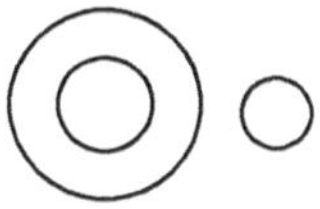
(b)
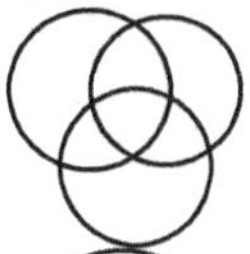
(c)

(d)
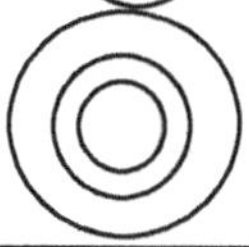

DIRECTIONS (Qs. 34 & 35): Study the following information carefully to answer the questions.

In a certain code language ' Sue Re Nik' means 'She is brave', 'Pi Sor Re Nik' means 'She is always smiling' and 'Sor Re Zhi' means 'Is always cherrful'.

34. What is the code for smiling?

(a) Nik (b) Re
(c) Pi (d) Sor

35. What is the code for cheerful?

(a) Sor (b) Zhi
(c) Re (d) Pi

36. Find the missing term.

m c _ m _ a _ c a _ c a

(a) a c m m (b) a c m a
(c) c m a m (d) a c c m

37. Find the odd one out.

(a) Cholera (b) Health
(c) Cancer (d) Jaundice

38. Consider five people A, B, C, D and E, each having different age. A is younger than only B. C is older than D. D is not the youngest. Who amongst the following are older than C?

(a) A and B (b) E, B and A
(c) A and E (d) E and B

39. Sunita is the 11th from either end of a row of girls. How many girls are there in that row?

(a) 19 (b) 20
(c) 21 (d) 22

40. Identify the one which is different from the others?

(a) 1003 (b) 2003
(c) 3004 (d) 3211

Space for Rough Work

OLYMPIAD Mock Test 5

Name : ________

Number of Questions : 40

Max. Marks : 40

Time : 2 Hours

There is no negative marking in the test.

DIRECTIONS (Qs. 1 to 3): Study the following information carefully to answer the questions.

Six persons are sitting in a circle. A is facing B. B is to right of E and left of C. C is to the left of D. F is to the right of A. Now, D exchanges his seat with F and E with B.

1. Who will be sitting to the left of D?

   (a) B (b) F

   (c) E (d) A

2. Who will be sitting to the left of C?

   (a) E (b) F

   (c) D (d) A

3. Who will be sitting opposite to C?

   (a) E (b) D

   (c) B (d) A

4. 'Doctor' is related to 'Patient'. In the same way 'Lawyer' is related to____.

   (a) Customer

   (b) Criminal

   (d) Magistrate

   (d) Client

5. Consider the relationship given below

   Road : Bus : Driver

   Now choose the group of words from the following which shows the same relationship as given above.

   (a) Water : Ship : Diver

   (b) Sky : Aeroplane : Pilot

   (c) Paper : Letter : Reader

   (d) Track : Train : Passenger

Space for Rough Work

DIRECTIONS (Qs. 6 & 7): Find the odd one out.

6. (a) Marigold (b) Tulip
 (c) Lotus (d) Rose

7. (a) DACB (b) EBCD
 (c) SPQR (d) XUVW

8. Number of unit cubes in the given figure is ________.

 (a) 25 (b) 26
 (c) 27 (d) 28

DIRECTIONS (Qs. 9 & 10): There are three forms, X, Y and Z of a sheet of paper. Figures X and Y respectively show the two consecutive folds of the sheet. And the figure Z shows punch on the folded sheet. Choose one figure from the four options (a), (b), (c) and (d), that is similar to the unfolded form of the sheet.

9. 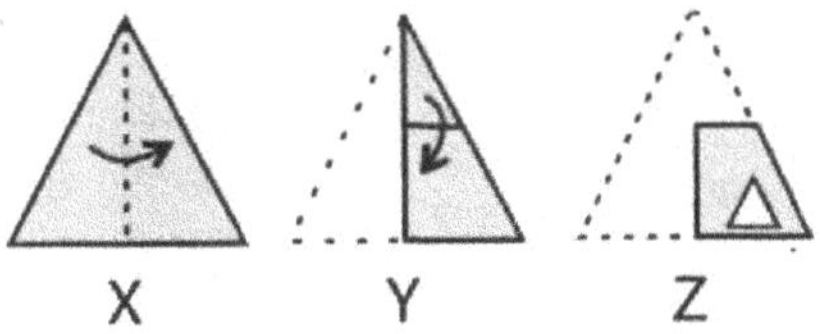

(a)  (b) 

(c)  (d) 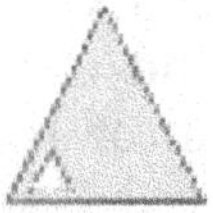

10. 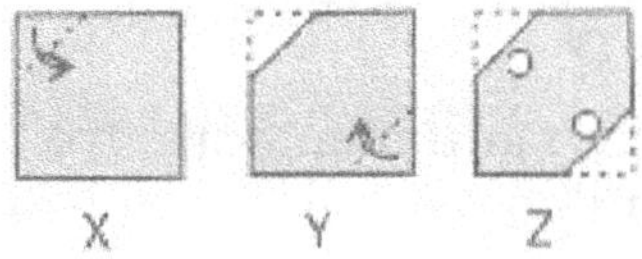

(a) 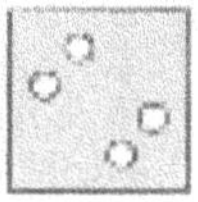 (b) 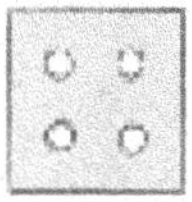

(c) 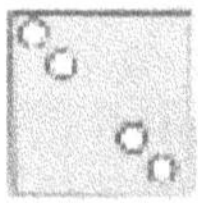 (d) 

11. Find the total number of C's each of which is immediately followed by a vowel in this sequence?

 B C C D E E C E A C E A C E A B C A B C A C A C A C B C

 (a) 4 (b) 6
 (c) 7 (d) 8

12. Kim ranks twelfth from the top in a class of forty six. What will be her rank from the last?

 (a) 33rd (b) 34th
 (c) 35th (d) 37th

Space for Rough Work

DIRECTIONS (Qs. 13 to 15): Study the following information and answer the questions that follow:

All the six members of a family P, Q, R, S, T and U are travelling together. Q is the son of R but R is not the mother of Q. P and R are married couple. T is the brother of R. S is the daughter of P. U is the brother of Q.

13. How many male members are there in the family?
    (a) 1 (b) 2
    (c) 3 (d) 4
14. How many children does P have?
    (a) 1 (b) 2
    (c) 3 (d) 4
15. How is T related to S?
    (a) Father
    (b) Uncle
    (c) Brother
    (d) Cannot be determined

DIRECTIONS (Qs. 16 & 17): Find the number which will replace the mark '?'.

16.

1	$\frac{1}{2}$	$\frac{3}{2}$
2	$\frac{2}{3}$	$\frac{8}{3}$
3	$\frac{3}{4}$	?

(a) $\frac{3}{4}$ (b) $\frac{2}{3}$

(c) $\frac{15}{4}$ (d) $\frac{6}{7}$

17. 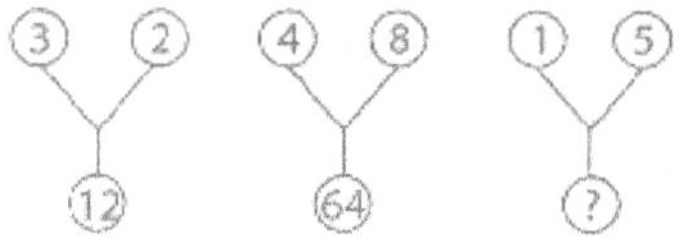

(a) 10 (b) 12

(c) 14 (d) 20

DIRECTIONS (Qs. 18 & 19): In each of the following questions, a series is given. One figure of this series is missing. Fill in the blanks to complete this series.

18. 

(a) 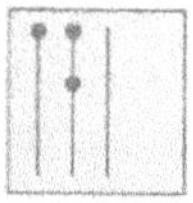 (b) 

(c) 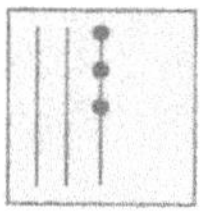 (d) 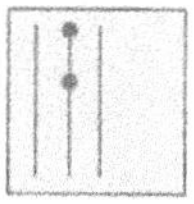

Space for Rough Work

19. 

(a)  (b) 

(c) 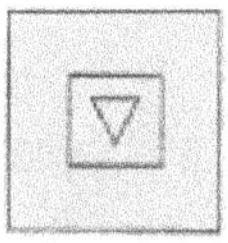 (d) 

20. How many such pairs of letters are there in the word 'JOURNEY', each of which has as many letters between them in the word (in both forward and backward directions) as they have between them in the english alphabetical order?

(a) None (b) One

(c) Two (d) Three

21. In the following question, a word has been given, followed by four other words, one of which cannot be formed by using the letters from the given word. Find that word.

C O M M U N I C A T I O N

(a) ACTION

(b) UNION

(c) NATION

(d) UNISON

22. Which single letter can be prefixed to the following words in order to obtain entirely new word?

(Same letter has to be prefixed in all five words of each)

EAT OUR IS AS AT

(a) S (b) H

(c) C (d) B

DIRECTIONS (Qs. 23 & 24): In each of the following questions, choose the correct water image of the figure (X).

23. 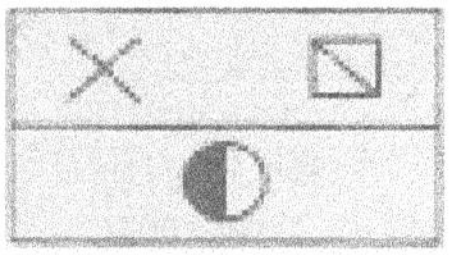

(X)

(a) 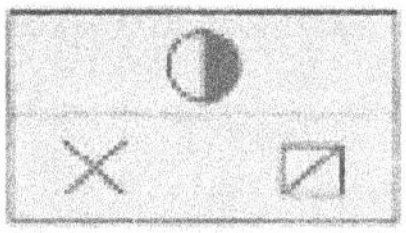

(b) 

(c) 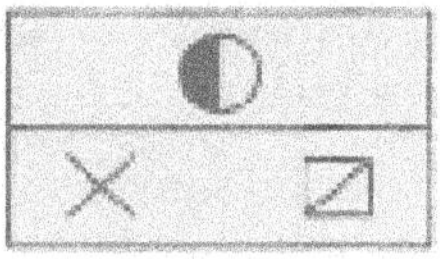

(d) 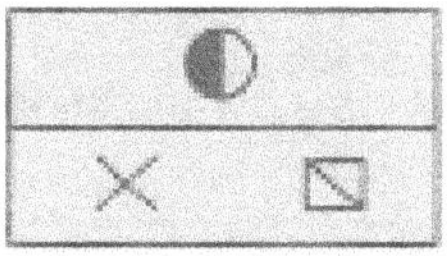

Space for Rough Work

24. 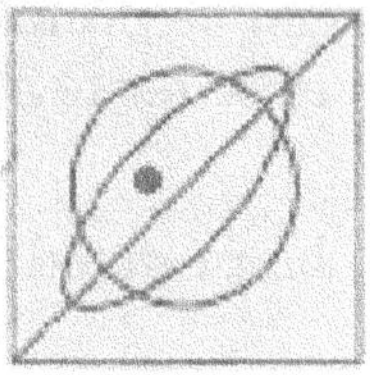

(X)

(a) 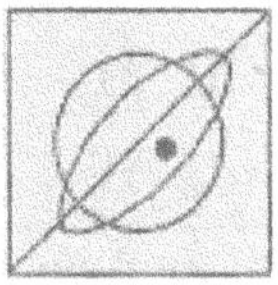 (b) 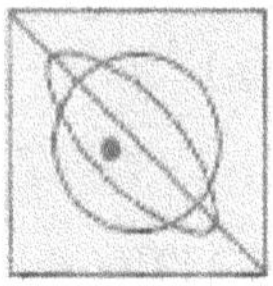

(c) 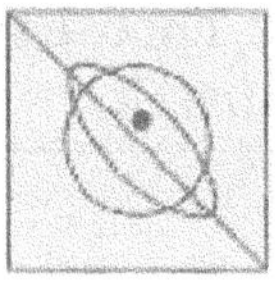 (d) 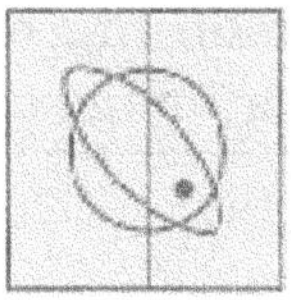

25. In a row of 62 persons. Rahul is 36th from left side of the row and Nitesh is 29th from the right side of the row. Find out the number of persons sitting between them?

(a) 1 (b) 2
(c) 3 (d) 4

26. In a certain code language, '123' means 'bright little boy', '145' means 'tall big boy' and '637' means 'beautiful little flower'. Which digit in that language means 'bright'?

(a) 1 (b) 2
(c) 3 (d) 4

DIRECTIONS (Qs. 27 & 28): Find the next term in the given series.

27. 5,6,9,14,21,?

(a) 28 (b) 30
(c) 31 (d) 29

28. R,O,L,I,F,?

(a) C (b) A
(c) E (d) I

29. Arrange the words in a meaningful order.

1. District 2. Village 3. State 4. Block

(a) 2,1,4,3 (b) 2,3,4,1
(c) 2,4,1,3 (d) 3,2,1,4

30. Arrange the following words as per order in the dictionary?

1. Divide 2. Division 3. Devine 4. Divest 5. Direct

(a) 5,4,3,2,1 (b) 5,4,1,3,2
(c) 1,2,3,4,5 (d) 3,5,4,1,2

31. A person walks towards his house at 8:00 am and observes his shadow to his right. In which direction he is walking?

(a) North (b) South
(c) East (d) West

32. The age of father is thrice of his son. If the sum of their ages is 48 yrs. What is the age of father?

(a) 30 yrs (b) 32 yrs
(c) 36 yrs (d) 40 yrs

Space for Rough Work

DIRECTIONS (Qs. 33 & 34): Study the figure given below carefully and answer the questions that follow.

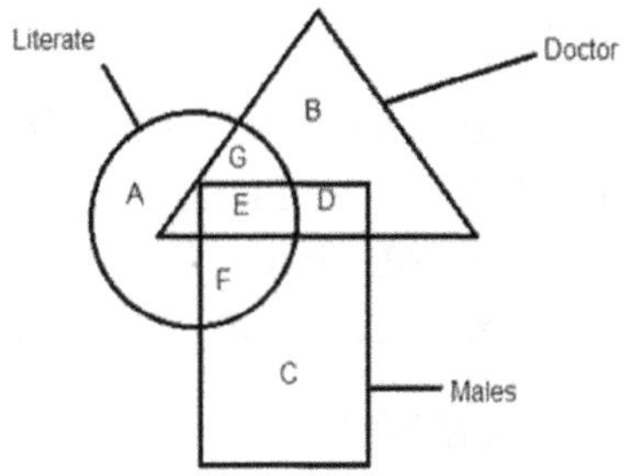

33. Which part shows Literate Males, who are Doctors?
    (a) G (b) E
    (c) D (d) F
34. Which part shows Males, who are neither Doctors nor Literate?
    (a) A (b) B
    (c) C (d) F
35. Select a figure from the options which would closely resemble the unfolded form of paper.

X Y Z

(a)  (b) 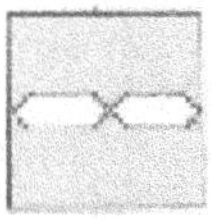

(c) 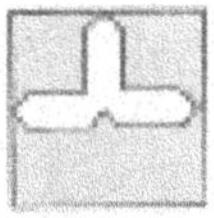 (d) 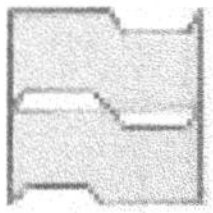

36. According to the given figure of dice, which option is correct.

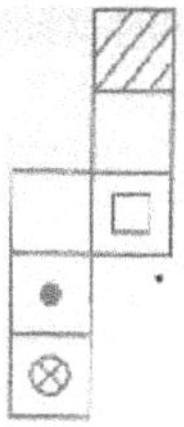

(X)

(1) (2) (3) (4)

(a) 1 only
(b) 2 and 3 only
(c) 1 and 3 only
(d) 1, 2, 3 and 4

37. Complete the figure matrix?

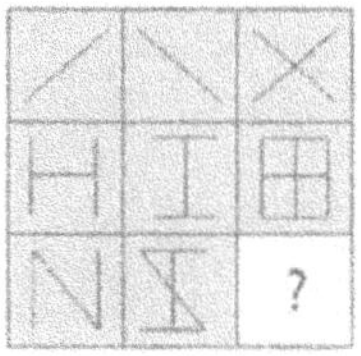

Space for Rough Work

(a)  (b) 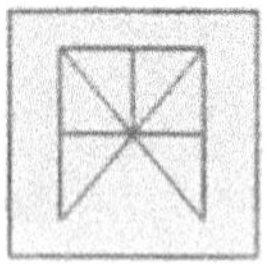

(c) 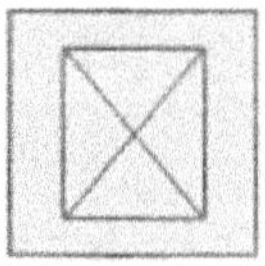 (d) 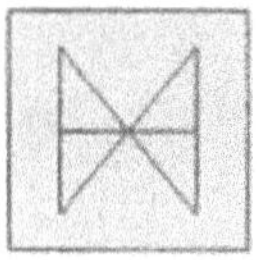

38. If 'p' denotes '÷', 'q' denotes '+', 'r' denotes '–' and 't' denotes '×', then 11 q 15 r 8 p 4 t 5 = ?

(a) 36 (b) 20

(c) 26 (d) 16

39. If the letters in the word UNDERTAKING are rearranged in the alphabetical order, which one will be exactly in the middle after the rearrangement?

(a) K (b) I

(c) G (d) N

40. By following a certain logic MTUXTRVN is written as NUVXTQUM. How is ASUMNJKL written in that logic?

(a) BTVMNIJK

(b) BTVMNKLM

(c) BTVNMIJK

(d) ZRTMNIJK

Space for Rough Work

CYBER OLYMPIAD

Mock Test 1

Name : ________

Max. Marks : 25

Number of Questions : 25

Time : 1 Hour

There is no negative marking in the test.

1. The basic goal of computer process is to convert data into
   (a) files (b) tables
   (c) information (d) graphs
2. Which of the following is the fastest type of computer?
   (a) Laptop (b) Notebook
   (c) Personal computer
   (d) Supercomputer
3. A printer is _______.
   (a) input (b) word processing
   (c) processing (d) output
4. Which contents are lost when the computer is turned off ?
   (a) storage (b) input
   (c) output (d) memory
5. Sending an e-mail is similar to
   (a) picturing an event
   (b) narrating a story
   (c) writing a letter
   (d) creating a drawing
6. Files deleted from the hard disk are sent to the–
   (a) recycle bin (b) floppy disk
   (c) clipboard (d) motherboard
7. The main component of a desktop PC which houses the computer's critical parts is called the _______.
   (a) processor (b) memory
   (c) hard Disk (d) system unit
8. Which of the following devices can sense hand-drawn marks such as small circles or rectangles made on pre-printed forms?
   (a) OCR (b) OMR
   (c) MBR (d) MICR
9. Which of the following is NOT true in the case of software?
   (a) It is a physical device.
   (b) It enables the computer to perform certain tasks for the users.
   (c) It enables the user to interact with the computer.
   (d) It is a collection of instructions.
10. A storage device can be ________.
    (a) a built device that holds information
    (b) the main storage area in a computer which stores data
    (c) an external hardware device used by the computer to store data
    (d) all of these

Space for Rough Work

11. A secondary storage device is also known as ________.
(a) auxiliary memory
(b) main memory
(c) available memory
(d) primary memory

12. BIOS of a computer is stored in _____.
(a) RAM (b) ROM
(c) cache (d) hard disk

13. Which of the following is NOT associated with fifth generation of computers?
(a) ULSI (b) CUI system
(c) Electronic-commerce
(d) WWW

14. Which among the following was the first electronic general purpose computer?
(a) UNIVAC (b) EDVAC
(c) ENIAC (d) None of these

15. On-screen work area which contains window icons, menus and dialog boxes is called _____?
(a) Desktop (b) Frame
(c) Screen (d) Display

16. The time is shown in the _____ on the taskbar.
(a) start menu (b) scrollbar
(c) desktop
(d) notification area or System Tray

17. In an MS-Word Table, which key is used to move to the next cell?
(a) Tab (b) Function
(c) Space (d) Alt

18. Which of the following Chart elements helps you to distinguish between series and data points and depicts the color or pattern assigned to series?
(a) Data Table
(b) Chart Title
(c) Legend
(d) Gridlines

19. In the current presentation, if we want to insert a new slide, we can choose which of these?
(a) Ctrl + F (b) Ctrl + O
(c) Ctrl + M (d) None of these

20. Which of these refers to the PowerPoint view used for displaying only the text (title and bullets)?
(a) Slide sorter show(b) Slide view
(c) Outline view (d) Notes page view

21. The QBASIC window has the following Components:
(a) Menu Bar
(b) Name of the current program
(c) Status Bar
(d) All of these

22. Which command is used to clear the output screen?
(a) CLS (b) CLEAR
(c) RUB (d) ERASE

23. Which of the following is not an internet connection service?
(a) ISDN (b) DSL
(c) UPS (d) Wi-Fi

24. In the web address
http//: www.myhomepage.com/pictures/myschool/ClassVI.jpg
what does/myschool/ indicate?
(a) The name of the image on the website.
(b) It is the URL
(c) The folder where Class VI. jpg will be found.
(d) The homepage image for the website www.myhomepage.com.

25. The digital payment system from Google is known as ________.
(a) Google Payments
(b) Google Wallet
(c) Google Money
(d) Google Cheques

Space for Rough Work

OLYMPIAD

Mock Test 2

Name : ________ **Max. Marks : 25**

Number of Questions : 25 **Time : 1 Hour**

There is no negative marking in the test.

1. The first computer made available for commercial use was:
   (a) MANIAC (b) ENIAC
   (c) UNIVAC (d) EDSAC
2. Help Menu is available at which button?
   (a) End (b) Start
   (c) Turnoff (d) Restart
3. Which of the following can be used to select the entire document?
   (a) CTRL+A (b) ALT+ F5
   (c) SHIFT+A (d) CTRL+K
4. Which of the following groups consist of only input devices?
   (a) Mouse, Keyboard, Monitor
   (b) Mouse, Keyboard, Printer
   (c) Mouse, Keyboard, Plotter
   (d) Mouse, Keyboard, Scanner
5. Using output devices one can
   (a) input data (b) store data
   (c) scan data (d) view or print data
6. Which of the following is not an example of hardware?
   (a) Scanner (b) Printer
   (c) Monitor (d) Interpreter
7. DVD is an example of
   (a) hard disk (b) optical disk
   (c) output device
   (d) solid-state storage devices
8. Letters, numbers and symbols found on a keyboard are –
   (a) icon (b) screen
   (c) keys (d) m,enu
9. Which of the following is a type of non-volatile memory, retaining stored data even when powered-off?

(i) (ii)

Space for Rough Work

(iii)

(iv)

(a) Only (i)
(b) Only (i) and (ii)
(c) Only (ii) and (iv)
(d) (i), (ii) and (iii)

10. A CPU's clock speed is measured in ________.
(a) gigahertz
(b) megahertz
(c) bits/bytes per second
(d) both (a) and (b)

11. Which of the following is a type of non-impact printer?
(a) Laser Printers
(b) Line Printers
(c) Dot-Matrix Printers
(d) Daisy-Wheel Printers

12. A CD-R is also known as _______.
(a) worm (b) woro
(c) wmro (d) wmrm

13 Match the following

Column-I	Column-II
(A) USB Flash drive	(i) 
(B) Hard disk drive	(ii) 
(C) Optical disk drive	(iii) 

(a) (A) - (ii), (B) - (iii), (C) - (i)
(b) (A) - (iii), (B) - (i), (C) - (ii)
(c) (A) - (i), (B) - (iii), (C) - (ii)
(d) (A) - (i), (B) - (ii), (C) - (iii)

14. Which one of the following technology was developed during Fourth Generation of Computers?
(a) Artificial Intelligence
(b) VLSI
(c) Integrated Circuits
(d) VALVE

15. In the given image, Windows needs your confirmation by displaying three buttons: Save, Don't Save and Cancel before closing any file. It is called _______.

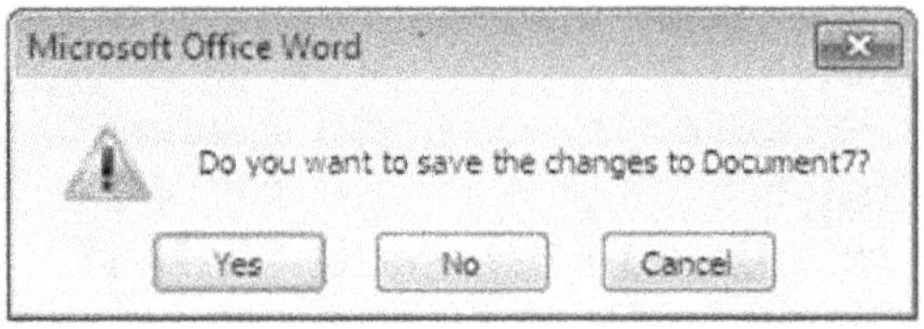

(a) mail box (b) question box
(c) info box (d) dialog box

16. When a computer is idle for sometime, it goes into the _______ mode to save energy.
(a) sleep (b) shut down
(c) slowdown (d) hibernate

Space for Rough Work

17. How can you format a Table?
    (a) By changing the row height
    (b) By changing the column width
    (c) By applying borders and shading
    (d) All of these
18. What does a ruler show?
    (a) Page width
    (b) Position of tabs, columns, etc.
    (c) Length of the document
    (d) All of these
19. The brightness and contrast of an image can be adjusted using the ________ command available under Format tab of Picture Tools.
    (a) color
    (b) compress Pictures
    (c) corrections
    (d) crop
20. Which of these is a valid numeric variable name?
    (a) M8 (b) 8M
    (c) $M (d) 2B43
21. Which of the following operators will combine two string constants?
    (a) – (b) +
    (c) * (d) ++
22. Identify the following:
    – It is a free mobile browser developed by the chinese mobile Internet company.
    – It is available on number of platform including Android, iOS and Windows phone.

    (a) KC browser (b) TC browser
    (c) UC browser (d) DM browser
23. Opera mini is a ________.
    (a) search engine
    (b) news reader
    (c) graphing package
    (d) none of these
24. The image shown here is displaying a ________.

    (a) pda
    (b) smartphone
    (c) notepad
    (d) convertible laptop
25. What is 'Google Now'?
    (a) It is an intelligent personal assistant.
    (b) It is a web browser.
    (c) It is a new version of Google Chrome web browser.
    (d) It is a play for smartphones.

Space for Rough Work

OLYMPIAD

Mock Test 3

Name : ________ **Max. Marks : 25**

Number of Questions : 25 **Time : 1 Hour**

There is no negative marking in the test.

1. Personal computers can be connected together to form a
   (a) server
   (b) supercomputer
   (c) network
   (d) enterprise
2. Information on a computer is stored as ______.
   (a) analog data (b) digital data
   (c) modem data (d) watts data
3. The rectangular area of the screen that displays a program, data and / or information is a
   (a) title bar (b) button
   (c) dialog box (d) window
4. You can keep your personal files/ folders in
   (a) my folder
   (b) my Documents
   (c) my Files
   (d) my Text
5. A chat is
   (a) an internet standard that allows users to upload and download files
   (b) a typed conversation that takes place on a computer or Mobile.
   (c) an online area in which users conduct written discussions about a particular subject
   (d) the transmission of messages and files via a computer network
6. The process of trading goods over the Internet is known as
   (a) e-selling-n-buying
   (b) e-trading
   (c) e-finance
   (d) e-commerce
7. In Word you can force a page break _____.
   (a) by positioning your cursor at the appropriate place and pressing the F1 key
   (b) by positioning your cursor at the appropriate place and pressing Ctrl+Enter

Space for Rough Work

(c) by using the insert /section break
(d) by changing the font size of your document

8. Which of the following computers are primarily used by government organizations for critical applications like bulk data processing - like census, consumer statistics, etc.?
(a) Microcomputers
(b) Minicomputers
(c) Mainframe computers
(d) Embedded computers

9. The given program is an example of ________.

```
Program SUM 2 (Input output)
VAR
NUM 1. NUM2.SUM : INTEGER
BEGIN
READ (NUM1. NUM2)
SUM=NUM1+NUM2
WRITEIN(SUM)
END
```

(a) Machine level language
(b) Assembly level language
(c) High level language
(d) None of these

10. Which of the following statements is NOT true about System Software?
(a) It is designed to operate the computer hardware.
(b) It provides basic functionality to the computer.
(c) They are simple programs designed to accomplish certain tasks.
(d) It is responsible for managing a variety of independent hardware components

11. Arrange the following units of memory from the smallest to the largest.
1 nibble, 1 terabyte, 1 byte, 1 petabyte, 1 bit, 1 exabyte
(a) 1 exabyte < 1 petabyte < 1 terabyte < 1 byte < 1 nibble < 1 bite
(b) 1 exabyte < 1 petabyte < 1 terabyte < 1 bit < byte < 1 nibble
(c) 1 bit < 1 nibble < 1 byte < 1 terabyte < 1 petabyte < 1 exabyte
(d) 1 bit < 1 byte < 1 nibble < 1 exabyte < 1 petabyte < 1 terabyte

12. Complete the given diagram by replacing the X, Y and Z with the following options

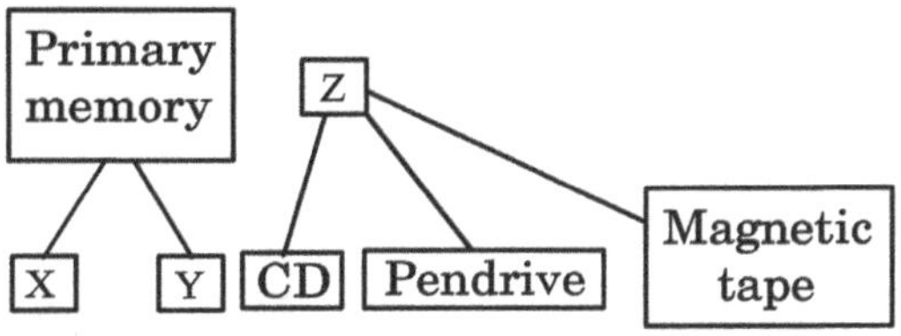

(a) X - RAM
Y - ROM
Z - Auxiliary memory
(b) X - RAM
Y - ROM
Z - Secondary memory
(c) X - Hard disk
Y - RAM
Z - Secondary memory
(d) Both (a) and (b)

13. Which of the following memories must be refreshed many times per second?
    (a) Static RAM
    (b) Dynamic RAM
    (c) EEPROM
    (d) Flash memory
14. Identify the computer generation.
    _ Microprocessor based systems.
    _ Development of computer languages like C, PASCAL, BASIC
    – Computer networking was inntroduced.
    – APPLE II is its example.
    (a) First (b) Third
    (c) Fifth (d) Fourth
15. Match the names of the early calculating devices with their corresponding pictures.

Column-I **Column-II**

(A) Difference Engine (i) 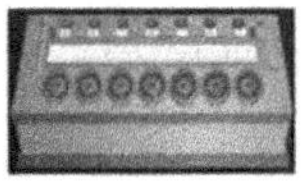

(B) Napier's Bones (ii) 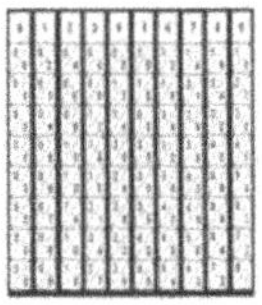

(C) Pascaline (iii) 

(a) (A) - (i), (B) - (iii), (C) - (ii)
(b) (A) - (i), (B) - (ii), (C) - (iii)
(c) (A) - (iii), (B) - (ii), (C) - (i)
(d) (A) - (iii), (B) - (i), (C) - (ii)

16. Identify the Windows start mode:
    – In this mode, Windows starts with a limited set of files and drivers.
    – This mode is useful for troubleshooting problems with programs and drivers which might not start correctly and prevents Windows from starting correctly.
    (a) Safe mode
    (b) Start mode
    (c) Error free mode
    (d) Troubleshoot mode
17. Complete the given steps by replacing '?' to turn off this feature.
    Steps : Right click the taskbar → Taskbar and Start Menu properties dialog box appears → ? → Uncheck 'Use Aero Peek to preview the desktop' option.
    (a) Start Menu tab
    (b) Taskbar tab
    (c) Toolbars tab
    (d) None of these
18. _______ Key combination is used to show paragraph marks and other

Space for Rough Work

hidden formatting symbols.

(a) Ctrl + Shift + S

(b) Ctrl + Shift + H

(c) Ctrl + Shift + * 8

(d) Ctrl + Shift + K

19. The given pane shown here is of 'Selection and Visibility'. If displays the name of the shapes that you have inserted in the document. Which of the following is the CORRECT step to open this pane?

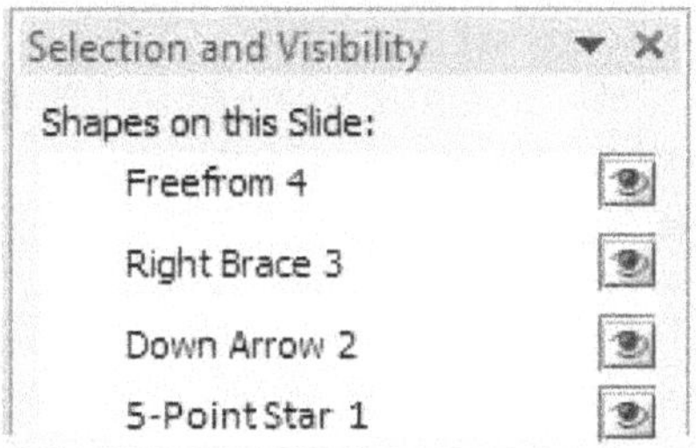

(a) Page Layout tab → Paragraph group → Selection pane
(b) Page Layout tab → Arrange group → Selection pane
(c) Page Layout tab → Page Setup group → Selection pane
(d) Page Layout tab → Themes group → Selection pane

20. While resizing, to maintain the height and width ratio of an object, you should ________.

(a) press and hold the Shift key while dragging a corner sizing handle
(b) press and hold the Enter key while dragging a middle handle
(c) drag a middle size handle
(d) all of these

21. Given below is an arithmetic expression. Which of the following parts of the expression will be calculated first in QBASIC?

A + B / 5 * C – D ^ 2

(a) B/5
(b) D^2
(c) A+B
(d) 5*C

22. Identify the following internet service:

– It is an American electronic commerce and cloud computing company founded by Jeff Bezos.
– It is an online shopping site that sells the variety of products.

(a) skype
(b) amazon.com
(c) Google
(d) ebay

Space for Rough Work

23. __________ is a web browser developed by Apple Inc.

(a)

(b)

(c)

(d) msn

24. The input device to be used to get a printed diagram into a computer, is called ____
(a) Touch pad
(b) Scanner
(c) Mouse
(d) Printer

25. Which of the following statements holds true about the given logo?

Statement 1 :
It is an instant messaging and video chat platform by Google.
Statement 2 :
Its name is Google communication.
(a) Only Statement 1
(b) Only Statement 2
(c) Neither Statement 1 nor Statement 2
(d) Both Statement 1 and Statement 2

Space for Rough Work

OLYMPIAD

Mock Test 4

Name : ________ **Max. Marks : 40**

Number of Questions : 40 **Time : 2 Hours**

There is no negative marking in the test.

1. BCC in the Email refer to
   (a) Blind Carbon Copy
   (b) Black Carbon Copy
   (c) Blank Carbon Copy
   (d) Blue Carbon Copy
2. Which function key is used to refresh the current window?
   (a) F1 (b) F5
   (c) F3 (d) F6
3. Which of the following shortcut is used to repeat the last action performed?
   (a) F3 (b) F4
   (c) F5 (d) F6
4. Which key launches the start button?
   (a) Windows (b) Esc
   (c) Shift (d) Function key
5. What is the permanent memory built into your computer called?
   (a) RAM (b) Floppy
   (c) CD-ROM (d) None of these
6. The computer abbreviation KB usually means
   (a) Key Block (b) Kernel Boot
   (c) Key Byte (d) Kilo Byte
7. Which of the following is the largest unit of storage?
   (a) GB (b) KB
   (c) MB (d) TB
8. A device that provides emergency power to your computer, conditions the voltage, and protects against power surges is called a ________.
   (a) PSU = Power Supply Unit
   (b) USP = Universal Surge Protector
   (c) UPPS = Universal Power Protection and Supply
   (d) UPS = Uninterruptible Power Supply
9. Mobile Commerce is best described as
   (a) the use of kiosks in marketing
   (b) transporting products
   (c) buying and selling goods/services through wireless handheld devices
   (d) using notebook PCs in marketing
10. An e-mail address typically consists of a user ID followed by the________

Space for Rough Work

sign and the name of the e-mail server that manages the user's electronic post office box.

(a) @ (b) #
(c) & (d) «

11. Microsoft Word is an example of
    (a) an operating system
    (b) a processing device
    (c) application software
    (d) an input device
12. Identify the following type of printer with the help of given information.
    X : They use typewriting printing mechanism, wherein a hammer strikes the paper through a ribbon in order to produce output.
    Y : They do not touch paper while printing. They use chemical, heat or electric signal to etch the symbols on paper.
    (a) X - Impact printer, Y - Non-impact printer
    (b) X - Non-impact printer, Y- Impacter printer
    (c) X - Common printer, Y- Uncommon printer
    (d) X - Uncommon printer, Y- Common printer
13. What do you mean by debugging?
    (a) It is the process of identifying all errors from a computer program.
    (b) It is the process to translate binary code into digital code.
    (c) It is the process to translate digital code into binary code.
    (d) All of these
14. Which of the following statements hold(s) true regarding EEPROM?
    Statement 1 : It can be reprogrammed and erased by applying special programming signals.
    Statement 2 : Its full form is Electrically Erasable Programmable Read Only Memory.
    (a) Only Statement 1
    (b) Only Statement 2
    (c) Both Statement 1 and Statement 2
    (d) Neither Statement 1 nor Statement 2.
15. What is the difference between Volatile and Non-Volatile Memory?
    (a) They are both same types of memory.
    (b) Volatile loses its contents when there is no electricity while non-volatile retains its content with or without electricity.
    (c) Non-volatile loses its contents when there is no electricity while volatile retains its content with or without electricity.
    (d) None of these
16. Apple computers were first developed in the 1970s. Who invented the first Apple computer?
    (a) Bill Gates
    (b) John von Neumann
    (c) Steve Wozniak
    (d) Larry Page

Space for Rough Work

17. Match the following

	Column-I		Column-II
(A)	Lady Augusta Lovelace	(i)	British mathematician and considered as a father of computers
(B)	Charles Babbage	(ii)	Mechanical calculator
(C)	John von Neumann	(iii)	The first lady Programmer
(D)	Gottfried Wilhelm Leibniz	(iv)	Suggested stored program concept

(a) (A) - (iv), (B) - (ii), (C) - (i), (D) - (iii)
(b) (A) - (i), (B) - (ii), (C) - (iii), (D) - (iv)
(c) (A) - (iii), (B) - (i), (C) - (iv), (D) - (ii)
(d) (A) - (iv), (B) - (iii), (C) - (ii), (D) - (i)

18. Identify the following feature of Windows 7.
– By simply dragging the title bar of the Window (you want to work with) to the left and right - just give it a few quick shakes and Windows 7 will automatically drop all the other windows down to the taskbar, leaving your main window in place.
(a) Aero Main (b) Title Shake
(c) Aero Shake (d) Shake Drop

19. Windows 10 is designed to run on _______.
(a) 32-bit processors
(b) 64-bit processors
(c) 128 bit processors
(d) Both (a) and (b)

20. The button shown here is used to insert a ______.

(a) blank page (b) page break
(c) cover page (d) picture

21. The command button 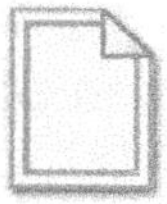 is used to _______.
(a) add or change border around a page
(b) choose a background color for a page
(c) merge cells
(d) display Table properties

22. Which of the following statements is correct regarding text boxes?
(a) You can insert boxes from the Insert Tab of the ribbon
(b) Text boxes once inserted cannot be relocated
(c) Text boxes are provided when you select a layout. They cannot be inserted after you have selected a layout
(d) None of these

23. Header and Footer placeholders are by default present in ______ view.
(a) Title Master
(b) Normal
(c) Handout Master
(d) Page Master

Space for Rough Work

24. QBASIC is a programming language developed by ______.
(a) MIT (b) Microsoft
(c) Wayne (d) Stanford

25. Character set on QBASIC includes __________.
(a) Numeric digits
(b) Letters
(c) Special characters
(d) All of these

26. Which of the following statements hold(s) true regarding spam?
Statement 1 : It means following the internet with the message, in an attempt to force the message on people who would not otherwise choose to receive it.
Statement 2 : Most spam are commercial advertising.
(a) Only Statement 1
(b) Only Statement 2
(c) Both Statement 1 and Statement 2
(d) Neither Statement 1 nor Steatomata 2

27. Which of the following steps is CORRECT if you want to see all the images you have downloaded from the Internet from Google Chrome?
(a) Go to 'Cutomize and Control Google Chrome' (present at the extreme right side of the window) → Downloads
(b) Go to 'Customize' button → Image
(c) Go to 'Customize button → Image download
(d) Both (a) and (b)

28. Which of the following statements hold(s) true about the given icon?

Statement 1 : Its make is One Drive, a cloud storage service by Microsoft.
Statement 2 : It allows you to create, edit and share documents regardless of the type of the device.
(a) Only Statement 1
(b) Only Statement 2
(c) Neither Statement 1 nor Statement 2
(d) Both Statement 1 and Statement 2

29. Multi-touch is a technology that enables touch screen devices to recognize touch gestures on multiple points on the surface of a device. Which among the following is a multi-touch gesture?
(a) Tap (b) Slide
(c) Pinch (d) Swipe

30. Microsoft's personal cloud storage service is called _______.
(a) OneNote (b) SoftDocs
(c) MicroDocs (d) OneDrive

31. You can talk to the computer using which of the following?
(a) Voice response system
(b) Speech recognition System
(c) Voice recorder system
(d) Multimedia Player

32. What type of webpage provides an overview of all the pages on a website?
(a) Home page (b) About page
(c) Link page (d) Site map

Space for Rough Work

33. What characteristic of read-only memory (ROM) makes it useful?
    (a) ROM information can be easily updated
    (b) Data in ROM is nonvolatile, that is, it remains there even without electriical power
    (c) ROM provides very large amounts of inexpensive data storage
    (d) ROM chips are easily swapped between different brands of computers
34. How many different documents can you have a open at any one time?
    (a) Not more than three
    (b) Only one
    (c) As many as your computer memory will hold
    (d) No more than your Taskbar can display
35. The software program that acts as an interface between the user and the www is ______.
    (a) e-mail (b) internet
    (c) web browser (d) protocol
36. Which company developed the chrome web browser?
    (a) Google
    (b) YAHOO!
    (c) Microsoft
    (d)
37. Which of the following computer is related to PDP-8 (the first successful commercial computer)?
    (a) Mainframe computer
    (b) Supercomputer
    (c) Microcomputer
    (d) Minicomputer
38. Identify this icon in MS-power point

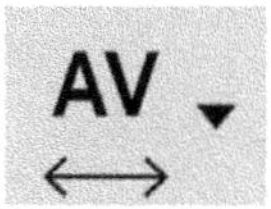

    (a) Text shadow
    (b) Font Color
    (c) Font Size
    (d) Character Spacing
39. Identify this icon in MS-power point

    (a) It is used to open a new slide
    (b) It is used to insert a slide
    (c) It is used to delete a slide
    (d) None of these
40. Identify this icon in MS-power point

    (a) It is used to change the layout of the slide
    (b) It is used to insert the new slide
    (c) It is used to delete the selected slide
    (d) None of these

Space for Rough Work

OLYMPIAD

Mock Test 5

Name : ________ **Max. Marks : 40**

Number of Questions : 40 **Time : 2 Hours**

There is no negative marking in the test.

1. A central computer that holds collections of data and programs for many PCs, workstations and other computers is a ——
   (a) supercomputer
   (b) minicomputer
   (c) laptop
   (d) server
2. A personal computer is designed to meet the computing needs of a(n)
   (a) individual (b) department
   (c) company (d) city
3. The ________ is responsible for performing calculations and contains decision-making mechanisms.
   (a) central processing unit
   (b) memory unit
   (c) arithmetic and logic unit
   (d) output unit
4. ________key is the example of Toggle key
   (a) Alt (b) Shift
   (c) Control (d) Caps Lock
5. What type of device is a 3½ inch floppy drive ?
   (a) Input (b) Output
   (c) Software (d) Storage
6. On a CD-RW you can
   (a) read and write information
   (b) only read information
   (c) only write information
   (d) read, write and rewrite information
7. Window 10 is an _____ developed by _____
   (a) Utility Software , Apple
   (b) Operating System, Google
   (c) Operating System, Microsoft
   (d) Network, Microsoft
8. An error is also known as
   (a) bug (b) debug
   (c) cursor (d) icon
9. Restarting a computer that is already on is referred to as

Space for Rough Work

(a) shut down (b) cold booting
(c) warm booting (d) logging off

10. What is the other name of LAN card?
(a) Modem
(b) Network connector
(c) Internet card
(d) NIC (Network Interface Card)

11. 'Bluetooth' technology allows
(a) satellite communication
(b) signal transmission on mobile phones only
(c) wireless communication between equipments
(d) landline phone to mobile phone communication

12. What is m-commerce?
(a) machine commerce
(b) mobile commerce
(c) money commerce
(d) marketing commerce

13. Which of the following is the valid domain name extension?
(a) .edu (b) .org
(c) .com (d) All of these

14. To restart the computer _________ key is used.
(a) Del + Ctrl
(b) Backspace + Ctrl
(c) Ctrl + Alt + Del
(d) Reset

15. What device separates a single network into two segments but lets the two segments appear as one to higher protocols?
(a) Switch (b) Bridge
(c) Gateway (d) Router

16. Identify the following:
– It is a device that provides functionality for other devices.
– It connects many other computers and provides access to resources like printers, Internet, files and programs.
(a) Mainframe (b) Server
(c) Laptop (d) Workstation

17. Which of the following devices is used to supply power to the computer system?
(a) Jumper
(b) Microprocessor
(c) SMPS
(d) Motherboard

18. Which of the following is true?
(a) 4 Nibbles = 1 Byte
(b) 4 Bytes = 1 Nibble
(c) 4 Bits = 1 Nibble
(d) 4 Nibbles = 1 Bit

19. Identify the following:
– It uses Integrated Circuit assemblies as memory to store data persistently.
– It has no moving mechanical components and it is typically more resistant to physical shock.
(a) Hard disk drive
(b) Solid-state drive
(c) Magnetic tape drive
(d) All of these

20. Which of the following statements hold(s) true regarding UNIVAC 1?
Statement 1 : It was the first commercial electronic computer developed by J. Presper Eckert and John Mauchly.

Space for Rough Work

Statement 2 : It was also the first computer to handle both numeric and text data.
(a) Only Statement 1
(b) Only Statement 2
(c) Both Statement 1 and Statement 2
(d) Neither Statement 1 nor Statement 2

21 Identify the following:
– It was the web browser with support of multiple internet protocols.
– This programe was developed in 1993.
– It is often known as the first graphical web browser to display images online.
– It was navigation tool for interactive material.
(a) Mosaic
(b) Internet Explorer
(c) Safari
(d) Netscape Navigator

22. The icon shown here is used to _____.

(a) Set the size of a page
(b) Split text into columns
(c) Add page break
(d) all of these

23. You can use different page format within the same document by a separating the differently formatted area with ____________.
(a) Document breaks
(b) Line breaks
(c) Section breaks
(d) Format breaks

24. Which of the following statements is CORRECT?
(a) You can apply transition only to first and last slide.
(b) You cannot hide slide.
(c) You can create custom animations using Animation Pane.
(d) You cannot provide more than one animations to a single object.

25. When the Draw Table feature is selected, the mouse pointer appears as a/an _______.
(a) solid plus sign
(b) Solid arrow
(c) I-beam
(d) Pencil

26. What would be the output of the given code?

```
CLS
LET b = 4
IF b MOD 2 = 0 THEN
PRINT "Even number"
ELSE
PRINT
PRINT "ODD Number"
END IF
```

(a) Even Number
(b) ODD Number
(c) ODD Number
Even Number
(d) Even Number
ODD Number

Space for Rough Work

27. Which among the following is an invalid numeric constants and why?

0.75	–99.09	48/A
(i)	(ii)	(iii)

(a) (i) only because decimals are not allowed
(b) (ii) only, because negative integers are not allowed
(c) (iii)only, because alphanumeric are not allowed
(d) None of these

28. Web addresses can be written as words or as numbers.
For example: www.sofworld.org might have an address number of 63.141.53.0. What are these numbers called?
(a) Uniform Resource Locator Number
(b) Internet Protocol Address
(c) File Transfer Protocol Address
(d) ISP Number

29. This word art

is commonly seen during verification. This is known as ________.
(a) Crypt (b) Auto Text
(c) Code (d) Captcha

30. _______ is a mobile payment and digital wallet service by Apple Inc.
(a) Apple Pay
(b) Apple Money
(c) Apple Digipurse
(d) Apple Wall

31. Which of the following is/are the parts of e-mail address?
(a) Username
(b) @
(c) Host server name
(d) All of these

32. What can be used with a PRINT statement for printing multiple values in a single line in QBASIC?
(a) Comma (b) Semicolon
(c) Tab (n) (d) All of these

33. Which of the following options is/are used in QBASIC to stop and get information from a user using a question mark?
(a) QUERY (b) GET
(c) QUESTION (d) PUT

34. In MS-Word 2010, to insert the header and footer in a document, which tab should you go to?
(a) View (b) Page Layout
(c) Home (d) Insert

35. To switch between the running applications, _______.
(a) press F1
(b) press ALT + F4
(c) press TAB
(d) press and hold down ALT and press TAB

36. Which of the following computer is related to **PARAM**?
(a) Mainframe computer
(b) Supercomputer
(c) Microcomputer
(d) Minicomputer

Space for Rough Work

37. Which of the following statements is/ are correct about the Micro computer?
    (a) Large and complex machines for I/O processing
    (b) Single user device used in home or office environment
    (c) It is a device that can be seen only by a microscope.
    (d) None of these
38. FLOPS Stands for........
    (a) Fast processing operations per second
    (b) Flowing power operations per second
    (c) Floating point operations per second
    (d) None of these.
39. The speed of a computer is measured in ....
    (a) Pixels
    (b) Nibble
    (c) Bits
    (d) Hertz (Hz)
40. Match the following terms with what they stand for.

Column-I	**Column-II**
(A) .in	(i) Australia
(B) .edu	(ii) India
(C) .au	(iii) commerce
(D) .com	(iv) education

    (a) (A)-(ii), (B)-(iv), (C)-(i), (D)-(iii)
    (b) (A)-(iii), (B)-(iv), (C)-(i), (D)-(ii)
    (c) (A)-(iv), (B)-(iii), (C)-(i), (D)-(ii)
    (d) (A)-(ii), (B)-(i), (C)-(iv), (D)-(iii)

Space for Rough Work

HINTS AND EXPLANATIONS

ENGLISH

MOCK TEST 1

ANSWER KEY									
1	(c)	11	(a)	21	(a)	31	(a)	41	(c)
2	(a)	12	(a)	22	(b)	32	(c)	42	(a)
3	(a)	13	(c)	23	(b)	33	(c)	43	(a)
4	(a)	14	(c)	24	(b)	34	(b)	44	(b)
5	(c)	15	(b)	25	(a)	35	(d)	45	(c)
6	(b)	16	(c)	26	(a)	36	(a)	46	(a)
7	(a)	17	(b)	27	(d)	37	(c)	47	(c)
8	(b)	18	(c)	28	(c)	38	(c)	48	(b)
9	(b)	19	(d)	29	(d)	39	(a)	49	(c)
10	(c)	20	(b)	30	(a)	40	(b)	50	(b)

1. (c) He liked my painting at first sight.

2. (a) Gradually the forests are decreasing. Humankind is being very hard on them.

3. (a) What's happening? Why are you making so much noise.

4. (a) The expert lawyer tried to cite many cases to prove his point.

5. (c) The number of girls is less than the number of boys in my class.

6. (b) During the interrogation I didn't remember anything, my mind went blank.

7. (a) We must not eat too much sugar, it is not good for our health.

8. (b) He had been complaining of fever for a long time. After a number of tests he was diagnosed with malaria.

9. (b) They always keep calculating lions' population.

10. (c) During summers we must drink a lot of water, it prevents dehydration.

11. (a) You need not take your goggles, as it is cloudy.

12. (a) 2 **13. (c)** 3 **14. (c)** 2

15. (b) You must leave before it starts raining.

16. (c) If you will press this red button, the alarm bell will start ringing.

17. (b) I finished the work that you told me to do.

18. (c) Everyone praised him for his perseverance but Ram did not praise him.

19. (d) 'Get the taste of one's own medicine' would mean get the ill-treatment which one gave others.

20. (b) Resha and Kiya can't stand each other as they thoroughly dislike each other.

21. (a) If bread is to sandwich, cotton is to dress.

22. (b) He broke the news of the terrorist attack on the border.

23. (b) We must make a room for everyone's views.

24. (b) 2, 1, 4, 3

25. (a) 2, 3, 1, 4

26. (a) Abraham Lincoln did what he thought was best for his country.

27. (d) He has been without work for a year.

28. (c) Avoid

29. (d) Ignorant

30. (a) Hideous

31. (a) All the developing countries have low sex ratio.

32. (c) Sex ratio is measured as the number of females per thousand males.

33. (c) Low sex ratio is not an indicator of stereotype against_women.

34. (b) Federation here would mean a federation of states joined together.

35. (d) By stopping female infanticide.

36. (a) Sam: Why are you sleeping so much? Are you not well?
Brian: Yes, I have fever.

37. (c) Rohan: Our answers were similar but he was given more marks than me.
Gautam: That's unfair.

38. (c) Sam: He is never late for his work.
Forge: He is very punctual.

39. (a) Kavita: I couldn't understand what you said. Could you please repeat?

40. (b) Viren: I was trying your number. But I couldn't get_through.

41. (c) Direct speech: Sam said, "I am going tomorrow."
Indirect speech: Sam said that he will be going tomorrow.

42. (a) The doctor said to the patient, "How are you feeling today?"

43. (a) Sweta said to her father, "Have you invited our relatives for the party?"
Father: Yes, I have.

44. (b) The inspector said to the witness, "Can you recognise them?"

45. (c) Mr. Pathak said to the students, 'Do you know that you will be required to fill in the examination form today?'

46. (a) It is a chemical science that claims to change ordinary into special.

47. (c) Manual

48. (b) Because it is manufactured there.

49. (c) Modern

50. (b) Would look at the sun and tell the time as people did in older times.

MOCK TEST 2

ANSWER KEY									
1	(b)	11	(a)	21	(d)	31	(c)	41	(a)
2	(c)	12	(b)	22	(a)	32	(b)	42	(a)
3	(b)	13	(a)	23	(d)	33	(c)	43	(b)
4	(d)	14	(c)	24	(c)	34	(a)	44	(a)
5	(b)	15	(c)	25	(b)	35	(b)	45	(b)
6	(b)	16	(c)	26	(c)	36	(d)	46	(b)
7	(b)	17	(b)	27	(a)	37	(d)	47	(a)
8	(b)	18	(a)	28	(a)	38	(a)	48	(b)
9	(a)	19	(a)	29	(b)	39	(b)	49	(a)
10	(b)	20	(a)	30	(b)	40	(c)	50	(b)

1. (b) concept
2. (c) when
3. (b) orator
4. (d) set out
5. (b) makes excuses
6. (b) bunch
7. (b) leap
8. (b) reporter
9. (a) vocal
10. (b) with
11. (a) among
12. (b) 2
13. (a) 1
14. (c) 2
15. (c) still
16. (c) was elected
17. (b) as honest as the day is long
18. (a) smokes like a chimney
19. (a) at
20. (a) If
21. (d) Irritating
22. (a) 3421
23. (d) All of the above
24. (c) They sowed trees
25. (b) clench
26. (c) Short
27. (a) Increasing use of chemicals to meet the demands of overgrowing populations
28. (a) I am David. I am your cousin.
29. (b) short of
30. (b) I don't mind hard work. The experience will help me in my career.
31. (c) You must answer all the questions.
32. (b) Congratulations! That's a great achievement.
33. (c) May I interrupt?
34. (a) Can I taste this?
35. (b) Yes, thanks for that wonderful gift.
36. (d) Encore !
37. (d) Hello, is this room service ? I wanted to place an order for dinner.
38. (a) Telephone
39. (b) Fax
40. (c) Mixed
41. (a) Voice message, Text message, Instant messenger, Fax.
42. (a) Survey
43. (b) below
44. (a) good
45. (b) luck
46. (b) distribution
47. (a) damage
48. (b) stocks
49. (a) still
50. (b) cereals

MOCK TEST 3

ANSWER KEY									
1	(b)	11	(a)	21	(b)	31	(b)	41	(b)
2	(b)	12	(d)	22	(a)	32	(a)	42	(a)
3	(a)	13	(b)	23	(a)	33	(d)	43	(b)
4	(a)	14	(a)	24	(c)	34	(c)	44	(d)
5	(d)	15	(a)	25	(a)	35	(c)	45	(b)
6	(b)	16	(a)	26	(a)	36	(b)	46	(a)
7	(a)	17	(a)	27	(a)	37	(c)	47	(a)
8	(b)	18	(c)	28	(a)	38	(b)	48	(b)
9	(b)	19	(d)	29	(b)	39	(b)	49	(b)
10	(b)	20	(b)	30	(b)	40	(c)	50	(b)

1. (b) We can meet the doctor only at six in the evening.

2. (b) The earthquake in Nepal took place in 2015.

3. (a) My teacher knows interesting facts about animals.

4. (a) Dry weather conditions are unsuitable for cultivating paddy.

5. (d) Let them rest a little, for they have just finished painting the wall.

6. (b) He addressed the Minister politely.

7. (a) The expedition through the old city was held up because of several delays in the delivery of food supplies.

8. (b) The hostess invited the guests to sit down.

9. (b) The teacher ordered him to go and polish his shoes right away.

10. (b) They have laid the foundation stone at the proposed site.

11. (a) Every time the stand up clown did something hilarious, the audience laughed.

12. (d) Let someone off would mean excuse or punish someone very lightly.

13. (b) My mother made me to study hard.

14. (a) We have to protect our environment at any cost.

15. (a) 2

16. (a) 1

17. (a) Rashi was driving a car that looked really old.

18. (c) The last we heard from him was on Sunday.

19. (d) There are so many good books that it becomes difficult to decide which one to buy.

20. (b) People living in slums suffer from many ailments.

21. (b) The movie was not at all interesting, the storyline was run-of-the-mill.

22. (a) He is such a coward, he is yellow-bellied.

23. (a) He is driving for the first time, keep your fingers crossed.

24. (c) He has a keen interest in birds. He wants to become a/ an ornithologist.

25. (a) Hideous

26. (a) Conflict

27. (a) To praise him of his efforts towards non-violence

28. (a) United Nations

29. (b) Gandhiji used non-violence till the other person was also not-violent.

30. (b) We should try to resolve the conflict by peaceful means.

31. (b) Leave your shoes outside in the Sun so that they can dry.

32. (a) Please hurry up for your school or you will reach late.

33. (d) Despite his best efforts to conceal his anger, people came to know that he was annoyed.

34. (c) Wow! I love it too!

35. (c) Sorry! I didn't see it.

36. (b) I'll be back by 5:30.

37. (c) "Even if it rains I shall come" means I will certainly come whether it rains or not.

38. (b) She never visits any zoo because she is strong opponent of the idea of holding the animals in captivity for our joy.

39. (b) I felt somewhat more relaxed and tension-free as compared to earlier.

40. (c) Rama's brother

41. (b) Its lead was damaged.

42. (a) We should never touch naked wires.

43. (b) To prevent electric current passing from the wires to human body.

44. (d) All of the above

45. (b) resistance

46. (a) courage

47. (a) whether

48. (b) strength

49. (b) yet

50. (b) street

MOCK TEST 4

ANSWER KEY

1	(a)	11	(b)	21	(c)	31	(c)	41	(b)
2	(b)	12	(a)	22	(a)	32	(c)	42	(a)
3	(a)	13	(b)	23	(b)	33	(c)	43	(d)
4	(a)	14	(c)	24	(b)	34	(b)	44	(b)
5	(b)	15	(a)	25	(a)	35	(a)	45	(b)
6	(b)	16	(b)	26	(c)	36	(a)	46	(b)
7	(b)	17	(a)	27	(c)	37	(a)	47	(a)
8	(c)	18	(a)	28	(b)	38	(b)	48	(a)
9	(d)	19	(c)	29	(c)	39	(d)	49	(c)
10	(c)	20	(c)	30	(a)	40	(c)	50	(b)

1. (a) by
2. (b) sent
3. (a) away
4. (a) fewer
5. (b) to buy
6. (b) understand
7. (b) apologise
8. (c) injured
9. (d) had left
10. (c) could
11. (b) gone
12. (a) have hurt
13. (b) hardly
14. (c) watch
15. (a) 1
16. (b) 2
17. (a) 1
18. (a) trip
19. (c) always
20. (c) remind
21. (c) founded
22. (a) avidly
23. (b) so well
24. (b) herd
25. (a) zero tolerance
26. (c) conclusion
27. (c) ripe
28. (b) most beautiful
29. (c) hatred
30. (a) horrendous
31. (c) go for swimming
32. (c) Painting the fence
33. (c) The sun was shining and the birds were singing.
34. (b) Because he realised that painting the fence would take a very long time
35. (a) He wanted Harry to become interested in painting and make him do it.
36. (a) laudatory
37. (a) provoke
38. (b) rare
39. (d) honorableness
40. (c) continuous
41. (b) Yes, he has acted in many popular plays.
42. (a) They must be somewhere on the table.
43. (d) No, I am not scared of ghosts.
44. (b) Thanks for the compliment.
45. (b) I am sorry, I don't know.
46. (b) Yes, I would be going in a little while.
47. (a) Why ? What happened?
48. (a) No, it isn't.
49. (c) Yes, I wanted a room in your hotel.
50. (b) Let's work towards it.

MOCK TEST 5

ANSWER KEY

1	(d)	11	(b)	21	(b)	31	(c)	41	(a)
2	(a)	12	(c)	22	(a)	32	(c)	42	(b)
3	(a)	13	(a)	23	(b)	33	(a)	43	(c)
4	(c)	14	(a)	24	(a)	34	(b)	44	(a)
5	(c)	15	(a)	25	(b)	35	(b)	45	(a)
6	(b)	16	(a)	26	(d)	36	(b)	46	(c)
7	(c)	17	(a)	27	(b)	37	(a)	47	(d)
8	(a)	18	(b)	28	(a)	38	(c)	48	(b)
9	(a)	19	(b)	29	(d)	39	(d)	49	(a)
10	(c)	20	(b)	30	(c)	40	(d)	50	(a)

1. **(d)** might

2. **(a)** to

3. **(a)** has

4. **(c)** If

5. **(c)** must

6. **(b)** can

7. **(c)** biggest

8. **(a)** sometimes

9. **(a)** about

10. **(c)** on

11. **(b)** and

12. **(c)** 3

13. **(a)** 1

14. **(a)** 1

15. **(a)** money

16. **(a)** gentle

17. **(a)** time

18. **(b)** worst

19. **(b)** so many

20. **(b)** extinguish

21. **(b)** chocolates

22. **(a)** to

23. **(b)** because

24. **(a)** has not paid

25. **(b)** up

26. **(d)** are taking

27. **(b)** realised

28. **(a)** suddenly

29. **(d)** world

30. **(c)** final

31. **(c)** The beautiful gardens and monasteries

32. **(c)** Sikkim

33. **(a)** Gangtok

34. **(b)** amidst the Himalayan ranges.

35. **(b)** Because he could not get leave from work

36. **(b)** West Bengal

37. **(a)** Telangana became a state in January 2014.

38. **(c)** Acute Respiratory Infections

39. **(d)** crores

40. **(d)** All of the above

41. **(a)** My sister is waiting for me to go home from college.

42. **(b)** I'd gone with my family to watch 'Spiderman'.

43. **(c)** Congratulations!

44. **(a)** stop her from eating.

45. **(a)** you worked hard today.

46. **(c)** Something cold, please.

47. **(d)** So is mine.

48. **(b)** Excuse me, may I get past?

49. **(a)** It is for ₹ 180.

50. **(a)** I'll surely come.

MATHEMATICS

MOCK TEST-1

ANSWERS KEY

1	(b)	11	(a)	21	(c)	31	(a)	41	(c)
2	(c)	12	(b)	22	(d)	32	(a)	42	(b)
3	(c)	13	(c)	23	(b)	33	(c)	43	(c)
4	(c)	14	(c)	24	(d)	34	(b)	44	(d)
5	(c)	15	(d)	25	(d)	35	(d)	45	(c)
6	(d)	16	(c)	26	(a)	36	(c)	46	(a)
7	(b)	17	(b)	27	(b)	37	(a)	47	(c)
8	(b)	18	(d)	28	(b)	38	(c)	48	(a)
9	(c)	19	(b)	29	(c)	39	(a)	49	(b)
10	(c)	20	(b)	30	(a)	40	(a)	50	(d)

1. (b) The difference between largest and smallest 5 digit number is 89999.

2. (c) 6034579 is the smallest number obtained by rearranging other digits.

3. (c) Length = 10 cm,
Breadth = 6 cm,
Height = 3 cm
Surface area of the chalk box
$= 2\ (lb + bh + hl)$
$= 2(10 \times 6 + 6 \times 3 + 3 \times 10)\ cm^2$
$= 2\ (60 + 18 + 30)\ cm^2$
$= 2(108)\ cm^2$
$= 216\ cm^2$

4. (c) ∵ Ratio of speeds = 2 : 3
Let the distance be D

$$\therefore \text{ Time taken by A} = \frac{\text{Distance}}{\text{Speed}} = \frac{D}{3x}$$

$$\text{Time taken by B} = \frac{D}{2x}$$

∴ Ratio of times taken

$$= \frac{D}{3x} : \frac{D}{2x} = 3 : 2$$

Given $3x - 2x = 10 \Rightarrow x = 10$
So, A would have taken 30 minutes.
But if *A* walks with double the speed, then he takes half the time, *i.e.*, 15 minutes.

5. (c) Case I
Let the numerator be x
then denominator = $3x + 1$

$$\therefore \text{Fraction} = \frac{x}{3x+1}$$

Case II
New numerator = x + 1
New denominator = 3x + 1 – 2
= 3x – 1

$$\text{New fraction} = \frac{x+1}{3x-1}$$

$$\text{Given } \frac{x+1}{3x-1} = 0.5$$

$$\frac{x+1}{3x-1} = \frac{5}{10}$$

$$\frac{x+1}{3x-1}=\frac{1}{2}$$

$$2(x+1)=3x-1$$

$$2x+2=3x-1$$

$$2x-3x=-1-2$$

$-x = -3$

$x = 3$

∴ Original fraction

$$=\frac{3}{3\times3+1}=\frac{3}{10}$$

6. (d) Distance covered by Vishal in one round is equal to the perimeter of the rectangle.
Perimeter of rectangle
= 2 (length + breadth)
=2(135 m+78 m) =426 m
Distance covered in 1 round
= 426 m
Distance covered in 4 round
= 426 m × 4 =1704 m

7. (b) $\frac{1}{4}+\frac{1}{4}=\frac{1+1}{4}=\frac{2}{4}=\frac{2\div2}{4\div2}=\frac{1}{2}$
Hence, both together picked fraction $\frac{1}{2}$ of the stones.

8. (b) 1 dozen = 12 items
∵ Cost of 12 pens = ₹180
∴ Cost of 1 pen = ₹$\frac{180}{12}$ = ₹15
∵ Cost of 8 ball pens = ₹56
∴ Cost of 1 ball pen = ₹$\frac{56}{8}$ = ₹7
∴ Ratio of cost of a pen to the cost of a ball pen = $\frac{15}{7}$ = 15 : 7.

9. (c) 90° + 30° + x° = 180°
x° = 180° – 120° = 60°
∠ACD = x° + 90°
= 60° + 90° = 150°

10. (c) Let the number of passengers alighted the bus is represented by negative sign and number of passengers boarded the bus is represented by the positive sign.
Total passengers after the stop
= 27– 6 + 9 = 30

11. (a) Let the monthly salary of Mr. Tan = x
Amount given to his parents

$$=\frac{2}{5}x$$

Remaining amount $=x-\frac{2}{5}x$

$$=\frac{3}{5}x$$

Amount given to his children

$$=\frac{3}{5}\left(\frac{3}{5}x\right)=\frac{9}{25}x$$

Amount remaining

$$=x-\frac{2}{5}x-\frac{9}{25}x=\frac{6}{25}x$$

12. (b) Let two unlike terms without constant terms are x and y.
The division of the terms = $\frac{x}{y}$
and it can not be reduced.

13. (c) CMXCIX = (1000 – 100) + (100 – 10) + (10 –1)
= 900 + 90 + 9 = 999

14. (c) LCM of 12, 15, 20 and 35 = 420

```
420) 1000 (2
      840
     -----
      160
```

∴ Required number
= 1000 + (420 – 160) = 1260.

15. **(d)** The circle has infinite number of lines of symmetry.

16. **(c)**

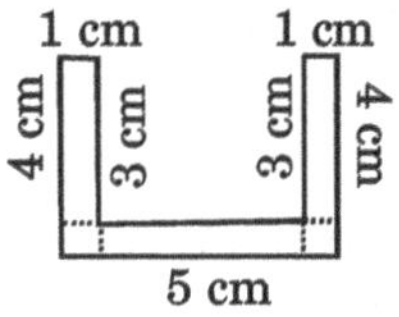

Area = (3 × 1) + (1 × 1) + (3 × 1) + (1 × 1) + (3 ×1)
= 3 + 1 + 3 + 3 + 1
= 11 sq cm.

17. **(b)** – 8 – 2 [6 + 4{7 – (4.2)}]
= – 8 – 2[6 + 4 {7 – 4.2}]
= – 8 – 2 [6 + 4{2.8}]
= – 8 – 2 [6 + 11.2]
= – 8 – 2 [17.2]
= – 8 – 34.4 = – 42.4

18. **(d)**

2	63, 70, 77
3	63, 35, 77
3	21, 35, 77
5	7, 35, 77
7	7, 7, 77
11	1, 1, 11
	1, 1, 1

∴ L.C.M. of 63, 70 and 77
= 2 × 3 × 3 × 5 × 7 × 11.
= 6930.
Hence, the minimum distance each should cover so that all cover the distance in complete steps is 6930 cm.

19. **(b)**

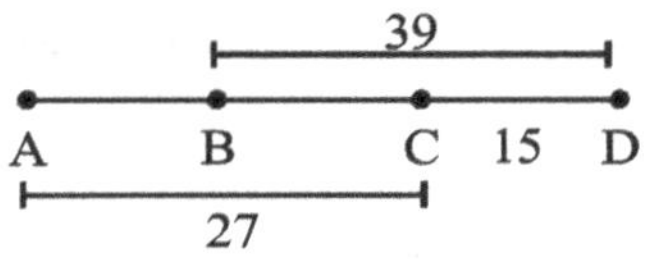

BC = BD – CD
= 39 – 15
= 24 km
∴ AB = AC – BC
= 27 – 24
= 3 km

20. **(b)** (i) $\dfrac{0.216+0.064}{0.36+0.16-0.24}$

$= \dfrac{0.28}{0.28} = 1$

(ii) $\dfrac{1}{0.0004175} = \dfrac{10000}{4.175}$
= 10,000 × 0.2395
= 2395

(iii) Given expression is equal to
[0.9 – {2.3 – 3.2 – (7.1 – 8.9)]
= [0.9 – {2.3 – 3.2 + 1.8}]
= [0.9 – {4.1 – 3.2}]
= [0.9 – 0.9] = 0

21. **(c)** Mean of a set of observations is the value which is a representative of the whole group.

22. **(d)** ∠ADE + ∠EDF = 180°
⇒ 13x + 20 + 40 – 20 = 180°
x = 10
∴ ∠EDF = 30° = ∠ABC.
(a) is true.
Also, ∠DBC + ∠ABC = 180° (Straight angle)
∠DBC = 180° – 30°
= 150°
and ∠EDF + ∠EDB = 180° (Straight angle)
∠EDB = 180° – 30°
= 150°
∵ ∠EDB = ∠DBC = 150°
BC || DE
∴ (c) is also true.
Also, ∠DBC + ∠EDF
= 150° + 30° = 180°
∴ (b) is also true.

23. **(b)** Required perimeter
= circumferences of both the circles + 2 radii of each of the circles.

$= 2\left[2\pi r - \frac{2\pi r}{4}\right] + (7 \times 4)$

$= 2\left[\frac{6\pi r}{4}\right] + 28 = 3\pi r + 28$

where $r = 7$

$= 3 \times \frac{22}{7} \times 7 + 28$

= 66 + 28 = 94 cm

24. (d) $\frac{3}{4} \times \frac{1}{4} = \frac{3}{16}$

$\frac{3}{16} \div 3 = \frac{1}{16}$

25. (d) 35x = 5 × 7 × x,
55x = 5 × 11 × x,
77x = 7 × 11 × x

∴ H.C.F = 24 = x

∴ Numbers are 35 × 24, 55 × 24, 77 × 24
i.e. 840, 1320, 1848

26. (a) Product

$= (3u^2v - 5uv^2)\left(\frac{1}{5}u^2 + \frac{1}{5}v^2\right)$

$= 3u^2v\left(\frac{1}{5}u^2 + \frac{1}{5}v^2\right)$

$- 5uv^2\left(\frac{1}{5}u^2 + \frac{1}{5}v^2\right)$

$= \frac{3}{5}u^4v + \frac{3}{5}u^2v^3 - u^3v^2 - uv^4$

27. (b) $\frac{1}{4} + \frac{1}{4} = \frac{1+1}{4} = \frac{2}{4} = \frac{2 \div 2}{4 \div 2} = \frac{1}{2}$

$1 - \frac{1}{2} = \frac{1}{1} - \frac{1}{2} = \frac{1 \times 2}{1 \times 2} - \frac{1}{2}$

$= \frac{2}{2} - \frac{1}{2} = \frac{2-1}{2} = \frac{1}{2}$

Hence, he put $\frac{1}{2}$ fraction of the covers on Wednesday.

28. (b) Distance travelled everyday
= 20 km 50 m
= 20 km + 50 m

$= 20 \text{ km} + \frac{50}{1000} \text{km}$

= 20 km + 0.050 km

$\left|\because 1 \text{ m} = \frac{1}{1000} \text{km}\right.$

= (20 + 0.050) km = 20.050 km

Distance travelled by bus
= 10 km 200 m
= 10 km + 200 m

$= 10 \text{ km} + \frac{200}{1000} \text{km}$

= 10 km + 0.200 km

$\left|\because 1 \text{m} = \frac{1}{1000} \text{km}\right.$

= (10 + 0.200) km = 10.200 km

∴ Distance travelled by auto
= 20.050 km – 10.200 km
= 9.850 km

29. (c) Height of A = $\frac{4}{3}$ × height of B

$= \frac{4}{3} \times 1.2 = 1.6$ m

30. (a) The figure given is a square. Square has four lines of symmetry.

31. (a) Let the breadth of rectangle be x

Then, length of rectangle = $\frac{6}{5}x$

∵ Perimeter of rectangle
= 132 m
2 (length + breadth) = 132

$$2\left(\frac{6}{5}x + x\right) = 132$$

$$2 \times \frac{11}{5}x = 132$$

$$x = 132 \times \frac{5}{2 \times 11}$$

$x = 30$

$\therefore$ Length $= \frac{6}{5}x = \frac{6}{5} \times 30 = 36$

Breadth = x = 30

$\therefore$ Area of rectangle
= length × breadth
= 36 × 30
= 1080 m^2

32. (a) Let the angle be x.
Then, the complementary angle = (90° – x).
According to the question.

$$x = \frac{4}{5}(90° - x)$$

$5x = 4(90° - x)$
$9x = 360°$
$x = 40°$

33. (c) L.C.M (40, 240, 480) = 480
H.C.F. (40, 240, 480) = 40
Let the number be x.
$\because$ Difference of L.C.M. and H.C.F. is eqal to twice of the number.
$\therefore$ 480 – 40 = 2x
440 = 2x

$$x = \frac{440}{2} = 220$$

Hence, required number is 220.

34. (b) The tenth place digit is 6, which is more than 5. So, the number at the hundred's place digit is increased by 1 and replaced by its right-most place digit of 0.Hence, required rounded off number is 45,700

35. (d) Length of the original piece of wire = $\frac{7}{8}$ metre

Length of one piece = $\frac{1}{4}$ metre

$\therefore$ Length of the other piece

$$= \left(\frac{7}{8} - \frac{1}{4}\right)\text{metre}$$

$$= \left(\frac{7}{8} - \frac{1 \times 2}{4 \times 2}\right)\text{metre}$$

$$= \left(\frac{7}{8} - \frac{2}{8}\right)\text{metre}$$

$$= \frac{7-2}{8}\text{metre} = \frac{5}{8}\text{metre.}$$

36. (c) $\because$ Distance covered by Karan in 2 hours = 8 km
$\therefore$ Distance covered by Karan in 1 hours = $\frac{8}{2}$ = 4 km

Distance covred by Karan in 4 hours = 4 × 4 = 16 km
$\therefore$ A = 16 km
$\because$ Distance covered by Kriti in 2 hours = 6 km
$\therefore$ Distance covered by Kriti in 1 hour = 3 km
Distance covered by Kriti in 4 hours = 4 × 3 = 12 km
$\therefore$ B = 3 km, C = 12 km

37. (a) $\because$ Drop in temperature in 30 days = 15°
$\therefore$ Drop in temperature in 1 day

$$= \frac{15}{30} \text{ degree}$$

$\therefore$ Drop in temperature in 10 day

$= \frac{15}{30} \times 10$ degrees = 5 degrees

Hence, the temperature will drop 5 degrees in the next ten days.

38. (c) Let first number be 'a'.
Second number = a + 2d + 5
Third number = a + 2d + 5 – 3d + 20
= a – d + 25
Sum: a + a + 2d + 5 + a – d + 25 = 10d + 9
⇒ 3a + d + 30 = 10d + 9
⇒ 3a + 30 = 9d + 9
⇒ a + 10 = 3d + 3
⇒ a = 3d – 7

39. (a) Second number = First number + 2d + 5 = 3d – 7 + 2d + 5
= 5d – 2
Third number = Second number – (3d – 20) = 5d – 2 – 3d + 20
= 2d + 18
∴ Sum = 3d – 7 + 2d + 18
= 5d + 11

40. (a) Second number = First number + 2d + 5

41. (c) We can divide the given figure into 12 equal parts

Shaded portion = $\frac{4}{12} = \frac{1}{3}$

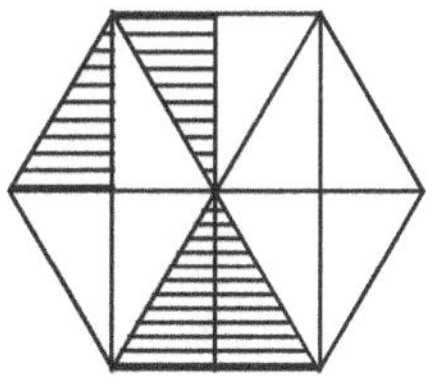

42. (b) x% of y + y% of x

$= \frac{xy}{100} + \frac{yx}{100}$

$= \frac{2xy}{100} = \frac{2}{100}xy$

= 2% of xy

43. (c) Smallest whole number other than 0 is 1.

Hence, $1 - \frac{5}{6} = \frac{1}{6}$

44. (d) If x is the quotient then the remainder is 125x + 82.
When this number is divided by 25, we get

$\frac{125}{25}x + \frac{82}{25} = 5x + 3 + \frac{7}{25}$

Hence the remainder will be 7.

45. (c) Both (i) and (ii)

46. (a) Time = $\frac{\text{Distance}}{\text{speed}} = \frac{240 \text{ km}}{80 \text{ km/h}}$

= 3 hours

47. (c) 5 : 120 : : 40 : x

$x = \frac{120 \times 40}{5} = 960$

48. (a) 400

49. (b) Patel

50. (d) Rao, Roy

MOCK TEST-2

ANSWERS KEY

1	(c)	11	(d)	21	(d)	31	(b)	41	(a)
2	(a)	12	(a)	22	(b)	32	(b)	42	(d)
3	(b)	13	(a)	23	(c)	33	(a)	43	(b)
4	(a)	14	(a)	24	(a)	34	(a)	44	(c)
5	(a)	15	(b)	25	(a)	35	(a)	45	(d)
6	(c)	16	(a)	26	(b)	36	(b)	46	(b)
7	(c)	17	(c)	27	(c)	37	(b)	47	(c)
8	(c)	18	(a)	28	(a)	38	(b)	48	(d)
9	(c)	19	(d)	29	(b)	39	(c)	49	(a)
10	(d)	20	(c)	30	(b)	40	(b)	50	(c)

1. (c) $63.3605 = 6 \times 10 + 3 \times 1 + 3 \times \frac{1}{10} + 6 \times \frac{1}{100} + 0 \times \frac{1}{1000} + 5 \times \frac{1}{10000}$

On comparing with the given expression we get

$A = 10, B = 1, C = \frac{1}{10}, D = \frac{1}{100}, E = \frac{1}{10,000}$

∴ Required expression

$= 40 + 7 + 0.6 + 100 + 0.0003$

$= 147.6003$

2. (a) Fractions can also be represented on the number line.

3. (b) $(34 + 20) \times 2 = 54 \times 2 = 108$.

Multiplicative inverse of 108 $= \frac{1}{108}$.

4. (a) Divisor = 555 + 445 = 1000

Quotient = 2 × (555 – 445) = 220

Remainder = 30

∴ Dividend = Divisor × Quotient + Remainder

= 1000 × 220 + 30 = 220030.

5. (a) Missing length = 23 – (4 + 5 + 8)

= 23 – 17 = 6 cm

6. (c) Given $a = 3, b = 5,$
$c = b - a = 5 - 3 = 2$

Putting these values, we will evaluate all the expressions

(a) $(a + c) \times b = (3 + 2) \times 5$
$= 5 \times 5 = 25 \neq 10$

(b) $(a + b) - c = (3 + 5) - 2$
$= 8 - 2 = 6 \neq 10$

(c) $(b + c) + a = (5 + 2) + 3$
$= 7 + 3 = 10$

(d) $(a - b) + c = (3 - 5) + 2$
$= -2 + 2 = 0 \neq 10$

7. (c) 54 km/h $= 54 \times \frac{5}{18}$ m/s = 15 m/s.

8. (c) (6x – 3by + 4cz) + (7by – 8ax –5cz) + (9cz – 2by + 2ax)

= 6x – 3by + 4cz + 7by – 8ax – 5cz + 9cz – 2by + 2ax

= 6x + 2by + 8cz – 6ax

9. (c) ∠x = 90° is vertically opposite to 90°.

∠b = 90° forms linear pair with ∠x.

So, ∠x = 90°, ∠b = 90°

10. (d) Number of sides of a square = 4
Number of edges of a cube = 12
Ratio = 4 : 12 = 1 : 3

11. (d) Let red marbles = 7x
Blue marbles = 4x
Total marbles = 7x + 4x = 11x
x can be 1, 2, 3.......
So, total number of marble can be 11, 22, 33......

12. (a) HCF (403, 434, 465) = 31
$\because$ The maximum capacity of a container that can measure the diesel of three containers exact number of times.
= HCF (403, 434, 465)
= 31

13. (a) Ribbon bought by Sarita = $\frac{2}{5}$m

Ribbon bought by Lalita = $\frac{3}{4}$m

$\therefore$ Total length of the ribbon they bought

$$= \frac{2}{5}m + \frac{3}{4}m = \left(\frac{2}{5} + \frac{3}{4}\right)m$$

$$= \left(\frac{2\times4}{5\times4} + \frac{3\times5}{4\times5}\right)m$$

$$|\text{L.C.M}(5,4) = 20$$

$$= \left(\frac{8}{20} + \frac{15}{20}\right)m = \frac{8+15}{20}m = \frac{23}{20}m$$

$$= 1\frac{3}{20}m$$

14. (a) The ratio of breadth and length of hall = 2 : 5
= 2 × 10 : 5 × 10
= 20 : 50
Then. A = 20.
Also, ratio of breadth and length
= 2 : 5
= 2 × 20 : 5 × 20
= 40 : 100
Then, B = 10,
Hence, the required values are A = 20, B = 100.

15. (b) (i) : John uses 12.5 litres of petrol in a day.
John uses (12.5 × 14) litres of petrol in 2 weeks (or 14 days)
= 175 litres
(ii) : Total distance travelled
= 204 km
time = 4 hours

Average speed = $\frac{204}{4}$

= 51 km/hr.

16. (a) Area of shaded portion
= $\pi(R^2 - r^2)$
= $\pi(224^2 - 210^2)$

$$= \frac{22}{7}(224 + 210)(224 - 210)$$

$$= \frac{22}{7} \times 434 \times 14 = 19096 \text{ sq. mm}$$

17. (c) The correct order of steps is CADB

18. (a) $\frac{2}{5} = \frac{2\times7}{5\times7} = \frac{14}{35}$

$$|\text{L.C.M.}(5,7) = 35$$

$$\frac{5}{7} = \frac{5\times5}{7\times5} = \frac{25}{35}$$

$$\therefore \frac{5}{7} - \frac{2}{5} = \frac{25}{35} - \frac{14}{35} = \frac{25-14}{35} = \frac{11}{35}.$$

19. (d) 10 (a + 3) – 2a = 18 + 3a
10a + 30 – 2a = 18 + 3a
10a – 2a – 3a = 18 – 30

$5a = -12$

$a = -\frac{12}{5}$

Hence, the given expression is true for one value of a.

20. (c) Figure 1 shows $= \frac{1}{3}$

Figure 2 shows $= \frac{4}{12} = \frac{1}{3}$

Figure 3 shows $= \frac{2}{6} = \frac{1}{3}$

21. (d) $(2a^3 - 3)(5a^3 - 2)$

$= 2a^3 (5a^3 - 2) - 3 (5a^3 - 2)$

$= 10a^6 - 4a^3 - 15a^3 + 6$

$= 10a^6 - 19a^3 + 6$

$= 10a^6 + (-19a^3) + 6$

22. (b) $x + 1 = 0$

$x = -1$

So, -1 is the solution of the equation.

23. (c) Distance travelled in one hour by an object is called speed.

$\text{Speed} = \frac{\text{Distance}}{\text{time}}$

For bus,

$\text{Speed} = \frac{160}{4} = 40$ km/hr

For train,

$\text{Speed} = \frac{320}{5} = 64$ km/hr

Ratio = 40 : 64 = 5 : 8

24. (a) Cake given to Naina $= 1\frac{1}{2}$ piece

$= \frac{(1\times2)+1}{2}$ piece

$= \frac{2+1}{2}$ piece $= \frac{3}{2}$ piece

Cake given to Najma $= 1\frac{1}{3}$ piece

$= \frac{(1\times3)+1}{3}$ piece

$= \frac{3+1}{3}$ piece $= \frac{4}{3}$ piece

∴ Total amount of cake given to both of them $= \frac{3}{2}$ piece $+ \frac{4}{3}$ piece

$= \left(\frac{3}{2}+\frac{4}{3}\right)$ piece

$= \left(\frac{3\times3}{2\times3}+\frac{4\times2}{3\times2}\right)$ piece

$|\text{L.C.M.}(2,3) = 6$

$= \left(\frac{9}{6}+\frac{8}{6}\right)$ piece $= \frac{9+8}{6}$ piece

$= \frac{17}{6}$ piece $= 2\frac{5}{6}$ piece

25. (a) A : $\frac{2}{5}\% = \frac{2}{500} = \frac{0.4}{100} = 0.004$

B : 25% of 75 $= \frac{25}{100}\times75 = 18.75$

C : Average of first eight natural numbers

$= \frac{1+2+3+4+5+6+7+8}{8}$

$= \frac{36}{8} = 4.5$

$$D: \frac{135}{45}\% = \frac{135}{4500} = 0.03$$

26. (b) Sale in June = 600

$$75\% \text{ of } 600 = 600 \times \frac{3}{4} = 450$$

Sale of April = 450 (From the graph)

27. (c) Add the number to the reverse of its digits.
For example : 163 + 361 = 524
Also 1898 + 8981 = 10879

28. (a) In the above figure
$41° + y + 113° = 180°$
$y + 154° = 180°$, $y = 180° - 154°$, $y = 26°$

29. (b)

30. (b) Let one number be x
then other number = 2x + 1
According to given condition,
x + (2x + 1) = 19

31. (b) Sum: $\frac{9}{22} + \frac{5}{22} = \frac{9+5}{22} = \frac{14}{22}$

$= \frac{7}{11}$

Difference:

$$\frac{9}{22} - \frac{5}{22} = \frac{9-5}{22} = \frac{4}{22} = \frac{2}{11}$$

32. (b) Square is a regular polygon.

33. (a) $(a^2 + ab + b^2)(a^2 - ab - b^2)$
$= a^2(a^2 - ab - b^2) + ab(a^2 - ab - b^2) + b^2(a^2 - ab - b^2)$
$= a^4 - a^3b - a^2b^2 + a^3b - a^2b^2 - ab^3 + a^2b^2 - ab^3 - b^4$
$= a^4 - a^2b^2 - ab^3 - ab^3 - b^4$
$= a^4 - a^2b^2 - 2ab^3 - b^4$

34. (a) Let the number of women in the garden is x.
The number of children = 84

According to the question.

$$\frac{9}{2} = \frac{x+84}{x} \Rightarrow 9x = 2(x+84)$$

$\Rightarrow$ 9x = 2x + 168
$\Rightarrow$ 9x – 2x = 168

$$\Rightarrow x = \frac{168}{7} = 24.$$

Hence the total number of children in the garden
= 84 + 24 = 108.

35. (a)
(a) HIDE / Mirror / HIDE
(b) CAKE / Mirror / CVKE
(c) SOON / Mirror / ƧOOИ
(d) SOUR / Mirror / ƧOՈꓤ

36. (b) Weight of apples = 2 kg 280 g
= 2280 g (Since 1 kg = 1000 g)
Weight of bananas = 3 kg 375 g
= 3375 g
Weight of grapes = 225 g
Weight of oranges = 5 kg 385 g
= 5385 g
Total weight = 2280 g + 3375 g + 225 g + 5385 g = 11265 g
Thus, total weight = 11265 kg

$$= \frac{11265}{1000} \text{kg}$$

= 11.265 kg

37. (b) Number of spokes = 48
Angle between two consecutive

$$\text{spokes} = \frac{360°}{48} = \left(7\frac{1}{2}\right)^0$$

38. (b) Required level = $1-\frac{2}{5}=\frac{3}{5}$.

39. (c) $\frac{3}{5}=0.6$

40. (b) $\frac{3}{5}+\frac{1}{5}=\frac{4}{5}$ is the required fraction.

41. (a) Reverse the previous number and add 1 to the first and second digit alternately.

42. (d) Let the breadth is x.
Perimeter of rectangle
= 2 (length + breadth)
70 = 2 (18 m + x m) x = 17 m

43. (b)

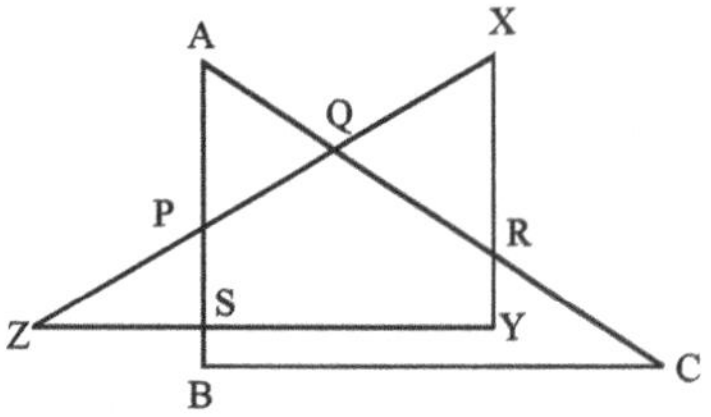

The five triangles are,
APQ, QXR, PZS, ABC and XYZ.

44. (c) We have

$\angle A + \angle B + \angle C + \angle D = 360°$

$(\angle A + \angle C) + (\angle B + \angle D) = 360°$

$180° + (\angle B + \angle D) = 360°$

$\angle B + \angle D = 180°$.

45. (d) $35x = 5 \times 7 \times x$,
$55x = 5 \times 11 \times x$,
$77x = 7 \times 11 \times x$

$\therefore$ H.C.F = $24 = x$

$\therefore$ Numbers are 35 × 24, 55 × 24, 77 × 24 i.e. 840, 1320, 1848

46. (b) To find the minimum number of square slabs to cover the floor, we have to find the greatest size of each such slab. For this purpose, we have to find the HCF of 450 and 300 (Since 4.5 m = 450 cm and 3 m = 300 cm)
Now HCF of 450 and 300 = 150
So the required size of the slab must be 150 cm × 150 cm.
Hence, the number of slabs required

$= \frac{\text{Area of the floor}}{\text{Area of one slab}}$

$= \frac{450 \times 300}{150 \times 150} = 6$

47. (c) As the sum is 47, the other integer is obtained by subtracting – 24 from 47. So, the required integer
= 47 – (– 24) = 47 + 24 = 71

48. (d) The number of students who obtained marks more than or equal to 5 is 17

49. (a) Cost of fencing per metre = ₹30
Total cost of fencing = ₹12000
So, the length of fencing (perimeter)

$= \frac{\text{Total cost}}{\text{Cost per metre}}$

$= \frac{1200}{30} = 400$ m

Now, length of fencing
= Perimeter of the square field
= 4 × side of the field
Therefore, 4 × side of the field
= 400 m
or, side of the field

$= \frac{400}{4}$ m = 100 m

So, area of the field
= 100 m × 100 m = 10000 sq. m.

50. (c) 7 + 5 = 12 students

MOCK TEST-3

ANSWERS KEY									
1	(d)	11	(d)	21	(b)	31	(b)	41	(b)
2	(d)	12	(b)	22	(b)	32	(b)	42	(c)
3	(c)	13	(b)	23	(b)	33	(a)	43	(d)
4	(c)	14	(d)	24	(c)	34	(a)	44	(d)
5	(c)	15	(c)	25	(c)	35	(b)	45	(d)
6	(d)	16	(b)	26	(b)	36	(a)	46	(d)
7	(a)	17	(a)	27	(a)	37	(c)	47	(c)
8	(a)	18	(c)	28	(b)	38	(c)	48	(b)
9	(d)	19	(c)	29	(a)	39	(b)	49	(d)
10	(c)	20	(c)	30	(d)	40	(c)	50	(c)

1. (d) 123 millions – 67,735
= 122 millions + 932 thousands + 265
= 12 crores + 29 lakhs + 32 thousands + 265.

2. (d)

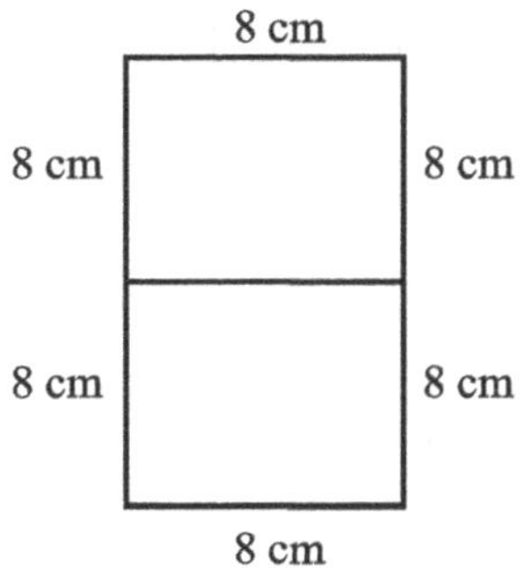

∴ Perimeter of the figure formed
= 8 + 8 + 8 + 8 + 8 + 8 = 48 cm.

3. (c) Required result $= \frac{1}{2}y - \frac{1}{3}y$

$= \frac{1}{6}y$

4. (c) $\frac{2}{5} = \frac{2\times7}{5\times7} = \frac{14}{35}$

$\frac{3}{7} = \frac{3\times5}{7\times5} = \frac{15}{35}$

$\therefore \frac{2}{5}+\frac{3}{7} = \frac{14}{35}+\frac{15}{35} = \frac{14+15}{35} = \frac{29}{35}.$

5. (c) L.C.M. (x, y, z) = z.

6. (d) Multiplicative inverse of –15 is $-\frac{1}{15}$

7. (a) Riya spent = ₹34.60
Money left with her
= ₹100.00
– ₹34.60
₹65.40

8. (a) Area of shaded portion
$= l \times b$
$= 6 \times 2 = 12 \text{ cm}^2$

9. (d) Time for the next flight
= 10 : 45 – 00.25 + 5 : 00
= 15 : 20 hours
= 15 : 20 – 12:00 = 3 : 20 pm.
Earlier flight took off at 10.45 – 25 minutes = 3 : 20 pm.

10. (c) (i) : Ratio 2 : 4 $= \frac{2}{4} = \frac{1}{2} = 1:2$

Ratio 12 : 24 $= \frac{12}{24} = 1:2$

(ii) : Number of games won = 6
Number of games loose
= 4 Ratio = 6 : 4 = 3 : 2

11. (d) Perimeter of equilateral triangle
= 3 × side
= 3 × 8 = 24 cm
∴ Perimeter of square = 24 cm

$$\text{Side of square} = \frac{\text{Perimeter}}{4}$$

$$= \frac{24}{4} = 6 \text{ cm}$$

∴ The area of square = $(\text{Side})^2$
= 6 × 6 = 36 cm^2

12. (b) Let cost of property by ₹x

$$\text{then } \frac{3}{5} \times x = 15000$$

$$x = 15000 \times \frac{5}{3} = 25000$$

Cost of $\frac{1}{2}$ of property

$$= \frac{1}{2} \times 25000 = ₹12500$$

13. (b)

14. (d) Length of land = 15 m
Breadth of land = 10 m
Area of the land
= Length × Breadth
= (150 × 10) sq. m = 150 sq. m
Area of 1 square flower bed
= side × side
= (2 × 2) sq. m = 4 sq. m
Area of 5 square flower bed 20 sq. m
= (5 × 4) sq. m
Area of the remaining part of land
= Area of land – Area of 5 square flower beds
= 150 sq. m – 20 sq. m = 130 sq. m

15. (c) Cost of ice cream = ₹20.50
Cost of chocolate = ₹10.50
Total cost = ₹20.50 + ₹10.50
= ₹31
Total money Rani had = ₹48.50
Money spent = ₹31
Money left = ₹48.50 – ₹31
= ₹17.50
Thus, ₹17.50 is left with her.

16. (b) Rehana : Rashmi = 2 : 3

$$\text{Rehana's share} = \frac{2}{5} \times ₹600$$

$$= ₹240$$

$$\text{Rashmi's share} = \frac{3}{5} \times ₹600$$

$$= ₹360$$

17. (a) The distance from Nandini's house to her school = $\frac{9}{10}$ km

The distance that Nandini traveled by bus = $\frac{1}{2}$ km

∴ The distance that Nandini walked far = $\frac{9}{10} - \frac{1}{2}$

$$= \frac{9}{10} - \frac{1 \times 5}{2 \times 5}$$

$$= \frac{9}{10} - \frac{5}{10}$$

$$= \frac{9-5}{10} = \frac{4}{10}$$

$$= \frac{2}{5} \text{ km}$$

Hence, the required distance that Nandini walked is $\frac{2}{5}$ km.

18. (c)

$$\begin{array}{r|l} & 0.25 \\ 12) & 3.00 \\ & 0 \\ \hline & 30 \\ & 24 \\ \hline & 60 \\ & 60 \\ \hline & \times \end{array}$$

Thus, $\frac{3}{12} = 0.25$

19. (c) (i) : Distance = Speed × Time
= 52 × 3 = 156 km
(ii) : Distance = Speed × Time
= 58 × 3 = 174 km

20. (c) 3

21. (b) Let the angle be x.
Then supplementary angle
= $180 - x$

Given $x = \frac{4}{5}(180 - x)$

$5x = 4(180 - x)$

$5x = 720 - 4x$

$5x + 4x = 720$

$9x = 720$

$x = \frac{720}{9} = 80°$

22. (b) Ratio of Parul's age to Priyam's age = 9 : 15

$= \frac{9}{15} = \frac{3}{5} = 3:5$

So, mother will divide ₹56 in the ratio of 3 : 5

Parul will get = ₹$\frac{3}{8} \times 56$ = ₹21
(as 3 + 5 = 8)

Priyam will get = ₹56 – ₹21
= ₹35

23. (b) Only (3) is correct. Every square is a rhombus but it is not necessary that every rhombus will be a square.

24. (c) Possible combinations of (A, B) such that AB = 64 are
(1, 64), (2, 32), (4, 16) and (8, 8)
∴ A + B cannot be 35.

25. (c) x is subtracted from 10.

26. (b) Since AB || CD

$\angle FCD = \angle ABF = 45°$
[alternate angles]

In ΔFCD,

$\angle FCD + \angle CDF + \angle CFD = 180°$
[Angle sum property]

$45° + \angle FDC + 110° = 180°$

$\angle FDC + 155° = 180°$

$\angle FDC = 180° - 155° = 25°$

27. (a) Distance travelled by bus
= 16.520 km
Distance travelled by auto
= 31.460 km
Distance walked = 1.450 km
Total distance
= 16.520 km + 31.460 km +1.450 km
= 49.430 km
So, Samson covered 49.430 km in total.

28. (b) Petrol filled on Monday
= 40 litres
Petrol filled the next day = 50 litres
∴ Total petrol filled on the two days
= 40 litres + 50 litres = 90 litres
∴ Cost of petrol per litre = ₹44
∴ Cost of 90 litres petrol
= ₹44 × 90
= ₹3960

29. (a) The cost of 1 kg of wheat

$= \frac{1756}{500} = ₹3.512.$

Hence, the cost of 125 kg of wheat

$= 125 \times 3.512 = ₹439$

30. (d) Weight of tablets = 2,00,000
Weight of 1 tablet = 20 mg
Weight of 2,00,000 tablets
= 2,00,000 × 20 mg
= 40,00,000 mg
Weight in gm

$= \frac{40,00,000}{1000} \text{gm} = 4000 \text{ gm}$

Weight in kg $= \frac{4000}{1000} \text{kg} = 4 \text{kg}$

31. (b) Group the positive and the negative integers together,
(–30) + (–20) + (–63) + (+75) + (65)
= (–113) + (140)
= (140 – 113) = 27

32. (b) Let the second term of the proportion be x then
$18 : x :: 27 : 36$
$18 \times 36 = x \times 27$
(Product of extremes = Product of mean)

$\frac{18 \times 36}{27} = x$

$24 = x$

Thus, second term of the proportion is 24.

33. (a) X has both horizontal and vertical lines of symmetry.

34. (a) Number of squares in the shaded portion = 15
Number of squares in the unshaded portion= 33
So, the ratio of the shaded portion to the unshaded portion
= 15 : 33

$= \frac{15}{33} = \frac{5 \times 3}{11 \times 3} = \frac{5}{11} = 5:11$

35. (b) Since AB is a straight line,
$\angle AOC + \angle COE + \angle EOB = 180°$
$50° + a + 30° = 180°$
$a + 80° = 180°$
$a = 100°$
$b = \angle EOB$ [vert.opp. angles]
$= 30°$
$\angle a - \angle b = 100° - 30°$
$= 70°$

36. (a)

37. (c) Let the length of the journey be x km.
Then,

$\frac{x}{45} - \frac{x}{60} = \frac{11}{2}$

$\Rightarrow \frac{4x - 3x}{180} = \frac{11}{2}$

$\Rightarrow \frac{x}{180} = \frac{11}{2}$

$\Rightarrow x = \frac{11 \times 180}{2} = 990 \text{ km.}$

38. (c) Wash room is in the form of a square.
∴ Perimeter = 4 × 3 = 12 m

39. (b) Bed room is in form of a rectangle.
∴ Area = 9 × 11 = 99 m^2.

40. (c) Lawn is in the form of a semicircle.
Perimeter of lawn
= circumference of semicircle

$= \frac{2\pi r}{2} = \pi r = \frac{22}{7} \times 4 = \frac{88}{7}$

41. (b)

2	40
2	20
2	10
5	5
	1

2	48
2	24
2	12
2	6
3	3
	1

3	45
3	15
5	5
	1

$40 = 2 \times 2 \times 2 \times 5$

$48 = 2 \times 2 \times 2 \times 2 \times 3$

$45 = 3 \times 3 \times 5$

L.C.M. of (40, 48, 45)

$= 2 \times 2 \times 2 \times 2 \times 3 \times 3 \times 5$

$= 720.$

42. (c) Area of rectangle I

= (2 × 1) sq. cm

Length of rectangle II

= (4 + 1) cm = 5 cm

Breadth of rectangle II = 3 cm

Therefore, area of rectangle II

= 5 × 3 sq. cm

= 15 sq. cm

Area of rectangle III

= (4 × 2) sq. cm

= 8 sq. cm

Area of rectangle IV

= (3 × 1) sq. cm

= 3 sq. cm

Thus, area of given figure

= Area I + Area II + Area III + Area IV

= 2 + 15 + 8 + 3 sq. cm

= 28 sq. cm.

43. (d) Since 21 ÷ 3 = 7, so multiply numerator and denominator of $\frac{3}{4}$ by 7.

$$\frac{3}{4} = \frac{3 \times 7}{4 \times 7} = \frac{21}{28}$$

Therefore, the required number is 28.

44. (d) A→(iii); B→(iv); C→ (i); D → (ii)

45. (d)

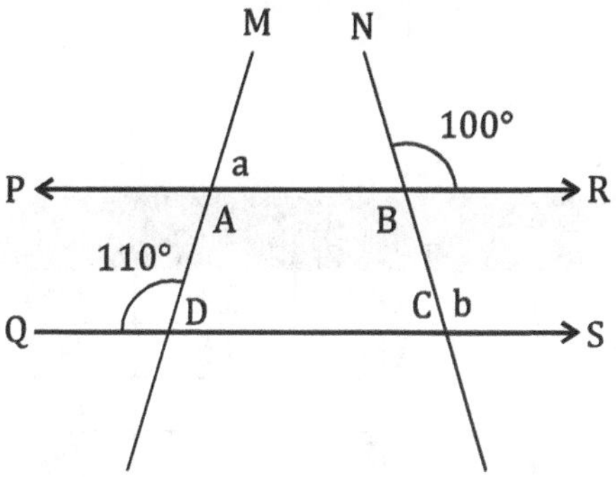

Since PR || QS

∠MAB = ∠ADC (Corresponding angles)

∠ADQ + ∠ADC = 180° (Linear pair)

∠ADC = 180° – 110° = 70°

∴ ∠MAB = ∠ADC = 70°

∠a = 70°

∠ABC = ∠NBR = 100° (Vertically opposite angles)

Since PR || QS,

∠BCS = ∠ABC (Alternate angles)

∠b = 100°

$$m\angle a + m\angle b = 70° + 100° = 170°$$

46. (d) Height of electric pole : length of its shadow

: : Height of tree : length of its shadow

x : 20 : : 6 : 8

x × 8 = 20 × 6

$$x = \frac{20 \times 6}{8} = 15 \text{ m}$$

Thus, height of the electric pole is 15 m.

47. (c) Time taken to travel 120 km
= 3hrs
Time taken to travel 1 km

$= \frac{3}{120}$ hrs.

Time taken to travel 360 km

$= \frac{3}{120} \times 360$ hrs

= 3 × 3 hrs = 9 hrs

48. (b) 100 × 5 = 500 cars

49. (d) Thursday

50. (c) 200 cars

MOCK TEST-4

ANSWERS KEY									
1	(a)	11	(b)	21	(d)	31	(b)	41	(b)
2	(b)	12	(c)	22	(c)	32	(b)	42	(a)
3	(a)	13	(d)	23	(c)	33	(d)	43	(a)
4	(d)	14	(b)	24	(c)	34	(d)	44	(b)
5	(a)	15	(d)	25	(c)	35	(c)	45	(c)
6	(c)	16	(c)	26	(c)	36	(d)	46	(b)
7	(d)	17	(c)	27	(b)	37	(c)	47	(d)
8	(c)	18	(d)	28	(c)	38	(b)	48	(c)
9	(b)	19	(c)	29	(b)	39	(b)	49	(d)
10	(d)	20	(b)	30	(c)	40	(c)	50	(a)

1. (a) $(2x+ 4y)(3x - 2y)$
$= 6x^2 - 4xy + 12xy - 8y^2$
$= 6x^2 + 8xy - 8y^2$

2. (b) Other integer = Sum of the integers – given integer
= (–396) – 64 = (–396) + (–64)
= –460.

3. (a) One side of a square

$= \frac{1}{4}$ (perimeter of the square)

So, side of the square whose perimeter is 80 cm

$= \frac{1}{4} \times 80 \text{ cm} = 20 \text{ cm}.$

4. (d) The HCF of an even and an odd number can be either even or odd.

5. (a) Time $= \frac{240 \text{ km}}{80 \text{ km / hr}} = 3$ hours

6. (c) To find the greatest number that will divide 328, 436 and 544 leaving remainder 7, 8 and 9, we find H.C.F. of 328 –7, 436 – 8 and 544 – 9, i.e, 321, 428 and 535.
Using division method we calculate the H.C.F. of 321 and 428.

```
321 ) 428 ( 1
     -321
     107) 321 ( 3
         -321
           ×
```

H.C.F. of (321, 428) = 107,

Now, we will calculate H.C.F. of 107 and 535.

$$107\overline{)535}(5$$
$$\underline{-535}$$
$$\times$$

So H.C.F. of (321, 428 and 535) = 107.

107 is the greatest number that will divide 328, 436 and 544 leaving remainder 7, 8 and 9 respectively.

7. (d) The sequence follows + 4, + 2, × 2. So, the question mark (?) will be replaced by 92.

8. (c) **Statement (i) :**

$2a + 3b = 2(-2) + 3(5)$
$= -4 + 15 = 11$

$2b - a = 2 \times 5 - (-2)$
$= 10 + 2 = 12$

$a - b = -2 - 5$
$= -7$

And,

$a^2 - b^2 = (-2)^2 - (5)^2$
$= 4 - 25$
$= -21$

$a^2 - b^2 = -21$ is least value.

Statement (ii) :

Anshi's present age (16 + x) years
After z years, Anshi will be
16 + x + z years old.

9. (b) $\frac{\text{smallest four digit number}}{\text{smallest prime number}}$

$= \frac{1000}{2} = 500$

Predecessor of the quotient
= 500 – 1 = 499

10. (d) $-12 - [(-15) + (-2) - 3]$
$= -12 - [(-15) + (-2) + (-3)]$
$= -12 - [(-20)] = -12 + 20 = 8.$

11. (b) Length = 8 m 25 cm = 825 cm
Breadth = 6m 75 cm = 675 cm
Height = 4m 50 cm = 450 cm
The required longest tape which can measure the three dimenssions of the room exactly
= HCF (825, 675, 450) = 75 cm

12. (c) Lunch interval = 30 minutes,
5 : 30 p.m. = 17 : 30 hours
Total period in office
= (17 : 30 – 9 : 00) hours
= 8 hours 30 minutes
= [(8 × 60 + 30)] minutes = 510 minutes

∴ Lunch interval : Total period in office
= 30 min : 510 min

$= \frac{30}{510} = \frac{1}{17}$ or 1:17.

13. (d) Total number of eggs = 400
Number of spoiled eggs
= 8 × 12 = 96
Number of good eggs left
= 400 – 96 = 304.

∴ Percentage of good eggs

$= \frac{304}{400} \times 100 = 76$

Thus, there were 76% of good eggs in the crate.

14. (b) 4 is the greatest number by which the product of the predecessor and successor of an odd natural number other than 1 is divided.

15. (d)

16. (c) Ratio of number of monkeys to the number of cats to the number of dogs = 30 : 25 : 20 = 6 : 5 : 4

17. (c) Let L and B be length and breadth of rectangle respectively.
Then, 2 (L + B) = 36

$L + B = \frac{36}{2} = 18$

We have to find number of pairs of natural numbers whose sum is 18. These are (1, 17), (2, 16), (3, 15), (4, 14), (5, 13), (6, 12), (7, 11), (8, 10), (9, 9), Which are 9 in number.

18 (d) The shaded portion comprises of four equal triangles

with base and height $\frac{25}{2}$ cm and

$\frac{18}{2}$ cm = 9 cm

Area of shaded portion

$= 4\left[\frac{1}{2}\times \text{base} \times \text{height}\right]$

$= 4\times\frac{1}{2}\times\frac{25}{2}\times 9 = 225$ sq. cm

19. (c) Percentage in math

$= \left(\frac{325}{500}\times 100\right)\% = 65\%$

Percentage in english

$= \left(\frac{240}{400}\times 100\right)\% = 60\%$

Percentage in geography

$= \left(\frac{84}{150}\times 100\right)\% = 56\%$

Percentage is science

$= \left(\frac{132}{200}\times 100\right)\% = 66\%$

$\therefore$ Rajeev obtained the highest percentage in science.

20. (b) Distance covered in one round = Perimeter of the field = 2 (90 + 70) m = 2 × 160 m

= 320 m

$\therefore$ Distance covered in 5 rounds

= 320 m × 5 = 1600 m

$\because$ The man walks 4 km (= 4 × 1000 m)

= 4000 m in 1 hour

$\therefore$ The man walks 1600 m in

$\frac{1}{4000}\times 1600$ hour

$= \frac{2}{5}$ hour $= \frac{2}{5}\times 60$ minutes

= 24 minutes

21. (d) There are 6 angles in the figure.

22. (c) Let one of the angles be of measure x in degrees and the other two y and z. Then, we are given that x = y + z.

By angle sum property, we have

x + y + z = 180.

$\Rightarrow$ x + x = 180 °

$\Rightarrow$ 2x = 180°

$\Rightarrow$ x = 90°

Hence, the required angle is of measure 90°.

23. (c) Both (i) and (ii)

24. (c) In case of any two or more numbers their HCF will always be the factor of their LCM. But 75 is not a factor of 180.

$\therefore$ 75 can not be HCF of the numbers.

25. (c) When the numerators are equal, the value of fraction is inversely related to the denominator. So

$\frac{5}{11}$ has the highest value and

$\frac{5}{17}$ has the lowest value among all.

But due to the negative sign,

with $-\frac{5}{11}$, it is the smallest

value and $-\frac{5}{17}$ is the largest.

26. (c) Remaining area

$= l^2 - \frac{\pi l^2}{4} = \frac{l^2(4-\pi)}{4} < \frac{l^2}{4}$

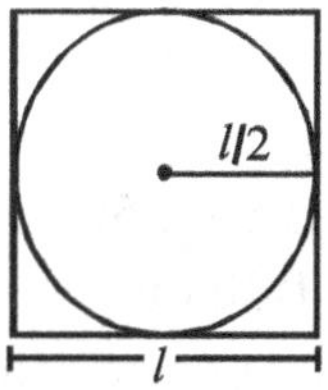

27. (b) Centroid divides the median in the ratio of 2:1.

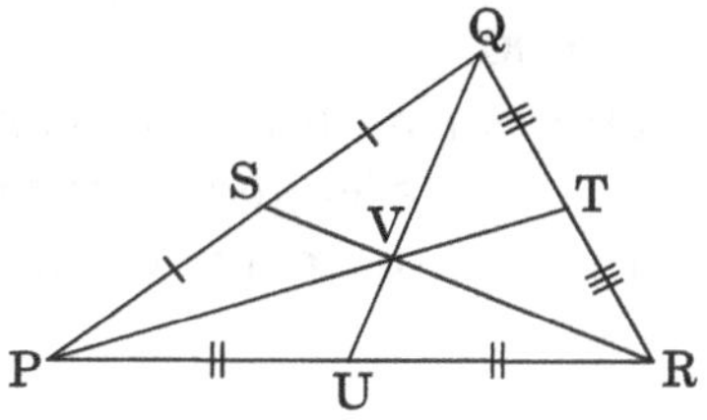

In the figure, V is the centroid of the triangle PQR.

28. (c) 80 –[20 – {175 ÷ 5 –(28 – 16 ÷ 4)÷ 6}]

= 80 – [20 – {35 – (28 – 4) ÷ 6}]

= 80 – [20 – {35 –24 ÷ 6}]

= 80 – [20 – {35 –4}]

= 80 – [20 – 31]

= 80 – (–11) = 80 + 11 = 91

29. (b) $\frac{\text{Peter's age}}{40} = \frac{2}{5}$

Therefore, age of Peter

$= \frac{40 \times 2}{5} = \frac{80}{5} = 16$ years

30. (c) $2 + 2 \div \left\{2 + 2 \div \left(2 + \frac{2}{3}\right)\right\}$

$2 + 2 \div \left\{2 + 2 \div \frac{8}{3}\right\}$

$2 + 2 \div \left\{2 + \frac{3}{4}\right\}$

$2 + 2 \div \frac{11}{4}$

$2 + \frac{8}{11}$

$\frac{30}{11}$

31. (b) A : length = 2 m = 200 cm

breadth = 28 cm

Ratio = 200 : 28 = $\frac{200}{28} = \frac{100}{14}$

$= \frac{50}{7}$ = 50 : 7

B : 60 hrs = 60×60 min

= 3600 min

3600 : 600 = $\frac{3600}{600} = \frac{6}{1}$ = 6: 1

C : 125 : 25 = $\frac{125}{25} = \frac{5}{1}$ = 5: 1

D : Number of consonant

= 5

= (N, G, L, S, H)

Number of vowels = 2 = (E, I)

Ratio of no. of consonants to the no. of vowels = 5 : 2

32. (b) A number is divisible by 6, if it is divisible by 2 as well as 3. The number 6979956 ends with an even number hence it is divisible by 2. The sum of digits of 6979956 is 51, which is divisible by 3, hence the number 6979956 is also divisible by 3. Therefore, it is divisible by 6 also.

33. (d) Product of two numbers

= HCF × LCM

Other number

$= \frac{\text{HCF} \times \text{LCM}}{1^{\text{st}} \text{ number}} = \frac{13 \times 1989}{117}$

= 221

34. (d) $0.0211788 \div 0.333$ is the same as

0.21.1788 ÷ 333. (Drop this zero as it is superfluous)

i.e., 21.1788 ÷ 333

$$\begin{array}{r} 0.0636 \\ 333 \overline{)\, 21.1788} \\ 19988 \\ \hline 1198 \\ 999 \\ \hline 1998 \\ 1998 \\ \hline 0 \end{array}$$

35. (c) C. P. of 50 dozen bananas

= ₹150.

Number of rotten bananas

= 5 dozen

∴ Bananas left

= 50 dozen – 5 dozen

= 45 dozen

Profit = 20% of ₹150

$$= \frac{20}{100} \times ₹150 = ₹30$$

∴ S.P. of 45 dozen bananas

= ₹150 + ₹30 = ₹180

∴ S.P. of 1 dozen bananas

$$= ₹\frac{180}{45} = ₹4.$$

36. (d) $(3a + 2b)(5a + 7b)$

$= 3a(5a + 7b) + 2b(5a + 7b)$

$= 15a^2 + 21ab + 10ab + 14b^2$

$= 15a^2 + 31ab + 14b^2$.

37. (c) Multiply each term by $\frac{3}{2}$ to get the next term. Then,

$$\frac{1}{24} \times \frac{3}{2} = \frac{1}{16}$$

38. (b) Area of one tile

$= 10 \text{ cm} \times 10 \text{ cm} = 100 \text{ cm}^2$.

Area of wall = 4 m × 2.5 m

= 400 cm × 250 cm

$= 1,00,000 \text{ cm}^2$.

∴ Number of tiles required

$$= \frac{\text{Area of wall}}{\text{Area of one tile}} = \frac{100000}{100}$$

= 1000.

39. (b) The perimeter or circumference of a circle is given by πd, where d is the diameter of the circle.

$\pi d = 44$ cm

$\frac{22}{7} d = 44$ cm

d = 14 cm

40. (c) Shaded face is a rectangle

Area of shaded face = 32

$\Rightarrow l \times b = 32$

Now, h = 4 cm.

∴ Volume $= l \times b \times h$

$= 32 \times 4$

$= 128 \text{ cm}^3$.

41. (b)

42. (a) ₹4.65 = 465 paise

The number of paise which is an exact number of rupees will be a multiple of 100. By the condition of the equation, the paise in the number of rupees saved by the boy will be a multiple of 465.

$$\begin{array}{r|l} 5 & 100,\ 465 \\ \hline & 20,\ \ 93 \end{array}$$

∴ L.C.M. of 100 and 465

= 5 × 20 × 93 = 9300

∴ The boy save 9300 paise.

∴ The required number of days

= 9300 ÷ 465 = 20.

43. (a) Denominator of fraction is 6 greater than numerator.
D = N + 6
The sum of denominator and numerator is 16.
D + N = 16
Add both sides 6, then
D + N + 6 = 16 + 6
D + D = 22
2D = 22
D = = 11
Since, D + N = 16
11 + N = 16
N = 16 – 11 = 5
Then, denominator = 11 and numerator = 5.

Hence, fraction is $\frac{5}{11}$.

44. (b) For a given proportion.
Product of extremes = Product of means
i.e., First term × Fourth term
= Second term × Third term
∴ Fourth term

$$= \frac{\text{2nd term} \times \text{3rd term}}{\text{1st term}}$$

$$= \frac{18 \times 40}{20} = 36$$

45. (c) Area of the sheet
= (125 × 85) cm^2.
Area of the paper required for one envelope
= (17 × 5) cm^2.
∴ No. of envelopes

$$= \frac{\text{Area of the sheet}}{\text{Area of piece of paper required for 1 envelope}}$$

∴ No. of envelopes

$$= \frac{125 \times 85}{17 \times 5} = 25 \times 5 = 125$$

46. (b) Square has 4 lines of symmetry.

47. (d) Average age of 5 children = 8 yrs 4 months
Total age of 5 children
= 5 × (8 yrs 4 months)
= 40 yrs 20 months
= 41 yrs 8 months
Average age of 4 children
= 7 yrs. 10 months
Total age of 4 children
= 4 × (7 yrs 10 months)
= 31 yrs 4 months
∴ Age of fifth child
= 41 yrs 8 months – 31 yrs 4 months
= 10 yrs 4 months

48. (c) The circulation of English new paper in 1200.

49. (d) The circulation of Hindi newspaper is 1600. The circulation of Bangali news paper is 800. Then, the circulation of Hindi news paper is more then circulaion of Bengali news paper by 1600 – 800
= 800

50. (a) The two langueses in which circulation of news paper is same are Marathi and Bengali.

MOCK TEST-5

ANSWERS KEY									
1	(b)	11	(a)	21	(c)	31	(d)	41	(b)
2	(d)	12	(c)	22	(c)	32	(a)	42	(a)
3	(d)	13	(b)	23	(d)	33	(b)	43	(a)
4	(b)	14	(b)	24	(d)	34	(d)	44	(d)
5	(c)	15	(b)	25	(c)	35	(c)	45	(c)
6	(b)	16	(d)	26	(b)	36	(c)	46	(a)
7	(a)	17	(b)	27	(b)	37	(c)	47	(b)
8	(a)	18	(d)	28	(a)	38	(d)	48	(b)
9	(a)	19	(a)	29	(c)	39	(c)	49	(a)
10	(a)	20	(b)	30	(b)	40	(c)	50	(c)

1. **(b)** $(10x^2y - 6xy + 15x - 25) - (4x^2y - 3xy + 5x)$

$= 10x^2y - 6xy + 15x - 25 - 4x^2y + 3xy - 5x$

$= 10x^2y - 4x^2y - 6xy + 3xy + 15x - 5x - 25$

$= 6x^2y - 3xy + 10x - 25$

2. **(d)** Chinmay had total money = ₹610000

He gave to Jyoti, Javed and John

= ₹87500 + ₹126380 + ₹350000

= ₹563880

Money left to him

= ₹610000 – ₹563880

= ₹46120

3. **(d)** $\left[\frac{3}{8}\right] \div \left[-\frac{24}{27}\right] = \frac{3}{8} \times \frac{-27}{24} = \frac{-27}{64}$

$\frac{-27}{64}$ is not amongst given options.

4. **(b)** To find minimum number of books required, we will find L.C.M. of 30, 35 and 40 by division method

$$\begin{array}{c|c} 5 & 30, 35, 40 \\ \hline 2 & 6, 7, 8 \\ \hline & 3, 7, 4 \end{array}$$

L.C.M. of (30, 35, 40)

$= 5 \times 2 \times 3 \times 7 \times 4 = 840$.

840 is the minimum number of books required for equal distribution in each class.

5. **(c)** Milk supplied in the morning = 32 litres

$\therefore$ Milk supplied in the evening = 68 litres

Total milk supplied

$= 32\,l + 68\,l = 100\,l$

$\because$ Cost of milk per litre = ₹15

$\therefore$ Money due to the vendor per day = Cost of 100 litres of milk

= ₹15 × 100 = ₹1500.

6. **(b)** Amount for x water cans

$= 1.50 \times x$

Amount for y biscuit packets

$= 2.70 \times y$

Total amount paid by Ravi

= ₹1.50 × x + ₹2.70 × y

$= 1.5\,x + 2.7\,y$

7. (a) Sum of $\frac{5}{7}$ and $\frac{2}{3}$

L.C.M. of (7, 3) = 21

So, $\frac{5}{7}+\frac{2}{3}=\frac{5\times3+2\times7}{21}$.

$=\frac{15+14}{21}=\frac{29}{21}=1\frac{8}{21}$

Now, $2\frac{1}{2}-1\frac{8}{21}=\frac{5}{2}-\frac{29}{21}$

$=\frac{5\times21-29\times2}{42}=\frac{105-58}{42}$

$=\frac{47}{42}=1\frac{5}{42}$.

8. (a) The minimum capacity of a container which can measure the petrol of either tanker in exact number of times = HCF (850, 680)
= 170 litres

9. (a) $2\frac{1}{4}\times\frac{3}{14}\div1\frac{2}{7}=\frac{9}{4}\times\frac{3}{14}\div\frac{9}{7}$

$=\frac{\cancel{9}^1}{4}\times\frac{3}{\cancel{14}_2}\times\frac{\cancel{7}^1}{\cancel{9}_1}=\frac{1\times3\times1}{4\times2\times1}$

$=\frac{3}{8}$

10. (a) Sum of the terms of the ratio
= 5 + 6 = 11
Sum of the numbers = 132

$\therefore$ One number = $\frac{5}{11}\times 132$

= 5 × 12 = 60.

Other number = $\frac{6}{11}\times132$

= 6 × 12 = 72
Hence, the numbers are 60 and 72.

11. (a) Four hundred ninety six is written as 496. 23 thousands is written as $\frac{23}{1000}$ or 0.023
Hence, 496 + 0.023 = 496.023

12. (c)

13. (b) $7\frac{11}{13}=\frac{102}{13}$

$\frac{102}{13}=7.84$

14. (b) We will add $\frac{5}{21}$ and $\frac{3}{21}$ to get the required fraction.

Thus, $\frac{5}{21}+\frac{3}{21}=\frac{8}{21}$.

So, $\frac{3}{21}$ should be subtrated from $\frac{8}{21}$ to get $\frac{5}{21}$.

15. (b) Greatest six digit number
= 765420
Least six digit number
= 204567
Sum = 765420 + 204567
= 969987

16. (d) Required rate
= H.C.F (68, 102, 51)
= 17 km per day

17. (b) Money given to the shopkeeper
= ₹ 100.00
Cost of book = ₹46.50
Money returned
= ₹100.00 – ₹46.50

₹100.00
–₹46.50
₹53.50

Thus, money he will get from the shopkeeper is ₹53.50.

18. (d) The time when all the three different traffic lights change again simultaneously after
= LCM (48, 72, 108)
= 432 seconds
= 7 minutes 12 seconds

19. (a) Let the expenditure be ₹x.
Then 21000 : x = 7 : 6
$\Rightarrow$ x × 7 = 21000 × 6

$$\Rightarrow x = \frac{21000 \times 6}{7} = 18000$$

∴ Expenditure = ₹18000
∴ Savings = income – expenditure
= ₹21000 – ₹18000 = ₹3000.

20. (b) Quotient

$$= \frac{-12a^3b + 18a^2b^2 - 24ab^3}{-6ab}$$

$$= \frac{-12a^3b}{-6ab} + \frac{18a^2b^2}{-6ab} - \frac{24ab^3}{-6ab}$$

= $2a^2 - 3ab - (-4b^2)$
= $2a^2 - 3ab + 4b^2$.

21. (c) Total number of males

$$= = \frac{6}{5} \times 560000 = 672000$$

22. (c) Ray $\overrightarrow{AB}$ and $\overrightarrow{BA}$ are not same.

23. (d) Boys : Girls : : Girls : Teacher
x : 180 : : 180 : 90
x × 90 = 180 × 180

$$x = \frac{180 \times 180}{90}$$

Thus, number of boys is 360.

24. (d) In ΔABC, 60° + 75° + x = 180°
$\Rightarrow$ 135° + x = 180°
$\Rightarrow$ x = 180° – 135° = 45°.

25. (c) Number of envelopes bought for ₹10.50 = 15

Number of envelopes bought for

$$₹1 = \frac{15}{10.50}$$

Number of envelopes bought for

$$₹70 = \frac{15}{10.50} \times 70$$

$$= \frac{15 \times 70 \times 100}{1050}$$

$$= \frac{15 \times 70 \times 100}{1050}$$

= 100 envelopes
Thus 100 envelopes can be bought for ₹70.
Cost of 15 envelopes = ₹10.50

Cost of 1 envelope = ₹$\frac{10.50}{15}$

Cost of 30 envelopes

$$= ₹\frac{10.50}{15} \times 30$$

$$= ₹\frac{1050}{1500} \times 30 = ₹21$$

26. (b) H.C.F of 18 and 12 is 6.

So, $\frac{18 \div 6}{12 \div 6} = \frac{3}{2}$ = 3 : 2

27. (b) $-7\frac{1}{2}$ will lie between –7 and –8.

28. (a) 50 – 42 ÷ 3 × 7 – (– 11 + 5) ÷ 4 × 2.
= 50 – 42 ÷ 21 – (– 6) ÷ 4 × 2

$$= 50 - 2 - \left(-\frac{3}{2}\right) \times 2$$

= 48 – (– 3) = 48 + 3 = 51

29. (c) In this problem you know a fractional part of a number and you have to find the whole number. You can do this by dividing the given number by the fraction.

$$540 \div \frac{5}{7} = \cancel{540}^{108} \times \frac{7}{\cancel{5}_1} = 756.$$

So there are 756 seats in the auditorium.

30. (b) 478) 40304.96 (84.32

```
  3824
  ----
   2064
   1912
   ----
    1529
    1434
    ----
     956
     956
    ----
       0
    ----
```

Move decimal 2 places to the right both in the divisor and the dividend. Then, the result is 84.32.

31. (d) $(3a + 2b)(5a + 7b)$

$= 3a(5a + 7b) + 2b(5a + 7b)$

$= 15a^2 + 21ab + 10ab + 14b^2$

$= 15a^2 + 31ab + 14b^2.$

32. (a) (i) : $\text{S. I} = \dfrac{P \times R \times T}{100}$

$$= \frac{900 \times 12 \times 3}{100}$$

S.I = ₹324

(ii) : $\text{S.I} = \dfrac{750 \times 6 \times 5}{100}$

S.I = ₹225

33. (b) 4 : m : 6 is in continued proportion

Hence, $\dfrac{4}{m} = \dfrac{m}{6}$

$\Rightarrow m^2 = 24$

$\Rightarrow m = 2\sqrt{6}$

34. (d) Let the breadth of rectangular plot be x

Then, length or rectangular plot $= 2x$

$\because$ Perimeter of rectangular plot $= 300$ m

$\therefore\ 2(x + 2x) = 300$

$2 \times 3x = 300$

$6x = 300$

$x = \dfrac{300}{6} = 50$

Then, length of rectangular plot is $= 2x = 100$ m

Breadth $= x = 50$ m

Hence, required area of plot

= length × breadth

$= 100 \times 50$

$= 5000\ m^2$

35. (c) Required perimeter =

$$28 + \frac{2\pi r_1}{2} + \frac{2\pi r_2}{4}$$

$$= 28 + \frac{22}{7} \times 14 + \frac{22}{7} \times 28 \times \frac{1}{2}$$

$= 28 + 44 + 44 = 116$ cm

36. (c) Let C and S denote car and scooter respectively. Then, the sequence of parking is

C S C S S C S S S C S
S S S C S S S / S S C S
S S S S S C S S S S S S
S C

The above sequence has been divided into two equal halves by a line. Clearly, number of scooters in second half of the line = 15.

37. (c) Given figure is a polygon.

38. (d) Let Radha's salary be ₹x.

40% of x + 20% of x + 4000 = x

$$\frac{40}{100}x + \frac{20}{100}x + 4000 = x$$

$$x - \frac{60}{100}x = 4000$$

$$\Rightarrow \frac{40}{100}x = 4000$$

$$x = \frac{4000 \times 100}{40}$$

x = ₹10,000

Her monthly salary is ₹10,000

39. (c) She spends on food

= 40% of 10,000

$$= \frac{40}{100} \times 10{,}000 = ₹4000.$$

40. (c) She spends on conveyance

= 20% of 10,000

$$= \frac{20}{100} \times 10{,}000 = ₹2000.$$

41. (b) $0.668 = \frac{668}{1000} = \frac{334}{500} = \frac{167}{250}$

42. (a) Using the formula, perimeter of a rectangle = 2 × (length + breadth), we have

breadth of the rectangle

$$= \frac{1}{2}\text{ (perimeter)} - \text{length}$$

$$= \frac{1}{2} \times 200\text{ cm} - 70\text{ cm}.$$

= 100 cm – 70 cm = 30 cm

43. (a) A→(iii); B→(i); C→(iv); D→(ii)

44. (d) Side of square

$$= \frac{\text{Perimeter}}{4} = \frac{56}{4} = 14\text{ cm}$$

Area of square = $(\text{Side})^2$

= $(14)^2$

= 196 sq. cm

Radius of circle = $\frac{14}{2}$ = 7 cm

Area of circle = πr^2

$$= \frac{22}{7} \times 7 \times 7$$

= 154 sq. cm

Area of shaded portion

= 196 – 154

= 42 sq. cm

45. (c) Length of the field = 350 m;

Breadth of the field = 240 m.

∴ Area of the field = $(350 \times 240)m^2 = 84000\ m^2$

$$= \frac{84000}{10000}\text{ha} = 8.4\text{ ha}$$

($\because$ 10000 m^2 = 1ha)

∵ Yield per ha = 25 quintal

∵ Yield from 8.4 ha = 8.4 × 25 q

= 210 q

Price of wheat = ₹160 per quintal

∴ Expected income = ₹(160 × 210)

= ₹33600.

46. (a) In ΔABD,

$y = 60° + 60° = 120°$

(Exterior angle property)

In ΔABD,

$20 + y + z = 180°$

$\Rightarrow 20° + 120° + z° = 180°$

$\Rightarrow z° = 180° - 140° = 40°$

Now, $x = 20° + z°$ (Exterior angle property)

$= 20° + 40° = 60°$

$x + y + z = 60° + 120° + 40°$

$= 220°$

47. (b) Original volume $= l \times b \times h$

$= lbh$

New volume $= 2l \times 2b \times 2h$

$= 8 \times lbh$

∴ New volume

= 8 (original volume)

Also, original surface area

$= 2\ [(2l)(2b)+(2b)(2h)+(2h)(2l)]$

$= 2 \times 4(lb + bh + hl)$

$= 4 \times 2\ (lb + bh + hl)$

∴ New surface area

= 4 × original surface area.

48. (b) LPG is used in maximum number of houses.

49. (a) 10 houses are using coal as fuel.

50. (c) Out of 100, houses using electricity = 5

∴ Out of 1, house using electricity $= \frac{5}{100}$

∴ Out of 1 lakh houses using electricity

$= \frac{5}{100} \times 1,00,000 = 5000$

SCIENCE

MOCK TEST-1

ANSWERS KEY									
1	(b)	11	(a)	21	(a)	31	(b)	41	(b)
2	(d)	12	(c)	22	(b)	32	(b)	42	(a)
3	(b)	13	(a)	23	(c)	33	(b)	43	(b)
4	(d)	14	(a)	24	(b)	34	(d)	44	(d)
5	(b)	15	(c)	25	(a)	35	(c)	45	(a)
6	(d)	16	(a)	26	(c)	36	(b)	46	(a)
7	(d)	17	(d)	27	(b)	37	(d)	47	(c)
8	(b)	18	(a)	28	(b)	38	(a)	48	(d)
9	(a)	19	(d)	29	(b)	39	(b)	49	(b)
10	(a)	20	(b)	30	(d)	40	(a)	50	(b)

PHYSICS

1. **(b)** Bulb will not light up if sufficient current is not provided
2. **(d)** The table classifies objects according to whether they are made of magnetic materials. Materials that can be attracted by a magnet are known as magnetic materials. Iron, nickel, cobalt and steel are magnetic materials. Brass button is made of non-magnetic material and it is the object that has been wrongly classified. Steel wire is made of magnetic material and is correctly classified. Thumbtack and key are usually made of magnetic material such as iron or steel and are correctly classified. Silver spoon, gold coin and copper plate are made of non-magnetic material and are correctly classified. Safety pin is usually made of magnetic material and has been wrongly classified. Therefore the answer is option (d).
3. **(b)** Objects made of a material that is a good conductor of electricity will light up the bulb when connected good electrical conductors. (B) and (D) are electrical insulators. An insulator does not allow electricity to flow through. Therefore, there is an open circuit and the bulb will not light up.
4. **(d)** Length of a curved line can be measured with the help of a thread and a meter scale.
5. **(b)** A $\rightarrow$ (r); B $\rightarrow$ (p); C $\rightarrow$ (q); D $\rightarrow$ (s)
6. **(d)** Muscular force is the example of Contact force.
7. **(d)** A shadow is an area of darkness and it is formed when an object blocks the path of light. For this question, the apple does not allow light to pass through it, which results in the formation of its shadow on the screen. It also demonstrates that light travels in a straight line.
8. **(b)** The speed of light (3×10^8 m/s) is more than speed of sound 332 m/s in air. So, we can see lightning before we hear thunder.
9. **(a)** The swinging pendulum of a wall clock performs both oscillatory and periodic motion.
10. **(a)** The attraction is maximum near magnetic poles

11. (a) When pure water was used, the bulb did not light up. This shows that pure water does not allow electricity to pass through it.

12. (c) A source of light, an opaque obstacle and screen behind the obstacle are necessary for shadow formation.

13. (a) Switch completes the circuit but does not act as a source of current

14. (a) Magnetic strength is equal at both the poles.

CHEMISTRY

15. (c) Cotton is obtained from plant.

16. (a) Saturated solution

17. (d) Plastic is water resistant and bad conductor of heat and electricity. Pliers have plastic handles so that they do not conduct electricity and are safe to use.

18. (a) No new substance is formed on melting of coaltar.

19. (d) Disposable cup has lower density than water therefore it floats on water.

20. (b) In chemical change molecules of substance undergo change and new substances are formed.

21. (a) Eggs will rotten to give foul smell. Bottle will remain the same whereas moth balls will sublime which is a physical change.

22. (b) In statement (i) state is changed whereas in statement (ii) new products are formed as a result of ignition.

23. (c) Nitrogen neither burns nor supports combustion. The gas controls burning in atmosphere.

24. (b) As one goes up in the atmosphere, the amount of oxygen in air decreases.

25. (a) Aquatic plants and animals use the oxygen dissolved in water to breathe.

26. (c) The part labelled W has to be made of waterproof material so as to keep water away when the umbrella is used in the rain. Plastic will be an ideal choice for making W. The part labelled X should be made of a strong material. Wood can absorb water and get wet, causing it to rot. Metal will be a better choice for making X. For making Y, wood will be a better choice than metal as metal is a good conductor of electricity and it can be dangerous during thunderstorms.

27. (b) A brittle material is one that can break easily upon impact. In this question, the property of brittleness is shown by the glass as it broke into smaller pieces when dropped on the floor.

28. (b) To hold $10L$ of water, the material must be strong. Materials P and Q satisfy this requirement. However, the material has to be waterproof also so that it can hold water. Thus, Ravi should choose material Q and not material P.

29. (b) Iron and nickel are magnetic while aluminium and silver are non-magnetic. Thus the property by which they are classified is the magnetic property.

30. (d) Separation of substances help in obtaining the useful component and improving the quality of substance by discarding harmful component

31. (b) Heat is required to change the state of water from liquid to gas. When water evaporates from the elephant's skin, heat from the elephant's body is used to change water into water vapour. This cools down the body of the elephant as heat is removed during this process.

BIOLOGY

32. (b) As the bee lands on the petal to drink the nectar from within the flower or to collect pollen, the stamen which hangs down from the top transfers pollen onto the bee's body. This pollen would be transferred to the stigma of another flower when the bee visits it. This process is pollination, the transfer of pollen grains from the anther to the stigma.
33. (b) Man-made materials such as plastics are usually non-biodegradable. In other words, they do not decay easily. We may bury them but because they do not break down easily, they will remain in the soil for a very long time. Thus, this increases land pollution on Earth. However, when these materials are burnt in incinerators, they produce harmful gases which then add to the air pollution on Earth.
34. (d) Structure A is stoma because gas exchange takes place via the small openings found on the underside of leaves. Structure B is chlorophyll because it absorbs light energy from the Sun. Structure C is the leaf vein where water and food can move in and out of the leaf. The vein consists of xylem and phloem which are tubes that transport water and food in plants.
35. (c) The bird, kiwi is found in New Zealand.
Its body is too heavy to fly. It is because the flight muscles cannot support the body weight when it flies.
36. (b) Paneer is made by this process this is called curdling of milk. Here, the milk protein separates out from the fat.
37. (d) Cuscuta is a parasitic plant because it gets its nutrition from another living plants.
38. (a) Zooplanktons are microscopic organisms found in water bodies. They are good nutritional source for aquatic animals.
39. (b) Haemoglobin of blood is a compound of iron.
40. (a) An annual plant completes its life cycle within one year and then dies such as – paddy, wheat and maize etc.
41. (b) Soil is a good medium for plant growth. It contains sufficient nutrients and minerals for plant life.
42. (a) Photosynthesis is the reverse process of respiration. Because in the process of photosynthesis the food is prepared and in respiration the stored food is oxidised releasing energy.
43. (b) Plants prepare their own food by the process of photosynthesis, so they are producers and animals depend upon plants for their food so they are consumers. Ozone layer is necessary for all living organism as it prevents the harmful U.V. rays from entering the earth.
44. (d) The seeds of fenugreek (methi) are used for cooking. The part of coconut which is used is its fruit drupe. The fibrous mesocarp of coconut is used to make fibre, whereas the endocarp is used as a source of oil and carbohydrate.
45. (a) On the earth the source of energy is sun. Plants use this energy for food preparation and animals depend upon plants for food. After death of animals, decomposers in soil use the dead bodies. After death of decomposers their body components are released in the

environment, mostly in soil. They are used by plants. This is path of flow of energy between organisms & environment. Living organisms are the biotic factors.

46. (a) Fin-like flippers used by divers help to move through water more efficiently. Since human feet are too small to provide much thrust.

47. (c) Through the process of excretion, animals eliminate excess water as well as waste products.

48. (d)

49. (b) Photosynthesis is carried out in the presence of sunlight. Chlorophyll is essential component. Carbon dioxide and water are utilized in this process. Carbohydrate is the main product.

50. (b) We should not burn dried leaves because it degrades the soil, produces fumes, destroys raw materials which can be used to prepare organic manure. Burning creates a lot of heat in the atmosphere which adds up to the global warming.

MOCK TEST-2

ANSWERS KEY									
1	(c)	11	(c)	21	(d)	31	(b)	41	(c)
2	(c)	12	(d)	22	(a)	32	(c)	42	(c)
3	(d)	13	(c)	23	(b)	33	(c)	43	(c)
4	(a)	14	(a)	24	(a)	34	(b)	44	(d)
5	(c)	15	(d)	25	(d)	35	(c)	45	(a)
6	(a)	16	(d)	26	(a)	36	(a)	46	(b)
7	(b)	17	(d)	27	(d)	37	(b)	47	(b)
8	(c)	18	(b)	28	(d)	38	(a)	48	(a)
9	(c)	19	(a)	29	(b)	39	(d)	49	(c)
10	(a)	20	(a)	30	(c)	40	(a)	50	(d)

PHYSICS

1. (c) In an electric circuit, the two terminals of the electric cell are always connected to the two terminals of the bulb.

2. (c) Multiple batteries arranged in series increase the current flowing through the circuit. Multiple batteries arranged in parallel do not increase the current flowing through the circuit. As more batteries are used, the current will increase if the batteries are arranged glow series and the bulb will glow brighter. When more bulbs are arranged in series, the brightness of each bulb decreases. Bulbs arranged in parallel increases the overall brightness of the circuit.

3. (d) Object Q is a magnet. Object Q and Magnet R have their like poles facing each another and the poles exert a force of repulsion. This force keeps them apart and Object Q floats above Magnet R.

4. (a) Distance = speed × time

$$40\text{kmph} \times \frac{10}{60}\text{hr} = 6.67\text{km}$$

5. **(c)** Since size of earth is bigger than that of moon. So the region of total darkness umbral is more than the region of partial darkness (penumbral) kind of eclipse is called total lunar eclipe.

6. **(a)** Sockets are made of electrical conductors while plug tops are made of insulators.

7. **(b)** 'One touch method' of preparing the magnet is shown in the figure. In this method the pole produced at the end of the nail, where the friction starts is same as the pole of the magnet which is in contact with nail. Hence north pole will be produced at A and south at B.

8. **(c)** When no force acts on a body, then it will either remain at rest or move in a straight line.

9. **(c)** Odometre is the device used to measure distance in vehicles.

10. **(a)** When switches X and Y are closed, the pathway containing bulb C and switch Z is still open. Thus, electricity will only flow in the closed path containing bulbs A, B and switch Y.

11. **(c)** The original glass windows allow all the light to pass through into the library and makes it too glaring. Frosted glass is a suitable substitute because it is translucent and allows only a little light to pass through. The amount of light passing through the library windows would be reduced and the library would not be too bright and glaring. Clear plastic and wired clear glass would not cut down the amount of light entering the library and are not good choices to use as substitutes. Soft wood is opaque and does not allow light to pass through at all. Thus, using soft wood does not meet the needs of the library.

12. **(d)** Time can be expressed only when there is starting point and an end point.

13. **(c)** Light falling on the tree changes with time.

14. **(a)** C is the positive terminal of the cell and D is the negative terminal of the cell.

CHEMISTRY

15. **(d)** The most amount of water left in the container indicates that the rate of evaporation in that container is the lowest. The rate of evaporation of water is affected by the exposed surface area of the water. Looking at the containers, container R has the smallest exposed surface area followed by container P, then container Q. This means that container R has the lowest rate of evaporation resulting in the most amount of water left in the container after two hours. Container Q has the largest exposed surface area and would therefore have the highest rate of evaporation and the least amount of water left behind after two hours. In other words, when the exposed surface area is bigger, the rate of evaporation is greater.

16. **(d)** Shiny appearance is the appropriate term for lusture.

17. **(d)** The body of the pot should be made of a good conductor of heat such as a metal. However, the chosen metal should not rust easily. Therefore, stainless steel is chosen to make the body of the pot. The handles of the pot should be made of a good insulator of heat so that it does not get too hot to hold the pot. A suitable material to make the handles would be plastic. The lid

should be made of a transparent material as the contents of the pot must be able to be seen. This transparent material needs to have a high melting point to withstand the heat from cooking. Therefore, glass is a suitable material.

18. (b) We use a hose to bring water from a tap to the place where water is needed. A hose needs to be long to reach places that are too far from the top. For storage purposes, a hose needs to be flexible so that it can be coiled up and would then only occupy a small space in storage. Since the hose transports water, it needs to be waterproof.

19. (a) A ductile material is one that can be stretched a long way before it breaks or fractures. It will also retain to shape that you stretch it to. In the above case, the rubber band returns to the original shape when the weight is removed. A rubber band is therefore not ductile but elastic. Elasticity is the ability of a material to return to its original shape after it has been stretched. Malleability is the ability of a material to be hammered into sheets without breaking. Durability is the ability of a material to withstand wear and tear or decay.

20. (a) Sieving is done to separate components of different sizes: Different sized sieves are available. .

21. (d) In both types of changes (i.e. reversible change and physical change) we can get back the original substance by reversing the conditions.

22. (a) It takes up nearly four-fifth of the space that air fills.

23. (b) Powerloom

24. (a) Formation of water by reaction of hydrogen and oxygen is a chemical change. Change of liquid water to water vapour is a physical change.

25. (d) Anaerobic bacterial digestion of animal waste and burning of biogas both are chemical changes as new products are formed in both the processes.

26. (a) The process of separating cotton fibres from the seeds is called ginning and the machines used for this purpose are called gins.

27. (d) The process of separation of gummy skin from jute fibre is called retting

28. (d) X = evaporation,
Y = condensation
Z = precipitation (rain fall, snow fall etc.)

29. (b) Dyeing or bleaching should be done in the last stage after the fabrics are made and before the clothes are cut out of it. This is done to avoid loss and inconvenience in handling materials.

30. (c) X particles are heavy and Y particles are light. These can be removed by using winnowing. In this process particles being lighter separated out and remaining mixture contains X and Z particles. Z being magnetic can be separately by magnetic separation.

31. (b) The label I in the figure represents a head light, made of glass.
The label II represents a seat, which is usually made of leather, while label III is made of metal.

BIOLOGY

32. (c) The African violet is an example of a plant that can reproduce from leaves.

33. (c) Statement (a), (b) and (d) reduce the burning of fossil fuels to produce electricity. When there is less burning, less carbon dioxide will be produced and this reduces air pollution. Statement (c) actually contributes to air pollution.

34. (b) White fur keeps the bodies of polar bear and arctic fox warm. White colour deceives enemies by giving a false look as a snowy structure.

35. (c) The landfill is the most common process of waste disposal. But burying a large amount of rubbish results in delay in decomposition process which in turn causes soil pollution.

36. (a) When we do something we use our hands and legs. During action, both skeletal and muscular system function together in hands or legs.

37. (b) It is not as hard as bones.

38. (a) Stomata are tiny openings present in leaves for gaseous exchange.

39. (d) Xerocoles are referred as those animals who are adapted for desert life. They can survive lack of water and excessive heat.

40. (a) The landfill is the most popularly used method of waste disposal. This process includes burying the waste material deep in soil for decomposition.

41. (c) Protozoa is a group of organisms that are motile and unicellular eukaryotic. They are not visible with naked eyes such as – *Amoeba* and *Plasmodium* etc.

42. (c) Obesity is the result of over eating of high calorie junk food. Junk foods contain very high levels of trans fats, salts and sugar.

43. (c)

44. (d) It is called dormancy.

45. (a) The formation of soil includes a process in which rock breaks into stones, stones break into gravels, gravels into silt and silt into sand. And finally sand breaks into fine particles forming soil.

46. (b) Pollen grains are produced within anther which is male part of the flower. Pollen grains are powdery in structure and are of different colour.

47. (b) Ghee is the best source of fat. In our body, the fat is stored under the skin. This stored fat is utilized when there is lack of fat in our food.

48. (a) When we go in desert area, generally we find that urine shows yellowish colour (due to concentration) and the quantity is also reduced.

49. (c) Beetroot is an underground root whereas potato and onion are underground stems.

50. (d) The characteristic features of living beings are respiration, reproduction, adaptation and excretion etc.

MOCK TEST-3

ANSWERS KEY									
1	(c)	11	(a)	21	(c)	31	(b)	41	(c)
2	(b)	12	(c)	22	(b)	32	(c)	42	(a)
3	(a)	13	(c)	23	(c)	33	(c)	43	(b)
4	(d)	14	(b)	24	(a)	34	(b)	44	(c)
5	(c)	15	(d)	25	(c)	35	(c)	45	(d)
6	(b)	16	(a)	26	(a)	36	(b)	46	(c)
7	(c)	17	(c)	27	(a)	37	(b)	47	(c)
8	(d)	18	(d)	28	(d)	38	(d)	48	(a)
9	(a)	19	(d)	29	(c)	39	(a)	49	(b)
10	(a)	20	(c)	30	(c)	40	(c)	50	(d)

PHYSICS

1. **(c)** Since, pressure is directly proportional to the depth of liquid column.
   So, container A will have more pressure.
2. **(b)** For magnets 2 and 3 to attract, the pole on the right of magnet 2 must be a S-pole and P must be a N-pole. For magnets 1 and 2 to repel each other, the two poles facing each other must be like poles. Thus Q must be a S-pole.
3. **(a)** An object which allows most of the light to pass through it is called as transparent object.
4. **(d)** Adding switches to the circuit allows the bulbs to be switched on and off at will. We can control the bulbs individually with Switch Y and Switch Z. Switch X is the main or master switch of the circuit. This is because it can switch on or off all the lights provided Switch Y and Switch Z are switched on.
5. **(c)** As there is the change is position of an object hence it has both distance and displacement.
6. **(b)** A rough surface diffuses incident beam of light. Therefore, option (b) is correct and rest of the options are incorrect.
7. **(c)** Silver is a good conductor of electricity but it is not used to make electric wires because it is expensive.
8. **(d)** Speed of a car = $\frac{\text{Distance travel}}{\text{Time taken}}$
9. **(a)** A horseshoe magnet has varying magnetic strengths at different positions. The magnetic strength is always the strongest at the poles. Therefore, a horseshoe magnet has the strongest magnetic strength at the poles which is at the two ends. The horseshoe magnet will pick up the greatest amount of magnetic objects at the ends than in the middle of the bar magnet. Points V and Z which are the poles of the magnet are have the greatest magnetic strength. These two points can attract the greatest number of pins. Point X, which is in the middle of the horseshoe magnet, has the weakest magnetic strength and can only attract the least number of pins. Points W and Y which lie between the poles and the middle of the magnet will attract more pins than Point X but less pins than Points V and Z.

10. (a) Force = mass × acceleration

11. (a) Current can flow through our body so it is a good conductor of electricity.

12. (c) Motion is along straight line. So it is rectilinear and it repeats itself after several time interval. So it is periodic.

13. (c) Shoe box can never form an circular shadow due to its rectangular of shape.

14. (b) The greatest concentration of iron filings will be at B as the strength is maximum at poles of the magnet and B is closest to the pole (N).

CHEMISTRY

15. (d) The given objects represent an iron nail and a needle. They both are hard and can be attracted by magnets.

16. (a) Washing powder is soluble in water.

17. (c) The melted wax undergoes combustion as the cotton thread gets burnt. The combustion produces carbon dioxide and water vapour. The burning of wax is a chemical change.

18. (d) A burning of matchstick is a chemical and irreversible change in which heat energy is released. It is an exothermic reaction and a fast change.

19. (d) The appearance of Halley's comet after every 76 years is a periodic change. The changes that occur at regular intervals of time are called periodic changes.

20. (c) Materials are grouped together on the basis of similarities and differences in their properties.

21. (c) Wood catches fire when heated directly over a flame. It is therefore the least suitable for making part labelled Q. The other materials, glass, steel and ceramics are able to absorb and retain heat from the fire.

22. (b) The mixture consists of sand, sugar and water. Sugar being soluble in water will form a sugar solution. During filtration, the sand will be separated by filter paper as residue while sugar solution will pass through. During distillation, pure water can be collected leaving the sugar separate. Distillation is the process to obtain pure form of liquid from a solution.

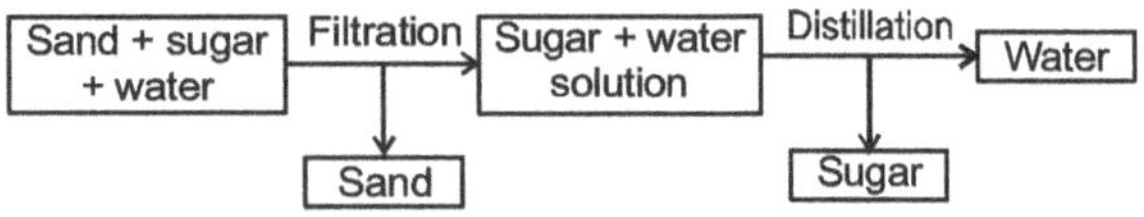

23. (c) All the given phenomen are example of periodic changes. Periodic changes are changes that occur at regular intervals of time.

24. (a) A-(ii); B-(i); C-(iv); D-(iii); E-(v)

25. (c) If we observe the classification chart carefully, we will see that the materials are classified according to sources they come from. Those materials that are grouped under X come from plants, whereas those that are grouped under Y come from animals.

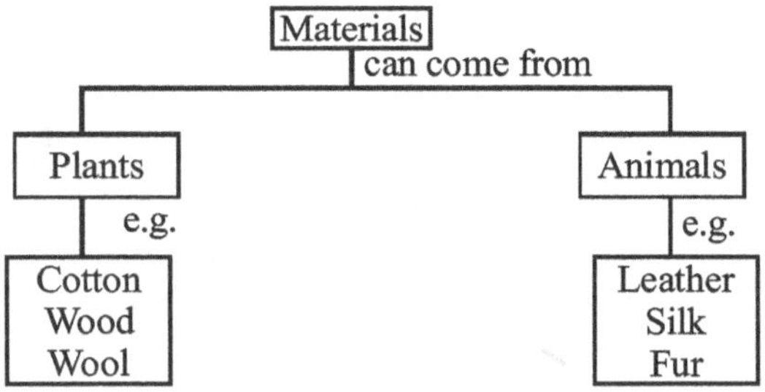

Wool is obtained from sheep. It should therefore be classified in Group Y. Silk comes from the cocoons of silkworms. Fur comes from the outer body covering of mammals. Leather comes from the skin or hide of animals.

26. (a) Fruit of cotton plant called cotton boll is used for obtaining cotton fibre. Cotton bolls on maturing open and give cotton.

27. (a) On tilting the bottle bubbles of air came out of bottle and some water entered the bottle.

28. (d) Melting of wax is a reversible change as melted wax can be solidified on cooling.

29. (c) Water droplets on the inner surface of the empty portion of the bottle is due to evaporation and condensation of the water.

30. (c) Magnifying glass and glass tumbler are transparent materials.

31. (b) Water is first filtered to remove solid impurities from water. Small suspended impurities are then removed by loading. Loading helps the suspended clay particles to settle down rapidly and clear water can be removed by decantation. Water is then boiled to remove harmful germs and to make water fit for drinking.

BIOLOGY

32. (c) The diagram shows a seedling. When a seed germinates, a seedling is produced. For germination to take place, the seed would require water, oxygen and the right temperature. Sunlight is not needed at this stage because no green leaves are present for the seedling to carry out photosynthesis.

33. (c) By practising reusing, recycling and reducing methods, less rubbish would be produced. Incineration and burying rubbish in landfills are not methods to reduce the production of rubbish. Incineration is a waste treatment method and a landfill is a site where waste materials are buried.

34. (b) These are the symptoms of night-blindness caused due to deficiency of vitamin A.

35. (c) The flower does not have large petals. Having large flower petals is a characteristic of insect-pollinated plants. The female parts that receive pollen grains are large. This is a characteristic of wind-pollinated flowers.

36. (b) The platypus has webbed feet and is likely to be found in a very wet environment. It does not have very thick fur coat hence it is probably adapted to moderate temperatures.

37. (b) The lines on the broad green part of leaf are called veins.

38. (d) Grass, giraffe and gold fish need essential living conditions such as nutrition and suitable atmosphere for proper growth.

39. (a) Bone marrow is a soft substance present inside bone.

40. (c) Respiration is an oxidation process because there is need of oxygen for this activity.

41. (c) Green plants prepare their food by the process of photosynthesis and there is occuring respiration in all living being for the evolution of energy.

42. (a) Aquatic habitats are concerned with ecosystem related with water bodies such as river, sea, lake and pond etc.

43. (b) The greenhouse effect is a process by which thermal radiation from earth surface is absorbed. It results in elevation of surface temperature.

44. (c) The process of photosynthesis can take place only in those living organisms that have chlorophyll such as algae, green plants etc.

45. (d) Rainforest habitat shows hot and wet climate with heavy rainfall. This results in rich vegetation.

46. (c) Hydrophytes are those plants that grow partly or wholly in water. Such as – lotus, lily and hyacinth etc.

47. (c) Nitrogen is an essential component of protein. In the absence of nitrogen protein cannot be formed.

48. (a) Soil fertility depends upon water holding capacity and humus availability. This quality is shown by clayey soil so it is more fertile in comparison to sandy soil.

49. (b) The leaves of aquatic plants do not have waxy coating on the surface because whole surface is required for gas exchange between plant and water.

50. (d) Desert plants lose very little water due to lack of stomata and roots grow very deep into the soil in search of water.

MOCK TEST-4

ANSWERS KEY									
1	(b)	11	(d)	21	(d)	31	(d)	41	(c)
2	(a)	12	(b)	22	(b)	32	(b)	42	(c)
3	(d)	13	(c)	23	(c)	33	(d)	43	(d)
4	(d)	14	(d)	24	(d)	34	(b)	44	(b)
5	(a)	15	(b)	25	(d)	35	(a)	45	(a)
6	(b)	16	(b)	26	(d)	36	(c)	46	(a)
7	(d)	17	(b)	27	(b)	37	(b)	47	(d)
8	(b)	18	(c)	28	(a)	38	(a)	48	(d)
9	(c)	19	(b)	29	(d)	39	(d)	49	(b)
10	(b)	20	(c)	30	(b)	40	(a)	50	(a)

PHYSICS

1. **(b)** The inside of the box is dark. The only light allowed into the box comes from the torch placed at the left side of the box. Light travels to the ball and is reflected into our eyes. Since light travels in straight lines, only the left half that is illuminated can be seen. The right half is in darkness and does not reflect any light, thus it cannot be seen.

2. **(a)** Brand X lasts for longest time.

3. **(d)** For experiments and investigations, besides the factors or condition to be tested, all other factor and conditions must remain the same. In the above experiment, the objective is to test if the surface of the inclined plane affect s the amount of force needed to move the object up the inclined plane. The material that is used for the ramp would determine the surface of the inclined plane. Therefore, the material of the ramp used must be the only variable that is changed and all the other variables must be kept the same.

4. **(d)** A → (s); B → (r); C → (p); D → (q)

5. **(a)** North pole points towards geographic north

6. **(b)** Since Object X moves towards the magnet in Richard's hand, it means that either Object X is a magnetic object or B and C are unlike poles of two different magnets.

7. **(d)** Pressure $P = h\rho g$
8. **(b)** Water is a good conductor of electricity
9. **(c)** On closing switch 'C' and 'D' the circuit becomes closed.
10. **(b)** Electronic watch is an modern day technology
11. **(d)** The essential conditions for the formation of shadow are:
    (i) A source of light
    (ii) An opaque substance
    (iii) A screen behind the obstacle
12. **(b)** Rubber is bad conductor of electricity
13. **(c)** 1 + 1 + 2 + 1 + 2 = 7 cm
14. **(d)** Steel spoon is good conductor of electricity.

CHEMISTRY

15. **(b)** Sohan will use material which is strong and flexible. It is because, a hammock should be strong enough to take the weight of person on it and also it should be flexible.
16. **(b)** Wood floats on water, is opaque and is used to make table, chair etc.
17. **(b)** One important property of the car windscreen is its degree of transparency. In other words, it is the ability of the material to allow light to pass through. We need to see where we are going when driving. Therefore, the windscreen needs to be transparent. The windscreen needs to be strong so that it does not break easily.
18. **(c)** Charkha (spinning wheel) is used to spin cotton to make yarn. Handloom and powerloom are used for weaving yarn to make fabric.
19. **(b)** A-(ii); B-(i); C-(iv); D-(v); E-(iii)
20. **(c)** Artificial ripening is an irreversible change as this process cannot be reversed.
21. **(d)** Both are chemical changes as new substances are formed.
22. **(b)** Cotton crop grow at places having black soil and warm climate.
23. **(c)** Dust and smoke are harmful to living beings.
24. **(d)**
25. **(d)** Winnowing method is based on the difference in weight of the component of a mixture. Lighter component of a mixture can be separated from heavier one with the help of wind.
26. **(d)** Oxygen dissolved in ocean is important for life of aquatic animals. Cold drinks have dissolved carbon dioxide in it.
27. **(b)** Evaporation is used to obtain a solid substance that has dissolved in water.
28. **(a)** A-(i), B-(iv), C-(iii), D-(ii)
29. **(d)** Metals expands on heating and contracts on cooling that is why iron rim is usually heated before fixing into the wooden wheel.
30. **(b)** Cotton fibres have less air spaces inside them, therefore they conduct the body heat, whereas woollen fibres have lot of air spaces inside them. Air being a very bad conductor of heat does not allow the body heat to escape and hence keeps us warm.
31. **(d)** Frying pan is strong and hard and is made up of metal. Hence, it is correctly paired.

BIOLOGY

32. **(b)** Narrow, long and thin leaves are present in submerged plants.
33. **(d)** Watering in mouth, closing of *Mimosa* leaves and shutting the eyes are example of response to stimulus. But a chick hatching out of an egg is phenomenon of reproduction.

34. (b) Cow and sheep provide milk for us.

35. (a) Grasses have parallel venation and fibrous roots. Due to this characteristic features they survive better in adverse conditions.

36. (c) Deficiency diseases are caused due to lack of balanced diet in our food. They can be controlled by taking carbohydrate, fats, protein, vitamins and minerals in proper ratio.

37. (b) Two muscles work together to move a bone one for contraction and other for relaxation.

38. (a) *Mimosa* (touch-me-not) is a very sensitive plant. When it is touched, its leaves fold inwardly.

39. (d) In a flower, stigma is situated at the upper part of a pistil and the bottom part of a pistil is called ovary.

40. (a) Cactus is a desert plant that can survive in scarcity of water and high temperature conditions.

41. (c) Lion and tiger are predators.

42. (c) Biotic components include living things such as plants, birds and insects etc. Abiotic components include non-living things such as air, water and soil etc.

43. (d) Skin cancer increases if thickness of ozone layer decreases.

44. (b)

45. (a) Sweet and fleshy fruits having bright colour of outer covering are preferred by all animals for their food. So they carry such fruits to different places and cause dispersal of seeds.

46. (a) The diagram shows a bisexual flower. The structure labelled X is the anther and the structure labelled Y is the filament. Thus, options (b) and (c) are false. This is because only the stigma receives pollen and the sepals hold the petals together.
Structures labelled X and Y make up the male reproductive part of a flower. Thus, option (d) is false because it is a bisexual flower with both stamens and pistil present.
Option (a) is true since it is a bisexual flower and has an ovary, it would be able to develop into a fruit.

47. (d) Inherited characters are called traits which pass from one generation to the other. For e.g. colour of hair, skin and eyes, and shape of nose.

48. (d) Milk has no dietary fibre. Besides it, fruits, vegetables, grains and whole pulse provide us dietary fibre.

49. (b) The female part of a flower consists of stigma, style and ovary. Collectively these make pistil.

50. (a) To prepare manure from kitchen garbage first of all we dig a pit then cover the bottom with sand, then put garbage into it. After this we cover the pit loosely with grass or gunny bag and in the last we add worms into the pit.

MOCK TEST-5

ANSWERS KEY									
1	(c)	11	(b)	21	(c)	31	(c)	41	(a)
2	(c)	12	(b)	22	(b)	32	(b)	42	(d)
3	(c)	13	(c)	23	(d)	33	(b)	43	(a)
4	(b)	14	(c)	24	(d)	34	(b)	44	(d)
5	(c)	15	(c)	25	(d)	35	(d)	45	(d)
6	(b)	16	(b)	26	(c)	36	(d)	46	(c)
7	(b)	17	(d)	27	(b)	37	(b)	47	(b)
8	(a)	18	(b)	28	(b)	38	(c)	48	(c)
9	(d)	19	(a)	29	(b)	39	(d)	49	(d)
10	(b)	20	(c)	30	(a)	40	(c)	50	(a)

PHYSICS

1. (c) Each tiny magnet having both North and South Poles. Poles of a magnet always exist in pairs.

2. (c) Distance = PQ + QR = a + a = 2a

3. (c) $F = m \times a = 1000 \times 8 = 8000$ N

4. (b) Magnets are commonly used to make electric motors and generators. With the help of magnets, electric motors can convert electricity (electrical energy) into motion (kinetic energy) and generators can convert motion (kinetic energy) into electricity (electrical energy). Many electrical appliances make use of electric motors to work. Among the given four options, the blender and the vacuum cleaner are two such examples. Therefore, the answer is Option (b). Other examples of electrical appliances that make use of electric motors are fan, washing machine and hair dryer.

5. (c) Since, $F = mg = 4 \times 10 = 40$ N

6. (b) Rotatory motion in which a body moves about fixed axis without changing its position.

7. (b) Insulators are bad conductor of electricity

8. (a) Unlike poles attract and like poles repel each other by this pole of a magnet can be identified

9. (d) Iron is a magnetic material.

10. (b) Circuit B have bulbs in parallel combination and circuit A and circuit C are in series combination

11. (b) A → (s); B → (r); C → (p); D → (q)

12. (b) Solar cell produces electricity from sunlight. In other words it converts light energy into electrical energy.

13. (c) Iron is a magnetic material due to which it can be used to make needle of a compass.

14. (c) A magnetic force can pass through the cardboard and attract magnetic objects to the magnet. Thus the paper clip moves towards the magnet. A magnetic force cannot pass through the iron sheet and magnetic objects cannot be attracted to the magnet. Magnetic materials such as iron and steel do not allow magnetic force to pass through them.

CHEMISTRY

15. (c) A-(r); B-(p); C-(s); D-(q)

16. **(b)** Silk is a natural fibres obtained from cocoon of silk worm.

17. **(d)** Molten ice cream when cooled gives ice-cream again.

18. **(b)** Both assertion and reason are true but reason is not correct explanation of assertion.

19. **(a)** Cotton fibre is obtained from fruit of cotton plant called cotton bolls. Rayon is obtained from cellulose.

20. **(c)** Fractional distillation method is used to purify mixture of liquids having different boiling point.

21. **(c)** Bubbles coming out of soil while watering the plants are due to presence of air in soil.

22. **(b)** Group A consists of objects that are transparent, Group B consists of objects that are translucent and Group C consists of objects that are opaque. A ceramic vase is made of ceramics which is an opaque material. Therefore, the ceramic vase can only be placed in Group C.

23. **(d)** It must have the ability to float in water. i.e., it should be water proof and should have low density so that it can float in water.

24. **(d)** Newspapers are made from papers which absorb water easily. Boots are made of plastics or rubber, both of which are waterproof or do not absorb water. Bottles and raincoats must be made of a material such as plastics that is waterproof. Bottles can be made of glass which is waterproof too.

25. **(d)** Opening of a bud is a chemical and irreversible process.

26. **(c)** Silk is smooth to touch and had vibrant colour and shine.

27. **(b)** P: Metal (Conductor of electricity)
Q: Plastic (does not conduct electricity)

28. **(b)** All the four gases— nitrogen, oxygen, carbon dioxide and argon are present in air. However, only oxygen is a reactive gas— it can cause metals, such as iron, to rust over a period of time. Oxygen is also required for things to burn. Green plants do not use oxygen to make food but they use oxygen to respire.

29. **(b)** Since new substance (i.e. magnesium oxide) is formed when magnesium is burnt in air so it is a chemical change. Since heat is produced so it is an exothermic change.

30. **(c)** Alum. The dissolved particles of alum load the fine clay particle in water and they become heavier and settle down quickly.

31. **(c)** Looms are used for weaving yarns to get fabric.

BIOLOGY

32. **(b)** The diagram shows a bisexual flower. Pollen grains land on the stigma of the flower represented by X. The other parts of the flower are labelled as shown.

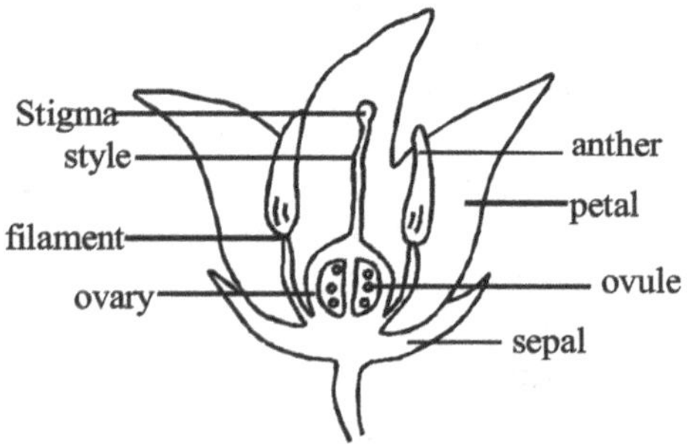

33. **(b)** After fertilisation, the ovary, represented by W, develops into a fruit. The ovule, represented by

Z, develops into a seed. Only A and D are correct.

34. (b) Because of hinge joint, lower jaw has the capacity for movement.

35. (d)

36. (d) They have a structure called 'gizzard' which helps them in grinding their food.

37. (b) Protein takes part in tissue building. It is an essential part of our food.

38. (c) Jackals eat the dead and decaying organic substance. They generally eat the left-over flesh of dead animals which are killed by larger animals such as – lion and tiger.

39. (d) Streamlined body and flexible backbone help fish for aquatic life. This adaptation provides help in search of food and safety.

40. (c) Besides vitamin C, other vitamins such as – vitamin A, vitamin B and vitamin D are not destroyed when we cook.

41. (a)

42. (d) Ball and socket joint is found between thigh bone and hip bone. This joint enables the bone to move in many planes.

43. (a) All the essential things are available in a particular habitat for a particular organism. Otherwise it will not be able to survive.

44. (d) All statements are ture.

45. (d) Due to seed dispersal, competition for space, nutrients and sunlight is minimized.

46. (c) The life cycle of annual plants is completed in one season. These are generally herbs. The example includes wheat, paddy, mustard etc.

47. (b) We use iodine to test the presence of starch in food. The starch and iodine combination gives violet colour.

48. (c) Plants with tap root system bear leaves which are generally broad and have criss-cross network of veins called reticulate venation.

49. (d) The adjacent vertebrae of the backbone have gliding joint between them. This joint provides flexibility to backbone.

50. (a) The label I represents plumule. During seed germination, the shoot develops from plumule, grows upward and forms the aerial part of the plant body.

GENERAL KNOWLEDGE

MOCK TEST 1

ANSWER KEY									
1	(b)	6	(c)	11	(d)	16	(a)	21	(a)
2	(c)	7	(b)	12	(c)	17	(a)	22	(a)
3	(b)	8	(b)	13	(a)	18	(c)	23	(c)
4	(b)	9	(a)	14	(a)	19	(b)	24	(c)
5	(a)	10	(a)	15	(a)	20	(a)	25	(b)

1. (b) Ostrich is the largest flightless bird native to Africa.

2. (c) Dinosaurs are omnivores as they eat both plants and animals.

3. (b) Darwin's finches referred to birds which were found on the Galápagos Islands.

4. (b) Whale is the largest mammal on the Earth.

5. (a) Herbs are plants with soft stems which grow up to five feet.

6. (c) Trees are leafless for a shorter or longer season of the year in scrub jungle forest.

7. (b) Oxygen liberated during photosynthesis comes from water.

8. (b) Maize has stilt roots which grow obliquely downwards from basal nodes of the main stem and fix firmly to the soil.

9. (a) Leaf of the pitcher plant modifies into a pitcher.

10. (a) Global warming leads to change in weather conditions on the Earth.

11. (d) Increase in human population impacts biosphere, hydrosphere, atmosphere, and geosphere.

12. (c) World Forest day- 21 March
World Environment day - 5 June
Earth day - 22 April
International Tiger day - 29 July

13. (a) Intergovernmental Panel on Climate Change aims to control greenhouse gas concentrations in the atmosphere.

14. (a) Silent Valley Movement started in the state of Kerala.

15. (a) World Environment Day is celebrated on 5th June every year.

16. (a) Tourism has been included from environmental assessment.

17. (a) White tiger was seen in the Nilgiris.

18. (c) Halley's Comet can be seen with the naked eye after every 76 years.

19. (b) Indira Gandhi was the only Indian woman Prime Minister.

20. (a) King Vijayalaya founded the imperial Chola Empire.

21. (a) Annie Ernaux won Nobel Prize in Literature in 2022.

22. (a) Ranbir Kapoor for Brahmastra: Part-1 won the Dadasaheb Phalke award in 2023.

23. (c) The first cricket match was held in Mumbai.

24. (c) Composite numbers have one factor.

25. (b) Rajiv Kumar Since May, 2022. Election commissioner of India.

MOCK TEST 2

ANSWER KEY									
1	(b)	6	(c)	11	(c)	16	(a)	21	(a)
2	(a)	7	(c)	12	(a)	17	(a)	22	(b)
3	(a)	8	(a)	13	(a)	18	(b)	23	(a)
4	(a)	9	(b)	14	(d)	19	(c)	24	(a)
5	(b)	10	(b)	15	(b)	20	(b)	25	(b)

1. (b) Millet is called coarse grain and can withstand drought conditions.

2. (a) Desert rat-kangaroo is an extinct marsupial found in desert area of Central Australia.

3. (a) Lava is molten rock that comes out during a volcanic eruption.

4. (a) Biomagnification is the accumulation of toxic substances in organisms across a food chain.

5. (b) Plastic is a non-biodegradable substance and remains in the environment for a long time.

6. (c) Species consists of sum total of the populations of the same type of organisms.

7. (c) Nitrogen is called pnictogens and lie in the group 15 of the periodic table.

8. (a) An acid tastes sour and when added to a base, the resulting solution is neutral.

9. (b) Venera 9 was an unmanned space mission launched by Soviet Union to record surface conditions of Venus.

10. (b) ISRO - Indian Space Research Organisation was responsible for this mission.

11. (c) Draupadi Murmu has been elected as the 15th President of India Since 2022.

12. (a) Pradhan Mantri Suraksha Bima Yojana is about accidental insurance cover.

13. (a) Swami Dayananda Saraswati founded the Arya Samaj.

14. (d) Calumniate means to accuse falsely.

15. (b) William Wordsworth is the poet of the poem, 'Daffodils'.

16. (a) Tang Dynasty is also known as 'The Age of 1000 Entertainments'.

17. (a) Sonal Mansingh is a dancer.

18. (b) 18th World Athletics Championship was held in Oregon, US in 2022.

19. (c) Elena Rybakina won the 2022 Women's Singles Wimbledon Championship.

20. (b) Tennis player Stan Wawrinka belongs to Switzerland.

21. (c) India's largest electric Vehicle (EV) charging station with a capacity of 100 charging points for four wheeler situated in Gurugram (HR).

22. (b) Infinity Bridge in Dubai, UAE.

23. (a) Values describes the beliefs of an individual or culture.

24. (a) The sign means slow down and prepare to stop if necessary.

25. (b) World TB Day is celebrated on 24 March.

MOCK TEST 3

ANSWER KEY									
1	(a)	6	(a)	11	(c)	16	(d)	21	(a)
2	(b)	7	(a)	12	(d)	17	(c)	22	(b)
3	(d)	8	(b)	13	(a)	18	(c)	23	(b)
4	(d)	9	(b)	14	(a)	19	(d)	24	(c)
5	(c)	10	(c)	15	(d)	20	(d)	25	(c)

1. (a) Earthworm breathes through skin.

2. (b) Pigeon has pneumatic bone which is hollow or contains many air cells.

3. (d) Wheat has fibrous roots which are branching roots growing from the base of the stem.

4. (a) Wet evergreen forests are present in the Western Ghats of India. Semi-evergreen forests which partially shed their leaves, occupy the Andaman and Nicobar Islands. Moist deciduous forests are found in Madhya Pradesh. Broad-leaved forests are present in the Eastern Himalayas.

5. (c) Air pollution is mainly caused by vehicular and industrial emission which contains gases like carbon dioxide, carbon monoxide, nitrogen dioxide, etc. Plants utilize carbon dioxide for photosynthesis and release oxygen, thus controlling air pollution. Acid rain contains sulphuric acid and nitric acid.

6. (a) It was first held in 1973 and has been an important campaign for raising awareness on emerging environmental issues due to marine pollution, human overpopulation, and global warming.

7. (a) In 1772, Daniel Rutherford discovered nitrogen which is an important element used by plants and animals. Nitrogen is a main component of amino acids which form proteins.

8. (b) The elements on the top and right-hand side like hydrogen and lithium have smaller radius and are lighter in weight.

9. (b) Solar system is made up of all the planets that orbit our Sun. Besides the planets, the Solar System also consists of moons, comets, asteroids, minor planets, and dust and gas.

10. (c) Isaac Newton is credited with building the first reflector in 1668 with a design that used a small flat diagonal mirror to reflect the light to an eyepiece mounted on the side of the telescope.

11. (a) D.Y.Chandrachud has succeeded U.U. Lalit as the 50th Chief Justice of India.

12. (d) Baffin Island, in the territory of Nunavut, is the largest island in Canada and the fifth largest island in the world. Its area is 507,451 km .

13. (a) Dayanand Saraswati was a Hindu religious leader and founder of the Arya Samaj, a Hindu reform movement of the Vedic tradition.

14. (a) President of India is the Head of State and the Supreme Commander of the Indian Armed Forces

15. (d) In the morning, the person wakes up and turns off the alarm clock. He then gets ready for school and hurries downstairs for breakfast. He reaches school and meets his friends.

16. (d) Neil Gaiman is an English author of short fiction, novels, comic books, graphic novels. He has not received any Nobel Prize. Bob Dylan, Mo Yan and Alice Munro received the Nobel Prize in Literature in 2016, 2012 and 2013, respectively.

17. (c) The film Soorarai Pottru won the Best Film Award at the 68th National Film Awards ceremony.

18. (c) Kuchipudi is the Indian classical dance from the Indian state of Andhra Pradesh.

19. (d) Iga Swiatek won the 2022 US Open Women's Single title.

20. (d) The national game of Spain is football.

21. (a) You should inform your parents when a stranger knocks at your door.

22. (b) We should plant more and more trees to protect our environment. Plants release oxygen and take in carbon dioxide.

23. (b) Svante Paabo won the Nobel Prize in Medicine in 2022. For his discoveries concerning "the genomes of extinct huminis and human evolution".

24. (a) Tashkent Uzbekistan will host the men's World Boxing Championship in 2023.

25. (c) The 18th edition of G20 summit will be held in New Delhi India.

MOCK TEST 4

ANSWER KEY

1	(a)	9	(a)	17	(b)	25	(b)	33	(d)
2	(a)	10	(c)	18	(c)	26	(b)	34	(c)
3	(b)	11	(d)	19	(b)	27	(a)	35	(c)
4	(a)	12	(b)	20	(d)	28	(d)	36	(a)
5	(c)	13	(b)	21	(a)	29	(a)	37	(d)
6	(a)	14	(a)	22	(c)	30	(c)	38	(a)
7	(b)	15	(a)	23	(b)	31	(a)	39	(b)
8	(d)	16	(b)	24	(a)	32	(b)	40	(d)

1. (a) Rice, wheat, onion, garlic are herbs because their bodies are clearly differentiated into roots, leaves and stems.

2. (a) Molars are large, flat tooth at the back of the mouth and are used primarily to grind food during chewing.

3. (b) Bengal Tiger is one of the endangered animal species in India.

4. (a) Anteaters are ant eating animals which catch their prey by inserting their tongue into insects' nests.

5. (c) Evolution of organisms involves change in both physical and genetic characters.

6. (a) American Pit Bull Terrier is a dog breed the ancestors of which came from the British Isles.

7. (b) Cashew nuts are used in dishes such as soups, meat stews, and some Indian milk-based desserts.

8. (d) Coffee is a tropical evergreen shrub which grows in mountain areas.

9. (a) Pine is an evergreen tree whereas Oak, maple and birch are deciduous trees.

10. (c) The branch of olive is a symbol of peace.

11. (d) A-q, B-p, C-s, D-r

12. (b) Chipko Movement was a forest conservation campaign. Antarctic Treaty was signed on an 1st December 1959. CNG is environment friendly gas. Plants and animals that are found in a particular location are referred to as an ecosystem.

13. (b) Global warming is caused by 'greenhouse effect'. The earth's atmosphere has numerous gases which allow solar radiation to pass through it and heat the surface of the earth.

14. (a) World Planting Day is celebrated on 21 March every year to promote planting of trees.

15. (a) Removal of a forest or trees is called deforestation. It leads to air pollution due to decrease in oxygen and increase in carbon dioxide in the atmosphere.

16. (b) Sodium bicarbonate or baking soda is primarily used in cooking and baking as a leavening agent, and as a very effective cleaning agent.

17. (b) Iron is a magnetic substance and will be attracted by magnets.

18. (c) Water, camphor and ether are volatile substances which escape into atmosphere when exposed to air. Wood is a non-volatile substance which remains in its place even when exposed to air for a long time.

19. (b) Gregor Mendel is called the 'Father of Genetics.' He was the first scientist to study plant heredity in pea.

20. (d) Ganymede is the largest natural satellite of our solar system. It is the moon of Jupiter.

21. (a) Christiaan Huygens discovered the moon 'Titan' and found that Saturn's rings are made of rocks.

22. (c) Andromeda Galaxy also known as Messier 31, is a spiral galaxy. It is the nearest large galaxy to the Milky Way.

23. (b) Venus is named after the Roman God and is the nearest planet to the earth.

24. (a) Kiran Bedi is the first IPS officer of India and is currently the Lieutenant Governor of Puducherry.

25. (b) Bharat Ratna is the highest civilian award of the Republic of India given in recognition of exceptional service/performance.

26. (b) Swachh Bharat Abhiyan was launched in the year 2014.

27. (a) Bishop Rock is the world's smallest island located off the western tip of the Scilly Isles, Great Britain.

28. (d) Mahatma Gandhi was not a member of the Constituent Assembly of India.

29. (a) Yellowstone National Park is the first national park of the United States.

30. (c) A mother frog lays her eggs in water after which the cells in the egg multiply and grow. Finally, the cells grow into a swimming tadpole.

31. (a) Nikhil Rao is a member of the rock band Indian Ocean. Other members of the band are Amit Kilam, Rahul Ram, and Himanshu Joshi.

32. (b) The film 'RRR' was released in 2022.

33. (d) Shahrukh Khan owns the film production company Red Chillies Entertainment.

34. (c) It is better to stay calm in case you are unhappy with someone's behavior.

35. (c) Akshay Kumar has been chosen as the brand ambassador for Swachh Bharat Mission in Uttar Pradesh.

36. (a) The Nal Sarovar Bird Sanctuary (NSBS) is located to the west of Ahmedabad near Sanand Village in Gujarat.

37. (d) The 34th edition of North Atlantic Treaty Organization (NATO) summit was held in Madrid, Spain.

38. (a) BS-IV vehicles cause less air pollution in comparison to BS-III vehicles.

39. (b) Jhulan Nishit Goswami, Indian women's team bowler, has become the highest wicket-taker in the history of women ODI cricket and broke the record of the Australian bowler Cathryn Fitzpatrick.

40. (d) The Union Government has launched a new countrywide campaign "Darwaza Band" in Mumbai on May 30, 2017 for promotion of toilet usage in the rural areas across the country. Amitabh Bachchan will lead the campaign.

MOCK TEST 5

ANSWER KEY

1	(d)	9	(d)	17	(a)	25	(a)	33	(a)
2	(b)	10	(a)	18	(c)	26	(d)	34	(b)
3	(a)	11	(a)	19	(a)	27	(c)	35	(b)
4	(c)	12	(b)	20	(a)	28	(b)	36	(a)
5	(d)	13	(a)	21	(b)	29	(d)	37	(a)
6	(d)	14	(c)	22	(c)	30	(a)	38	(a)
7	(a)	15	(b)	23	(b)	31	(d)	39	(a)
8.	(a)	16.	(a)	24	(c)	32	(c)	40	(b)

1. (d) Red Fox is the largest of the true foxes and found in the Northern Hemisphere from the Arctic Circle to North Africa.

2. (b) Pneumonia causes swelling of the lungs and includes symptoms like dry cough, chest pain, fever, and trouble breathing.

3. (a) Neem is a tree because it has well-defined woody stems, roots and leaves.

4. (c) Bats are nocturnal and produce sound to capture insects for feeding.

5. (d) Whales are warm-blooded animals and are very intelligent.

6. (d) Evolution is a genetic process in which organisms change their characteristics with time.

7. (a) Giant panda is an endangered species which is native to China. It eats bamboo and is a good climber.

8. (a) Plants store the prepared food in the form of starch in leaves.
9. (d) All the animals are nocturnal.
10. (a) 2nd February is celebrated across the world as the World Wetlands Day.
11. (a) The Bishnoi Movement took place in Rajasthan.
12. (b) Ozone depletion causes global warming. Water polluted with mercury causes Minamata disease. Hemoglobin has higher binding affinity with carbon monoxide. Fossil fuel is a non-renewable resource of energy.
13. (a) Increase in sulphur dioxide concentration in the atmosphere decreases the population of lichens.
14. (c) Great Barrier Reef is the biggest single structure made by living beings.
15. (b) Hebron, a city in Palestine, has been put on UNESCO's list of World Heritage in danger.
16. (a) Ramsar Convention signed in 1971 is regarding the conservation of wetlands.
17. (a) A gas expands on heating. A wood piece and an iron rod get heated at different rate. Water turns into ice on cooling. Ice when heated turns into water.
18. (c) An electric bell rings due to electric and magnetic effect of current.
19. (a) Archimedes gave the laws of floatation.
20. (a) Ball and bearings are used in machines to reduce friction.
21. (b) Carbon dioxide is used in beverages to produce fizz.
22. (c) Saturn has each season of Seven years.
23. (b) World's first artificial satellite Sputnik I was launched by Russia on October 4, 1957.
24. (d) Proxima Centauri is a red dwarf star.
25. (a) The currency of Argentina is Argentinian Peso.
26. (d) Virendra Shehwag is not the recipient of the Padma Vibhushan award.
27. (c) P.V. Sindhu won silver at Olympics in 2016, only Indian other than Saina Nehwal who got to have, won a bronze medal at Olympics.
28. (b) Mark Zuckerberg is the CEO of social media site Facebook.
29. (d) Kanpur, Allahabad and Haridwar are situated on the banks of river Ganges.
30. (a) Hindi is not declared an official language of the UN.
31. (d) The topic to be considered at a meeting is called agenda.
32. (c) 'Green with envy' is an idiom which means to grow jealous of something.
33. (a) Mallika Sarabhai is an activist and a Kuchipudi and Bharatanatyam dancer from Ahmedabad, Gujarat.
34. (b) Jhanvi Kapoor made her debut in the film 'Dhadak'.
35. (b) Virat Kohli became the first cricketer to 3000 runs Twenty20 Cricket match.
36. (a) Lianlian was the name of the Mascot at 19th south Asia Games 2022. It was held in Hangzhou, China
37. (a) An interview is an example of verbal communication which involves oral communication between people.
38. (a) Subodh Kumar Jaiswal is the current director of the Central Bureau of Investigation.
39. (a) Jairam Ramesh has written the book 'Indira Gandhi: A Life in Nature'.
40. (b) Neiphiu Rio is the new chief minister of Nagaland.

LOGICAL REASONING

MOCK TEST 1

ANSWER KEY									
1	(d)	6	(c)	11	(a)	16	(b)	21	(b)
2	(c)	7	(a)	12	(a)	17	(b)	22	(b)
3	(d)	8	(b)	13	(d)	18	(a)	23	(b)
4	(c)	9	(d)	14	(c)	19	(c)	24	(d)
5	(d)	10	(b)	15	(c)	20	(a)	25	(c)

1. **(d)** As,$12 = 3^2 + 3 : 30 = 5^2 + 5$
Similarly, $20 = 4^2 + 4$:
$? = 6^2 + 6$
$? = 36 + 6$
$? = 42$

3. **(d)** The numbers are 1, 1+2, 1+2+3. 1+2+3+4, 1+2+3+4+5
i.e., 1,3,6,10,15.

4. **(c)** Each next term = 3 × its preceding term.

5. **(d)** Each letter moves 4 steps ahead to get its code.

6. **(c)** We sleep at night and night is called sunshine. So, we sleep at sunshine.

7. **(a)** Lady's son's father is lady husband. So, the lady's husband is the son-in-law of Neelam's mother, i.e. the lady is the daughter of Neelam's mother. Thus, Neelam is the lady's sister. Hence, the correct option is (a).

8. **(b)** Y is the brother of Z who is the son of P. so, Z is also the son of P. When P is the father of Y and X is the wife of Y then P is the father-in-law of X.

9. **(d)** Clearly, comparing the figure, A is in southwest direction.

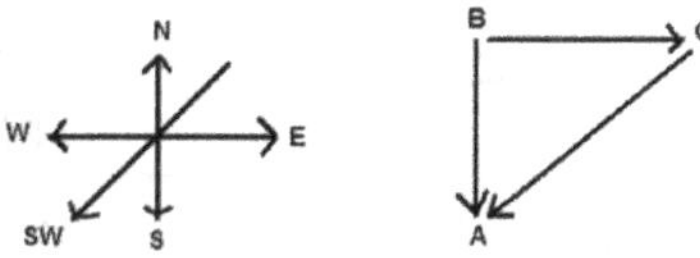

10. **(b)** As per the data, D faces North. A faces towards West. So, its partner B will face towards A and hence towards East. So, C who will face D will face towards South.

14. **(c)** The sitting arrangement of six persons is as following:

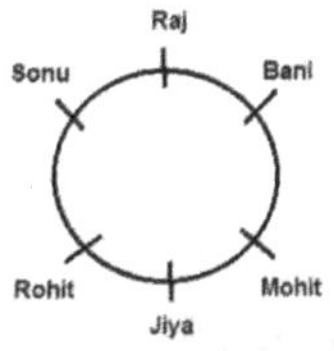

It is clearly shown from the above that Bani is in between Raj and Mohit.

15. **(c)**

Key	Lock	Door	Room	Switch on
1	3	2	4	5

16. **(b)** Given expression: 28 L 7 P 8 Q 6 M 4
$= 28 \div 7 \times 8 - 6 + 4 = 30$

17. **(b)** According to the given table from option (b).

18 S 30 R 6 Q 5 P 0 = 85

$18 \times 30 \div 6 - 5 + 0 = 85$

85 = 85

18. (a) Add the numbers of horizontal, vertical and slanting lines.

19. (c) There are 18 unit cubes in the given solid.

20. (a) Adjacent faces of 3 are 1,2,5 and 6. Therefore, faces 3 and 4 are opposite.

23. (b)

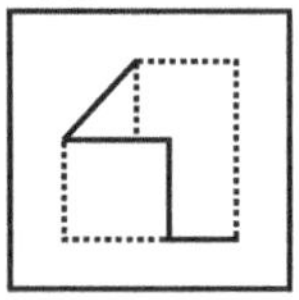

MOCK TEST 2

ANSWER KEY									
1	(d)	6	(d)	11	(d)	16	(b)	21	(a)
2	(b)	7	(b)	12	(b)	17	(d)	22	(a)
3	(d)	8	(d)	13	(b)	18	(c)	23	(b)
4	(d)	9	(c)	14	(c)	19	(c)	24	(a)
5	(a)	10	(b)	15	(a)	20	(d)	25	(d)

1. (d) The pattern is as follows:

$Z \xrightarrow{+4} D \xrightarrow{+4} H \xrightarrow{+7} O \xrightarrow{+1} P$

$A \xrightarrow{+4} E \xrightarrow{+4} I \xrightarrow{+7} P \xrightarrow{+1} Q$

So, O P is wrong in the series.

2. (b) As,

$4 + 5 = 9^2 = 81$

$9 + 8 = 17^2 = 289$

And,

$4 + 6 = 10^2 = 100$

Similarly,

$10 + 8 = 18^2 = 324$

3. (d) The second term is double the first term on the left of 'as'.

Hence $? = 9 \times 2 = 18$

6. (d) As, O is written as P, A as B, M as N, S as T and so on, then COMPANIES will be written as DPNQBOJFT.

9. (c) Amit's son's uncle — Amit's brother. So. the old man's son is Amit's brother i.e., the old man is Amit's father.

10. (b) M + J means M is the daughter of J.

$J \div K$ means J is the son of K.

So, M is the granddaughter.

11. (d) Earlier flight took off at 10:45 – 25 minutes = 10:20 a.m. The next flight will be after 5 hours i.e., at 3:20 P.M.

12. (b) Count the number of days from 2005 onwards to get 0 odd day.

Year	2005	2006	2007	2008	2009	2010
Odd days	1	1	1	2	1	1

= 7 or 0 odd days.

Therefore, calendar for the year 2005 is the same as that for the year 2011.

13. (b) The direction of ayan is as follows:

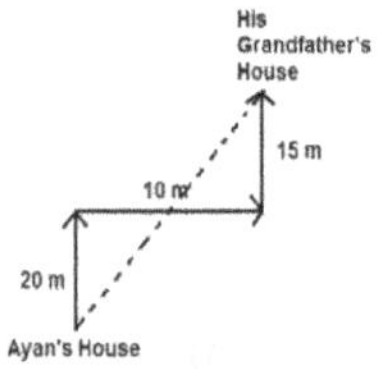

North-east direction is his grandfather's house from his house.

14. (c) The direction of Veena is as follows:

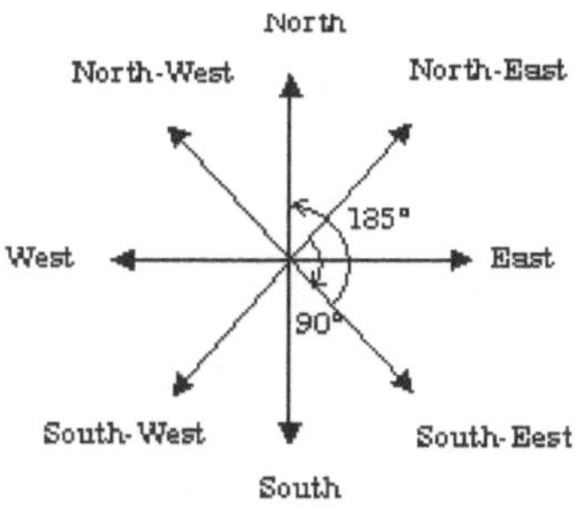

So, she is facing North direction.

17. (d) Number of plants = 6 + 6 – 1 = 11

18. (c) The greatest number = 839 + 1 = 840, second digit is 4.

The lowest number = 275 + 1 = 276 , second digit is 7.

$\therefore$ 7-4 = 3

20. (d) Given expression: 540 – 36 + 12 ÷ 75 × 55

After putting sign:

540 ÷ 36 × 12 + 75 – 55

= 15 × 12 + 75 – 55

= 180 +75 – 55

= 255 – 55 = 200

MOCK TEST 3

ANSWER KEY									
1	(b)	6	(d)	11	(d)	16	(a)	21	(d)
2	(c)	7	(c)	12	(b)	17	(c)	22	(b)
3	(a)	8	(a)	13	(c)	18	(c)	23	(a)
4	(d)	9	(b)	14	(d)	19	(d)	24	(b)
5	(c)	10	(c)	15	(c)	20	(a)	25	(a)

3. (a) Each term in the pattern is +8, +8, +16, +16, +24, +24.

4. (d) Each term except first two terms is equal to sum of preceding two terms.

7. (c) As,

S O F T W A R E

+1 +2 +3 +1 +2 +3 +1 +2

T Q I U Y D S G

Similarly, T Y P E

+1 +2 +3 +1

U A S F

8. (a) The blood relation is as shown below:

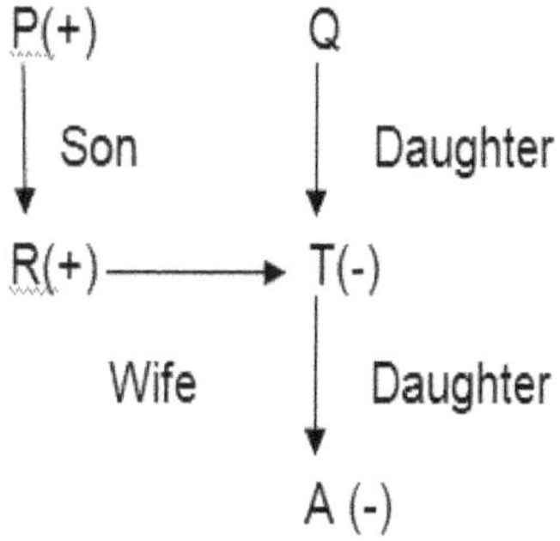

So, P is grandfather to A.

13. (c) Wife's mother-in-law = Mother

Daughter of mother = Sister

So, the woman is Sister to the man.

15. (c) The direction diagram is as shown below:

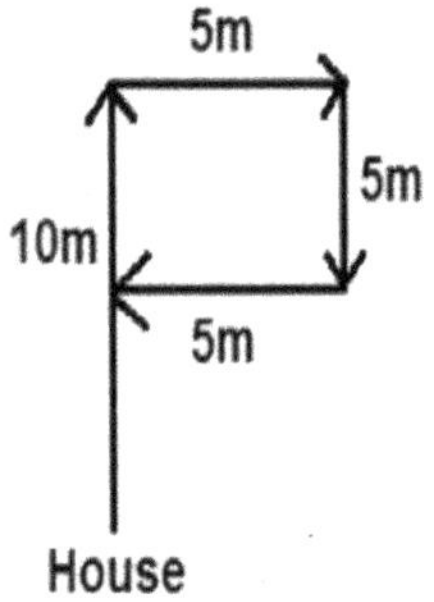

So, I am in North direction from my house.

16. (a) As,

A B | C D E F G H I J K L M | N O | P Q R S T U V W X Y Z |

Interchanging alphabets from C to M with P to Z

A B P Q R S T U V W X Y Z N O C D E F G H I J K L M

Now, Write in reverse order,

M L K J I H G F E D C O N [Z] Y X W V U T S R Q P B A

Midway between F and T

17. (c) Given numbers:

389 476 635 847 568

After interchanging the digits:

983 674 536 748 865

So, it is clear from the above arrangement that 536 is the smallest number after interchanging the digits. Hence, option (c) is correct answer.

24. (b) As,

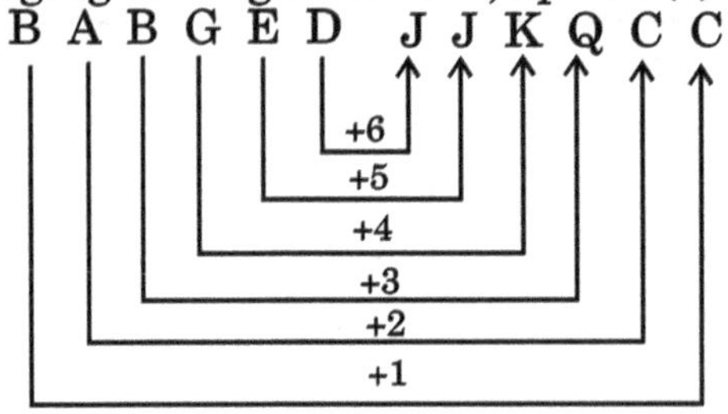

Similarly,

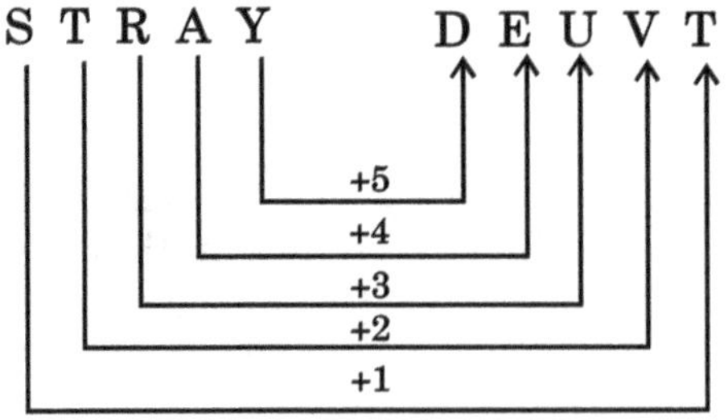

MOCK TEST 4

ANSWER KEY									
1	(b)	9	(b)	17	(c)	25	(a)	33	(b)
2	(a)	10	(a)	18	(d)	26	(c)	34	(c)
3	(b)	11	(d)	19	(d)	27	(c)	35	(b)
4	(b)	12	(d)	20	(d)	28	(c)	36	(a)
5	(b)	13	(c)	21	(d)	29	(c)	37	(b)
6	(c)	14	(c)	22	(b)	30	(d)	38	(a)
7	(a)	15	(a)	23	(b)	31	(a)	39	(c)
8	(a)	16	(b)	24	(b)	32	(c)	40	(d)

4. (b) As,

$10 + 14 + 2 = 26$

$5 + 7 + 1 = 13$

$24 + 28 + 4 = 56$

Simlialry,

$15 + 21 + ? = 39$

$? = 39 - 36$, $? = 3$

6. (c) The pattern is as follows:

$3 \xrightarrow[+3]{} 6 \xrightarrow[+5]{} 11 \xrightarrow[+7]{} 18 \xrightarrow[+9]{} 27$

$F \xrightarrow[+1]{} G \xrightarrow[+2]{} I \xrightarrow[+3]{} L \xrightarrow[+4]{} P$

7. (a) Son of Namrata's grand-father's only child is Namrata's brother.

8. (a) As, In 1st figure: $36 - 25 = 11$ and $64 - 49 = 15$

$11 + 15 = 26$

In 2nd figure: $16 - 9 = 7$ and $81 - 25 = 56$

$7 + 56 = 63$

Similarly,

In 3rd figure: $36 - 25 = 11$ and $144 - 64 = 80$

$11 + 80 = 91$

10. (a) As,

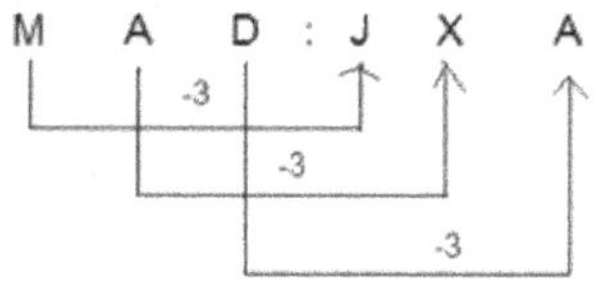

Similarly,

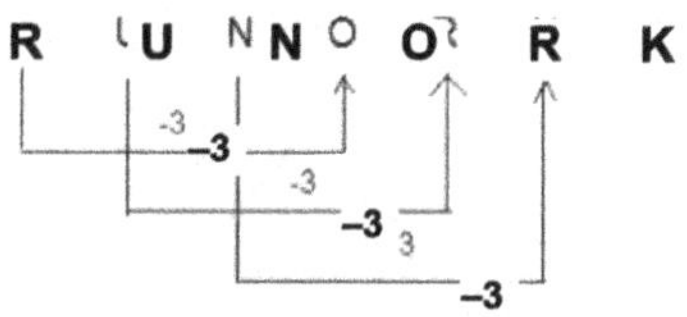

12. (d) Given word:

M A T H E M A T I C A L

After interchanging the letters:

T A M M E H I T A L A C

7th letter from the left end

13. (c) The arrangement of five friends is as following:

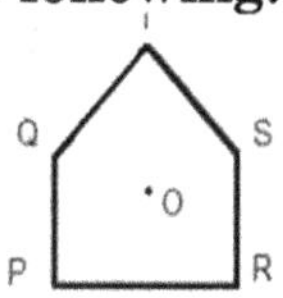

It is clearly shown that T is second to the left of P.

17. (c)

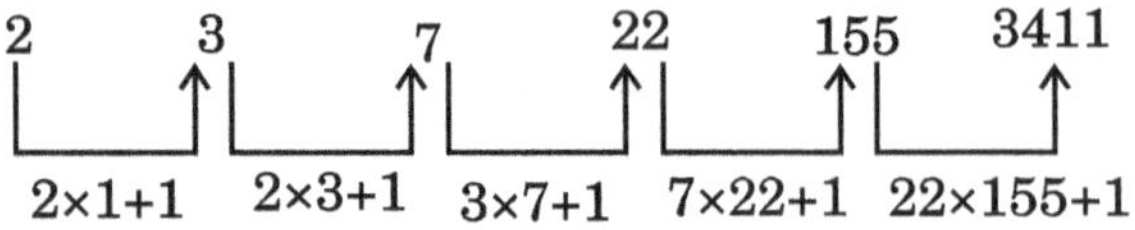

18. (d) The directiond diagram of a man is as following:

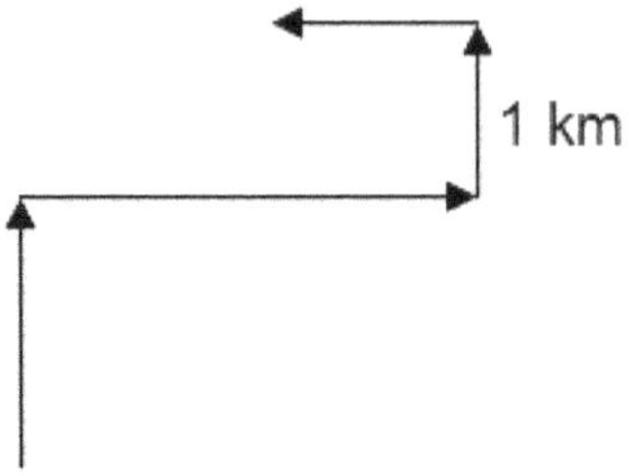

It is clearly shown from the above directions that the man is facing now West direction.

19. (d) The direction diagram is as follows:

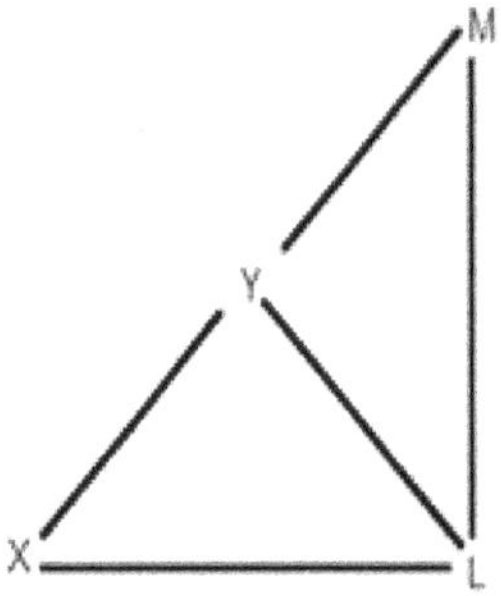

It is clear from the above diagram that M is located in North-east of Y.

20. (d) (7 z 3) y 6 x 5 = $(7 \times 3) - 6 + 5$ = 20

21. (d) As, $\left.\begin{array}{l}211 = 2+1+1 = 4 \\ 333 = 3+3+3 = 9\end{array}\right\} 5$

Similarly, $\left.\begin{array}{l}356 = 3+5+6 = 14 \\ 388 = 3+8+8 = 19\end{array}\right\} 5$

Sol. (24 & 25):

The blood relation diagram is as shown below:

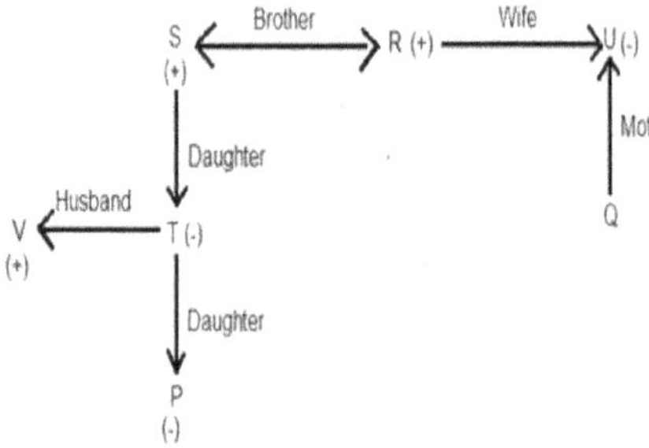

24. (b) It is clear from the above diagram, S is the grandfather of P.

25. (a) It is clear from the above diagram,T is cousin of Q.

26. (c)

27. (c)

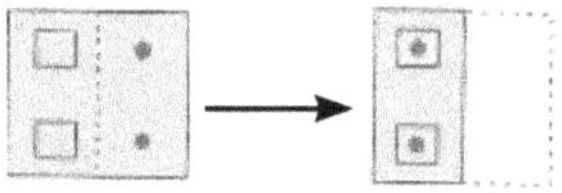

28. (c) Opposite pair are

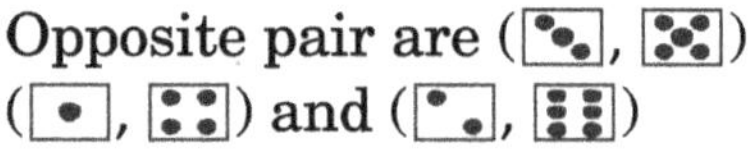

32. (c) If day before yesterday was Thursday, then today is Saturday and Tomorrow will be Sunday.

Sol. (34 & 35): According to the given information,

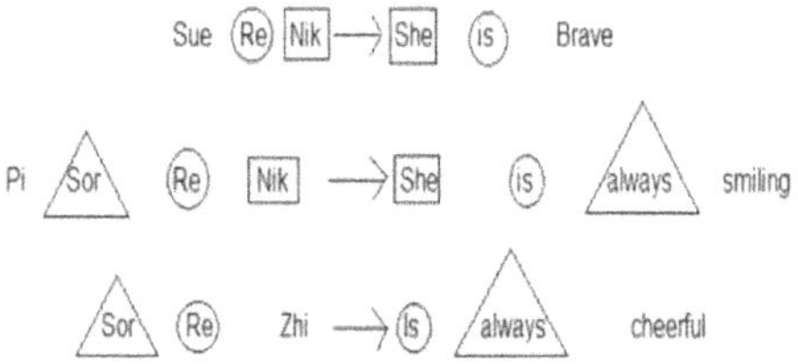

34. (c) The code for smiling is Pi.

35. (b) The code for cheerful is Zhi.

38. (a) Arrange the people according to their age,

B > A > C > D > E

So, A and B are older than C.

39. (c) The total number of girls

= 11 + 11 – 1 = 22 – 1 = 21

MOCK TEST 5

ANSWER KEY									
1	(d)	9	(c)	17	(a)	25	(a)	33	(b)
2	(a)	10	(c)	18	(c)	26	(b)	34	(c)
3	(b)	11	(c)	19	(b)	27	(b)	35	(b)
4	(d)	12	(c)	20	(d)	28	(a)	36	(c)
5	(b)	13	(d)	21	(d)	29	(c)	37	(a)
6	(c)	14	(c)	22	(b)	30	(d)	38	(d)
7	(a)	15	(b)	23	(c)	31	(b)	39	(a)
8	(c)	16	(c)	24	(b)	32	(c)	40	(a)

Sol. (1 to 3) The sitting arrangement of six persons is as following:

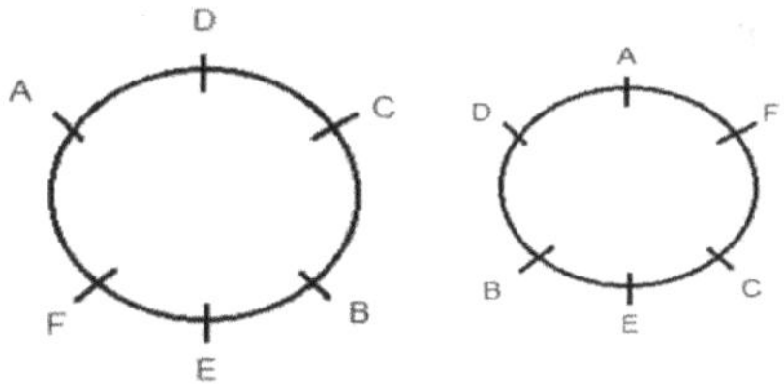

After interchange

1. **(d)** A will be sitting to the left of D.
2. **(a)** E will be sitting to the left of C.
3. **(b)** D will be sitting opposite to C.

7. **(a)** Option (a) shows different nature from the rest others as

$$D \rightarrow A \rightarrow C \rightarrow B$$
$$-3 \quad +2 \quad -1$$

$$E \rightarrow B \rightarrow C \rightarrow D$$
$$-3 \quad +1 \quad +1$$

$$S \rightarrow P \rightarrow Q \rightarrow R$$
$$-3 \quad +1 \quad +1$$

$$X \rightarrow U \rightarrow V \rightarrow W$$
$$-3 \quad +1 \quad +1$$

12. (c) Required rank = (46 – 12 + 1) = 35th.

Sol.(13 to 15) The blood relation is as follows:

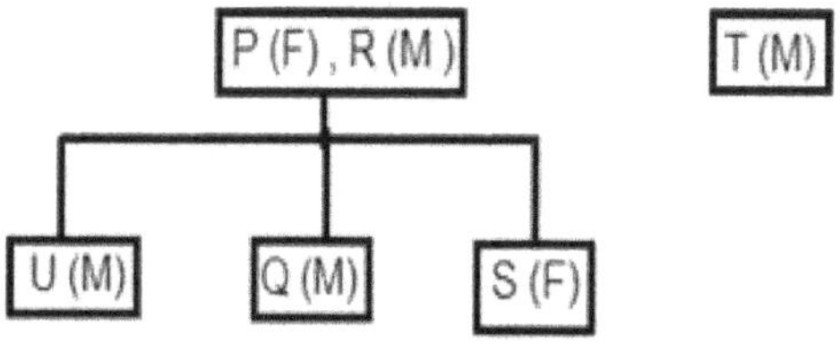

14. (c) Married couple P and R, has son Q, son of U and daughter S i.e. three children.

15. (b) T is the brother of R who is the father of S. So, T is the uncle of S.

16. (c) In each row, last term = sum of first two terms

$$\therefore ? = 3 + \frac{3}{4} = \frac{15}{4}$$

17. (a) Lower number = (Product of upper numbers) × 2

Required number = (1 × 5) × 2 = 10

25. (a) No. of Persons between Rahul and Nitesh

= (36 + 29) –62 – 2

= 65 – 62 – 2

= 1

26. (b) According to the given question,

1 2 3 → Bright little boy ....(i)

1 4 5 → tall big boy ....(ii)

6 3 7 → beautiful little flower ....(iii)

From eqs. (i) and (ii) , 1 → boy

From eqs. (i) and (iii), 3 → little

Hence, 2 → bright

Sol. (27 & 28)

27. (b) The pattern is as follows:

5 → 6 → 9 → 14 → 21 → 30

+1 +3 +5 +7 +9

28. (a) The pattern is as follows:

R → O → L → I → F → C

-3 -3 -3 -3 -3

31. (b) At 8:00 am the Sun is in the East direction.

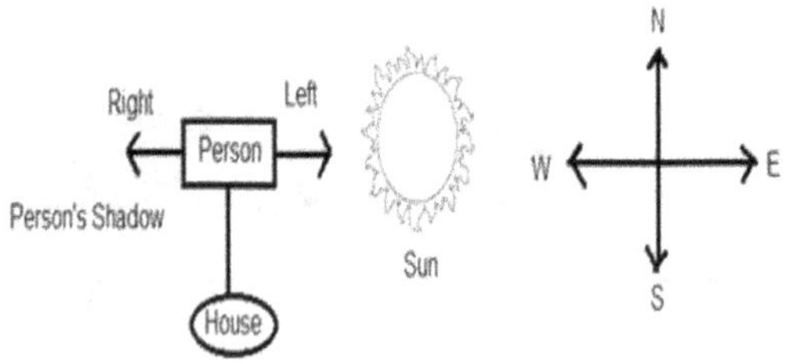

Clearly, the person is facing the south direction.

32. (c) Let the age of son = x yrs

Then, the age of father = 3x yrs

Now, 3x + x = 48

4x = 48

X = 12

Therefore, Age of father = 3 × 12 = 36 yrs.

38. (d) Given expression

= 11 + 15 – 8 ÷ 4 × 5 = 16

40. (a)

A	S	U	M	N	J	K	L
+1 ↓	+1 ↓	+1 ↓	↓	↓	–1 ↓	–1 ↓	–1 ↓
B	T	V	M	N	I	J	K

CYBER

MOCK TEST-1

ANSWERS KEY									
1	(c)	6	(a)	11	(a)	16	(d)	21	(d)
2	(d)	7	(d)	12	(b)	17	(a)	22	(a)
3	(d)	8	(b)	13	(b)	18	(c)	23	(c)
4	(d)	9	(a)	14	(c)	19	(c)	24	(c)
5	(c)	10	(d)	15	(a)	20	(d)	25	(b)

8. (b) OMR or **Optical Mark Recognition** collects data from people by identifying markings on a paper.

9. (a) Software is set of instructions required to perform specific tasks. You cannot touch or feel it.

11. (a) Examples of secondary storage are: CDs, DVs, pendrive, etc.

13. (b) CUI stands for Character User Interface, that means it enables the user to interact with computer with only text and characters rather than graphics, icons and menus.

20. (c) The outline view in PowerPoint shows a list with the whole text of all slides on the left of the screen. There are no images and graphics displayed in this view. It's useful for editing the presentation and can also be saved as a Word document.

22. (a) CLS command is used for 10 Clear the Screen.

23. (c) UPS stands for Uninterrupted Power Supply. It does not belong to the internet in anyway.

MOCK TEST-2

ANSWERS KEY									
1	(c)	6	(d)	11	(c)	16	(a)	21	(b)
2	(b)	7	(b)	12	(a)	17	(d)	22	(c)
3	(a)	8	(c)	13	(a)	18	(d)	23	(a)
4	(d)	9	(d)	14	(b)	19	(c)	24	(d)
5	(d)	10	(d)	15	(d)	20	(a)	25	(a)

9. (d) Device marked as (iv) is of RAM, which is the primary memory of the computer. It retains the data till when computer is switched ON. Device marked as (i), (ii) and (iii) are of Hard disk, Pendrive and CD respectively, which is a secondary memory of a computer. And they retain the data even when computer is switched OFF.

12. (a) In computer storage media, WORM (write once, read many) is a data storage technology that allows information to be written to a disc a single time and prevents the drive from erasing the data.

14. (b) Very-large-scale integration (VLSI) is the process of creating an integrated circuit (IC) by combining thousands of transistors into a single chip.

16. (a) Steps to go to sleep made:

Start menu → Click on drop-down menu of Shut down button → Sleep

23. (a) The given logo is of Opera Mini:

24. (d) A convertible laptop is a hand-held machine that provides the function and computing power of traditional laptops, with the hands-on, tactile user experience of a tablet. These devices incorporate touchscren interfaces with robust operating systems, powerful processors, and helpful accessories.

MOCK TEST-3

ANSWERS KEY									
1	(c)	6	(d)	11	(c)	16	(a)	21	(b)
2	(b)	7	(b)	12	(d)	17	(b)	22	(b)
3	(d)	8	(d)	13	(b)	18	(c)	23	(b)
4	(b)	9	(c)	14	(d)	19	(b)	24	(b)
5	(b)	10	(c)	15	(c)	20	(a)	25	(a)

10. (c) Example of System software are:
Windows 7, Windows 8.1, Android.

13. (b) Dynamic random access memory (DRAM) is a type of memory that is typically used for data or program code that a computer processor needs to function. DRAM is a common type of random access memory (RAM) used in personal computer (PCs), workstations and servers. It needs to be refreshed periodically.

18. (c) To show or hide paragraph marks, go to : Home tab → Paragraph group → Paragraph marks

24. (b) Scanner is a device that optically scans images, printed text, handwriting or an object and converts it to a digital image.

25. (a) The given logo is of Google Hangout.

MOCK TEST-4

ANSWERS KEY

1	(a)	9	(c)	17	(c)	25	(d)	33	(b)
2	(b)	10	(a)	18	(c)	26	(c)	34	(c)
3	(b)	11	(c)	19	(d)	27	(a)	35	(c)
4	(a)	12	(a)	20	(b)	28	(d)	36	(a)
5	(d)	13	(a)	21	(a)	29	(a)	37	(d)
6	(d)	14	(c)	22	(a)	30	(d)	38	(d)
7	(d)	15	(b)	23	(c)	31	(a)	39	(a)
8	(d)	16	(c)	24	(b)	32	(d)	40	(a)

15. (b) Example of volatile memory is RAM and example of non-volatile memory are hard disk, CDs, etc.

20. (b) The given feature is used to Insert Page and Section breaks, it can be accessed by going to Page Layout tab → Page Setup group → Breaks.

21. (a) To access the page borders feature, go to Page layout tab → Page Background group → Page Borders.

31. (a) A voice response system (VRS) is a computer interface which responds to voice commands, instead of responding to inputs from a mouse or a keystroke.

32. (d) A site map (or sitemap) is a list of pages of a web site accessible to crawlers or users.

37. (d) The 12-bit PDP-8, produced by Digital Equipment Corporation (DEC), was the first successful commercial minicomputer.

MOCK TEST-5

ANSWERS KEY									
1	(d)	9	(c)	17	(c)	25	(d)	33	(a)
2	(a)	10	(d)	18	(c)	26	(a)	34	(d)
3	(c)	11	(c)	19	(b)	27	(c)	35	(d)
4	(d)	12	(b)	20	(c)	28	(b)	36	(b)
5	(d)	13	(d)	21	(a)	29	(d)	37	(b)
6	(d)	14	(c)	22	(a)	30	(a)	38	(c)
7	(c)	15	(b)	23	(c)	31	(d)	39	(d)
8	(a)	16	(b)	24	(c)	32	(d)	40	(a)

16. (b) In the given architecture, Server device has been labeled.

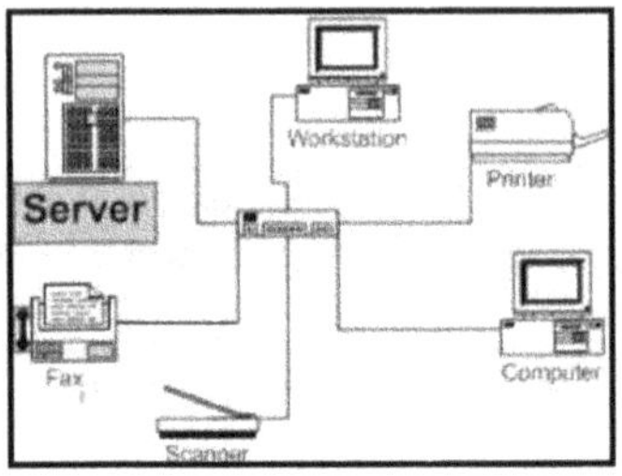

19. (b) A solid-state drive (SSD) is a non-volatile storage device that stores persistent data on solid-state flash memory.

22. (a) The given icon can be accessed by going to, Page layout tab → Page Setup group → size

25. (d) The given icon used for drawing table:

26. (a) MOD operation will give the remainder. So, 4/2 = 0, so it will print THEN statement, i.e. Even Number.

28. (b) An Internet Protocol address (IP address) is a numerical label assigned to each device (e.g., computer, printer) participating in a computer network that uses the Internet Protocol for communication.

29. (d) CAPTCHA stands for "Completely Automated Public Turing test to tell Computers and Humans Apart". It is a type of challenge-response test used in computing to determine whether the user is human or not.

36. (b) **PARAM** is a supercomputers designed and assembled by the Centre for Development of Advanced Computing (C-DAC) in Pune, India.

38. (c) In computing, floating point operations per second (FLOPS) is a measure of computer performance, useful in fields of scientific computations that require floating-point calculations.

39. (d) The speed that a CPU works at is measured in hertz (Hz). Modern processors often run so fast that gigahertz (GHz) is used instead. One gigahertz means one billion cycles per second.

www.ingramcontent.com/pod-product-compliance
Lightning Source LLC
Chambersburg PA
CBHW080857060426
42516CB00042B/1674
* 9 7 8 9 3 9 5 9 8 5 3 0 7 *